NUCLEAR
WASTE IN YOUR
BACKYARD

Other Books by the Authors

By Robert L. Ferguson

The Cost of Deceit and Delay: Obama and Reid's Scheme to Kill Yucca Mountain Wastes $Billions

By Michele S. Gerber

On the Home Front: *The Cold War Legacy of the Hanford Nuclear Site*

NUCLEAR
WASTE IN YOUR
BACKYARD

Who's to Blame and How to Fix It

To Evie,

This ~~overwsome~~ history we dis'cussed.

Best Wishes,
Bob

ROBERT L. FERGUSON
with Michele S. Gerber, Ph.D.

ARCHWAY
PUBLISHING

Archway Publishing books may be ordered through booksellers or by contacting:

Archway Publishing
1663 Liberty Drive
Bloomington, IN 47403
www.archwaypublishing.com
1-(888)-242-5904

Because of the dynamic nature of the Internet, any web addresses or links contained in this book may have changed since publication and may no longer be valid. The views expressed in this work are solely those of the author and do not necessarily reflect the views of the publisher, and the publisher hereby disclaims any responsibility for them.

Any people depicted in stock imagery provided by Thinkstock are models, and such images are being used for illustrative purposes only.
Certain stock imagery © Thinkstock.

ISBN: 978-1-4808-0859-1 (sc)
ISBN: 978-1-4808-0861-4 (hc)
ISBN: 978-1-4808-0860-7 (e)

Library of Congress Control Number: 2014913303

Printed in the United States of America.

Archway Publishing rev. date: 09/08/2014

Advance praise for
Nuclear Waste in Your Backyard

Bob Ferguson has written an important book—his analysis is right on target. I highly recommend his book to be read and acted upon by every American concerned about how partisan politics can trump good science. Such action is especially important for those in positions of policy development. President Obama's flagrant violation of the law, and the seriousness of its implications, is extremely damaging to the well-being of our nation.

—Dr. Alan Waltar, Past President, American Nuclear Society; Retired Professor and Department Head, Nuclear Engineering, Texas A&M University; and author of *America the Powerless*, and other books on science and energy

The American public needs to know that the Yucca Mountain Repository Project is a scientifically sound and robust engineering solution to nuclear waste management. Bob Ferguson and Dr. Gerber have done an impressive job writing a compelling narrative that describes the shrewd political wrangling used to block Yucca Mountain. This project, which is an essential part of a safe, secure, and clean energy future for the United States, is funded by the *electric utilities ratepayers* and *not the taxpayers*, and is required *by the law*.

—Donald Wall, Ph.D., is director of a research nuclear reactor facility in the Pacific Northwest, and teaches graduate courses in nuclear chemistry, reactor operations, and the fuel cycle. He created a course that prepares students to take the U.S. NRC Reactor Operator licensing examination

Nuclear Waste in Your Backyard is the most comprehensive treatise I've seen on nuclear power. Bob Ferguson provides clear evidence that other countries are moving ahead with their nuclear energy programs, while the U.S. continues to play political games. Ferguson's book is a must-read for Department of Energy officials, political leaders involved in making energy policy, and all of the Senators of states forced to indefinitely store nuclear waste in their backyards.

—Gary Petersen, Vice-President, Hanford Programs, Tri-Cities Development Council, Kennewick, Washington

When President Obama flouted the law by terminating the Yucca Mountain Project in 2009, Bob Ferguson stepped up as a private citizen to challenge him. As Bob's attorney, I had the rare chance to help ensure that the law is followed not just by ordinary citizens, but also by the President and his federal agencies.

—Barry Hartman, Partner, K&L Gates, Washington, D.C.

Nuclear Waste in Your Backyard builds on Bob Ferguson's previous book that reveals the real culprits responsible for the current dysfunction in U.S. efforts to dispose of nuclear waste—President Barack Obama and Senator Harry Reid. He likens the overarching strategy of the current administration to that of a stage magician, giving the American people "illusions in the form of truth." The basis for building the nation's first repository was at hand until Obama and Reid destroyed the Department of Energy's nuclear waste program and severely compromised the integrity of the Nuclear Regulatory Commission. This nation has the technical capability to build a safe repository. Now it needs the political will!

—Donald L. Vieth, Ph.D., former manager of the Yucca Mountain Project and U.S. representative to the International Atomic Energy Agency committee on Underground Disposal of Radioactive Waste. Vieth is principal author of the chapter on "Waste Repositories" for the *Mining Engineer's Handbook*.

Nuclear Waste in Your Backyard is the best one-volume analysis of the need for carbon-free energy (nuclear power) and a road map to achieve that goal by storage and disposal of high-level waste and used nuclear fuel. Bob Ferguson has done an outstanding job and performed a great service.

— Dick Hames, former general counsel for the Department of Energy and retired partner at Davis Wright Tremaine, Seattle, Washington

British Nuclear Fuels Limited, Board of Directors: Back row—left to right: Landy Langley, Lee Sillin, **Bob Ferguson** (author), Harold Bolter, Bill Wilkerson, Peter Green. Front row—left to right: **Elliott Richardson**, Neville Chamberlain, James Schlesinger.

Dedication

This book is dedicated to the memory of Elliott L. Richardson, who chose to resign his post as U.S. Attorney General for President Richard Nixon rather than carry out Nixon's dubious order to fire Special Prosecutor Archibald Cox and abolish his office. Cox was investigating Nixon's role in the "Watergate" scandal. Richardson had promised during his confirmation hearings before the Senate that he would assure the independence of the Special Prosecutor. In his letter of resignation, he told Nixon, "I could not in the light of these firm and repeated commitments carry out your direction." His legacy is an abiding example to all those who serve in public office that preserving individual integrity is more important than carrying out the orders of any president who does not respect the law.

I have always greatly admired Mr. Richardson's courage to do the right thing that night more than 40 years ago. His example embodies the enduring principles of our democracy and the importance of courageous individuals to serve as a bulwark against tyranny and corruption in our government.

I first met Elliott Richardson in 1990 when we were both being interviewed for positions on the Board of Directors of British Nuclear Fuels, Inc. During the ensuing years, I experienced first-hand his incredible integrity and brilliant wit.

Richardson was one of only two individuals to serve in four U.S. Cabinet positions: Secretary of Health, Education, and Welfare from

1970 to 1973; Secretary of Defense from January to May 1973; Attorney General from May to October 1973; and Secretary of Commerce from 1976 to 1977.

Our country needs more exemplary individuals like Richardson to re-establish public trust in our government, which has struggled under the weight of President Barack Obama's disrespect for the Constitution and the law.

Contents

Foreword

Bob Ferguson has written a book that describes in vivid detail the story of a lawsuit that he and two colleagues filed as private citizens against President Obama and Secretary of Energy Chu and won. The positive outcome of the lawsuit will benefit the Tri-Cities, which includes the Hanford Site where more high-level nuclear waste is stored than any other location in the United States.

Bob's previous book, *The Cost of Deceit and Delay*, focused in part on the challenges at the Hanford Site with legacy defense nuclear waste. This book addresses both defense waste and commercial spent nuclear fuel stored at nuclear power plants in 38 states across the nation. The Nuclear Waste Policy Act (NWPA) of 1982 required that the Department of Energy (DOE) take custody of this waste for storage at the Yucca Mountain deep geologic nuclear waste repository when it was licensed and constructed. Congress has voted to reaffirm this decision many times. However, President Obama and his administration chose to suddenly and illegally shut down the Yucca Mountain Project, which violated the NWPA. The Nuclear Regulatory Commission (NRC), which was required to perform a technical review of the Yucca Mountain license application, discontinued its review, which also violated the NWPA. These actions were the subject of Bob's lawsuit, which later was joined by the states of Washington and South Carolina, Aiken County, SC, Nye County, NV, and the National Association of Regulatory Utility Commissioners (NARUC). The court ruled in August 2013 that the president and the NRC did not have the authority to terminate the Yucca Mountain Project and ordered the NRC to resume the technical review of the license application. The court's written decision highlighted the constitutional requirements that Congress is responsible for making the laws and the president is responsible for implementing them—not ignoring or changing them and thus he should uphold the law as it is written. The NWPA has not been repealed or revised and is still the law of the land.

Nuclear Waste in Your Backyard addresses these actions to show how the president has created a political stalemate regarding the U.S. nuclear waste program, and then Bob proposes his recommendations for a path forward for the disposition of defense high-level waste as well as commercial spent fuel.

Bob has more than 50 years of career experience in the field of nuclear energy, both in the public and private sectors. He was in charge of building the experimental Fast Flux Test Facility reactor in the 1970s, and also Washington State's only commercial nuclear power plant, the Columbia Generating Station, which is still generating electricity for the region. He also founded a company that treats nuclear waste at Hanford and across the U.S., Canada, and Mexico. The book's co-author, Michele S. Gerber, is a scholar and historian with a long and distinguished career in World War II and Cold War history. She is the author of *On the Home Front: The Cold War Legacy of the Hanford Nuclear Site.*

While I don't agree with all of the assessments and recommendations in this book, it will be of interest to anyone wishing to learn more about nuclear waste in the United States, not only at Hanford, but in all the states currently obliged to store nuclear waste indefinitely in their backyards. Books like this play an important role on driving larger conversations about the federal government's defense waste cleanup responsibilities and the benefits of nuclear power.

Congressman Doc Hastings
Doc Hastings
Pasco, Washington
April 2014

Acknowledgments

In the dedication of this book to **Elliott L. Richardson**, I note that his integrity and courage in standing up to the U.S. president he served inspired me to make my own stand against President Barack Obama and a few members of his administration who have made a habit of ignoring laws passed by Congress for reasons of political self-interest.

I spent many thousands of dollars of my own money to mount a defense of the Nuclear Waste Policy Act (NWPA) against President Obama, Secretary of Energy Steven Chu, and the Nuclear Regulatory Commission. My lawsuit, which was joined by others directly affected by the shutdown of the Yucca Mountain Project, was finally decided in the court on August 13, 2013. These petitioners included the states of Washington and South Carolina; Aiken County, South Carolina; Nye County, Nevada; and the National Association of Regulatory Utility Commissioners (NARUC). Although we won our case, the stalemate for the U.S. nuclear waste program continues as of this writing. Therefore, I offer in this book a proposal with specific, easily implemented recommendations, which could put the U.S. back on track to solving the problem of nuclear waste storage and disposal. More important, the U.S. can then get back to expanding the use of nuclear energy to generate abundant clean energy without emitting the tons of carbon pollution derived from fossil fuel burning.

I want to express my appreciation to U.S. Representative **Richard "Doc" Hastings** (R-WA), not only for contributing the Foreword to this book, but for his unwavering support in Washington, D.C. for the Hanford Site and eastern Washington, through 10 terms as a member of the House of Representatives. I am honored to show my appreciation for his outstanding service as part of this book, especially because Doc has announced his retirement from politics at the end of his term in 2014. Doc's legacy includes the bipartisan Nuclear Cleanup Caucus he created in the House in 2000, which will continue to keep the focus on the Department of Energy's (DOE's) many environmental cleanup projects, including the Hanford Site. He has also served with distinction as chairman of the House Natural Resources Committee. Thanks also to **Jenny Gorski**, Doc's Chief of Staff, for her help with logistics and in getting timely approvals.

I have prevailed upon my friends and colleagues who are experts in the field of nuclear energy and nuclear waste management for a technical review of this book regarding its accuracy, fairness, and usefulness. In some cases, I cannot thank them by name because of their ongoing affiliations with some of the entities I criticize in the book. They have my gratitude and respect for the valuable assessments and recommendations they provided and my appreciation for their continued friendship.

There also are some experts in the nuclear field who provided essential technical analyses and critiques that I can thank by name—namely, **Dr. Don Wall**, Director of the Nuclear Radiation Center, Washington State University, Pullman, Washington; **Dr. Alan Waltar**, past president of the American Nuclear Society, and retired professor and head of the Department of Nuclear Engineering at Texas A&M University; **Dr. Donald Vieth**, who has been recognized for his more than 30 years of management and technical solutions to issues facing the U.S. Nuclear Weapons Complex including the selection of Yucca Mountain as the preferred site for the permanent disposal of high-level nuclear waste; and **Richard Hames**, former Chief Counsel for the DOE's Richland Operations Office at Hanford during the days of the Atomic Energy

Commission, the Energy Research & Development Agency, and the Department of Energy from 1970 to 1984; he also was a partner at Davis Wright Tremaine in Seattle, Washington, from 1984 to 2000.

I want to thank my good friends and colleagues **Bill Lampson** and **Gary Petersen**, who joined me as private citizens in filing the lawsuits against President Obama and Energy Secretary Chu for arbitrarily terminating the Yucca Mountain Project, and the Nuclear Regulatory Commission and its former chairman Gregory Jaczko for unlawfully stopping the Yucca Mountain license review. Bill is the CEO of Lampson International, a worldwide leader in the heavy lift and transport industry based in the Tri-Cities, Washington, with offices all over the world. Gary is vice-president for Hanford Programs at the Tri-City Development Council (TRIDEC), the economic development agency for the Tri-Cities, Washington.

I'd like to thank my co-author, **Michele S. Gerber**, for sharing her deep knowledge of the Manhattan Project, the Hanford Site, and nuclear waste history, as well as her research prowess and excellent writing. I am also grateful for her partnership as a spokesperson for the book and its recommendations for breaking the nuclear waste stalemate in this country. Thank you to our editor, **Sallie Ortiz**, who used her considerable expertise to keep us focused, grammatical, and stylistically correct, and who prepared this book for publication. Without the two of them, this book would not have been published.

In conclusion, I want to thank **Barry Hartman**, our attorney from K&L Gates, who represented us so brilliantly in our lawsuit, and **Tim Peckinpaugh**, the attorney at K&L Gates who recommended Barry for the job. Tim is a longtime friend who has represented the Tri-Cities' interests for many years. Being able to engage this prestigious law firm located in Washington, D.C., and having Barry as an attorney experienced in trying cases before the U.S. Court of Appeals for the District of Columbia Circuit, is the only way three private citizens could ever have had a voice in the outcome of this historic lawsuit. In appreciation, the attorneys who represented the state and county plaintiffs in our combined lawsuit are shown in the following photo, and I believe they would agree that Hartman made us, the three private citizen petitioners, true partners in this important case. AND WE WON!!!

The petitioners' representatives in the lawsuit are, from left to right: Ken Woodington, attorney for South Carolina; James Bradford Ramsey, attorney for the National Association of Regulatory Utility Commissioners (NARUC); Bob Ferguson, the author; Barry Hartman, attorney for Ferguson et al.; Andy Fitz, attorney for Washington State; Robert Anderson, attorney for Nye County, NV; Tom Gottshall, attorney for Aiken County, SC; Ross Shealy attorney for Aiken County, SC; and Mary Wilson, attorney for Washington State.

Acronyms and Abbreviations

AECL	Atomic Energy Limited of Canada
AFFF	Advanced Fuel Fabrication Facility
ANDRA	National Agency for Management of Nuclear Waste
AR4	IPCC's Fourth Assessment Report on Climate Change
AR5	IPCC's Fifth Assessment Report on Climate Change
ARIUS	Association for Regional and International Underground Storage
ASLB	Atomic Safety and Licensing Board
B&W	Babcock & Wilcox Company
BARC	Bhabha Atomic Research Centre
BNFL	British Nuclear Fuels Limited
BRC	Blue Ribbon Commission on America's Nuclear Future
BTEX	benzene, toluene, xylene, and ethylbenzene
BWR	boiling water reactor
CAB	Citizens Advisory Board
CANDU	Canada Deuterium Uranium
CB&I	Chicago Bridge & Iron Company
CEZ Group	České Energetické Závody Group
CIGEO	Centre Industrial de Stockage Geologique
CNNC	China National Nuclear Corporation
CO_2	Carbon dioxide

COGEMA	Compagnie Générale des Matières Nucléaires
CSA	Combined Statistical Area
CSS	carbon capture and storage
CVTR	Carolina-Virginia Tube Reactor
D&D	decontamination and decommissioning
DECC	Department of Energy and Climate Change
DOE	U.S. Department of Energy
DOJ	U.S. Department of Justice
EC	European Community
ECA	Energy Communities Alliance
EDF	Électricité de France
EIA	U.S. Energy Information Administration
EIS	Environmental Impact Statement
EM	Environmental Management
EnBW	Energie Baden-Württemberg AG
EPA	U.S. Environmental Protection Agency
EPRI	Electric Power Research Institute
ERDA	Energy Research and Development Administration
ERDO	European Repository Development Organisation
EU	European Union
FOIA	Freedom of Information Act
FY	fiscal year
GAO	Government Accountability Office
GDF-Suez Corp	Gaz de France-Suez Corporation
GDP	Gross Domestic Product
GEH	GE Hitachi Nuclear Energy
GNEP	Global Nuclear Energy Partnership
GNP	Gross National Product

HAB	Hanford Advisory Board
IAEA	International Atomic Energy Agency
IG	Inspector General
IHI	Ishikawajima-Harima Heavy Industries Co., Ltd.
INL	Idaho National Laboratory
IPCC	Intergovernmental Panel on Climate Change
IRS	Internal Revenue Service
ISFSI	licensed independent spent fuel storage installations
JAEA	Japan Atomic Energy Agency
JNFL	Japanese Nuclear Fuel Limited
KNNP	Kudankulam Nuclear Power Project
KURT	Korea Underground Research Tunnel
kWh	kilowatt hour
LINE	Leadership in Nuclear Energy
LLW	low-level waste
M&O	management and operations
METI	Ministry of Economy, Trade, and Industry
MHI	Mitsubishi Heavy Industries
MOX	mixed oxide
MRS	Monitored Retrievable Storage
MT	metric tons
MTU	metric tons uranium
MW	megawatt
MWe	megawatts electric
NAGRA	National Cooperative for the Disposal of Radioactive Waste
NARUC	National Association of Regulatory Utility Commissioners
NAS	National Academy of Sciences

NDAA	National Defense Authorization Act
NEA	Nuclear Energy Agency
NEI	Nuclear Energy Institute
NNSA	National Nuclear Security Administration
NRC	U.S. Nuclear Regulatory Commission
NRDC	Natural Resources Defense Council
NSA	National Security Administration
NTS	Nevada Test Site
NUMO	Nuclear Waste Management Organization
NWA	Nuclear Waste Administration
NWF	Nuclear Waste Fund
NWPA	Nuclear Waste Policy Act
OCRWM	Office of Civilian Radioactive Waste Management
OECD	Organization for Economic Cooperation and Development
OPEC	Organization of Petroleum Exporting Countries
PHMSA	Pipeline Hazardous Materials Safety Administration
PNNL	Pacific Northwest National Laboratory
ppm	parts per million
PWR	pressurized water reactor
RAWRA	Radioactive Waste Repository Authority
RPP	Rokkasho Reprocessing Plan
RWE	Rheinisch-Westfälisches Elektrizitätswerk AG
RWMC	Radioactive Waste Management Funding and Research Center
SAPIERR	Strategic Action Plan for Implementation of European Regional Repositories
SMR	small modular reactor
SNF	spent nuclear fuel

SRS	Savannah River Site
THORP	Thermal Oxide Reprocessing Plant
TPA	Tri-Party Agreement
TRIDEC	Tri-Cities Development Council
TRU	transuranic waste
TSPA	Total System Performance Assessment
UAE	United Arab Emirates
UK	United Kingdom
USGS	U.S. Geological Service
USSR	Union of Soviet Socialist Republics
WIPP	Waste Isolation Pilot Plant
WIR	Waste Incidental to Reprocessing
WMAC	Waste Management Area C
WNA	World Nuclear Association
WPPSS	Washington Public Power Supply System
WTP	Waste Treatment Plant
WVDP	West Valley Demonstration Project

Introduction

In the early morning of August 13, 2013, a phone call woke me out of a sound sleep. The voice on the telephone declared, "We won!"

"What?" Still half asleep, I recognized the voice as my attorney, Barry Hartman, from his office at K.L. Gates in Washington, D.C. He repeated the long-awaited good news that we had won the lawsuit that my two colleagues[1] and I had filed as private citizens against the Nuclear Regulatory Commission (NRC) for unlawfully stopping the technical review of the Yucca Mountain license application. The NRC's action was based on President Obama's unlawful order to shut down the Yucca Mountain nuclear waste repository. I was relieved that the court finally had ruled in favor of the law, and also reassured that the judicial branch of our government had defended ordinary citizens against the abuse of political power.

The U.S. Court of Appeals for the District of Columbia Circuit ruled that President Obama did not have the authority to terminate the Yucca Mountain Project and that the NRC had violated the law when its former chairman, Gregory Jaczko, stopped the technical review of the Yucca Mountain license application.

Unfortunately, much damage was done to the Yucca Mountain repository licensing process during the three years it has taken the court to hold the president and his administration accountable to the law. The Yucca Mountain project offices have been dismantled, the highly skilled workforce has been dismissed and scattered, and the U.S. nuclear waste program is in a political stalemate. Fifteen billion dollars spent on developing the site and researching and preparing the license application have been wasted and the repository project has been set back by decades. (This delay could be reversed if the project were restarted without constraints from funding or politics). The court's August 2013 decision to issue an order to the NRC to resume the technical review of the license application offers a glimmer of hope toward breaking the political nuclear waste stalemate.

In a two-to-one ruling, the three-judge panel of the D.C. Court of Appeals issued a "writ of mandamus" to the NRC in response to the suit we filed in July 2011. The writ directs the NRC to follow the law and resume the licensing process.[2]

Authority of the U.S. Constitution

The U.S. Department of Energy's (DOE's) action to withdraw its license application from the NRC was unlawful because it violated the Nuclear Waste Policy Act (NWPA), a law enacted by Congress and signed by two presidents—first in 1982 and again in 1987 in amended form. The NWPA expressly directs the DOE to submit a license to construct a nuclear waste repository at Yucca Mountain in Nevada, and requires the NRC to perform a technical review of the application within three years to make a recommendation to Congress as to whether or not the site is safe and suitable for licensing.

Under our Constitution, which has been governing the United States for 227 years, the founding fathers designed a democratic government with three branches to serve as a bulwark against corruption: an executive branch, a legislative branch, and a judicial branch.

The American people elect a president as the head of the executive branch. The president swears an oath to the country when he takes office to *"take Care that the Laws be faithfully executed."* These words are a direct quote from Article II, Section 3, of the U.S. Constitution.[3]

The people elect Representatives and Senators to serve in Congress as the legislative branch—to write and enact the laws by which we all live. Only Congress has the power to change or repeal laws.

Judges—who serve in the judicial branch of the federal government—are not elected because they must be impartial, beholden only to the law and not swayed by elections and politics.

The separation of powers among the three branches safeguards our democratic government by ensuring that neither the legislative nor the executive branch has all the power. A further safeguard ensures that judges will arbitrate when either branch disregards the law or the Constitution.

When a duly elected Congress passes a law, the president is not free to disregard it, even if he disagrees with it. Our whole system of governance—our democracy—would fall apart if presidents are allowed to ignore laws that are not convenient to their political agendas. Without the boundaries among the three branches of government, democracy could not exist. The D.C. Court of Appeals' ruling in our case successfully demonstrated that the safeguards provided by the separation of the branches are working, even during the apparent dysfunction in politics. The court ruled that the NRC, acting at the president's direction, was not allowed to disregard the law.

Regardless of the ruling in our legal case admonishing the president for disregarding the law, President Obama has since gained a reputation for making decisions without the benefit of consulting the other two branches of government. His actions in this regard have become the subject of political cartoons such as the clever one shown here, which was published in syndicated newspapers across the country in 2014.

By permission of Chip Bok and Creators Syndicate, Inc.

In President Obama's 2014 State of the Union address, he bragged that he would continue to act with or without Congress: "Wherever and whenever I can take steps without legislation to expand opportunity for more American families, that's what I'm going to do," he stated. He added, "I'll act on my own to slash bureaucracy and streamline the permitting process for key projects," and encouraged other elected officials to follow his lead, saying to "every mayor, governor, state legislator in America, I say, you don't have to wait for Congress to act."[4]

When I decided to sue the president, it wasn't on a whim or because I prejudged Yucca Mountain to be a safe place for a nuclear waste repository. I did it because I believed that an important Constitutional principle was at stake and Congress had not reacted as it should have to stop the president and some in his administration from violating the NWPA. The consequence of allowing a president or a federal agency to ignore the law and get away with it—even once—is to conclude that the rule of law does not exist in our country. Granted, there was much at stake for my state and 37 others forced to store nuclear waste indefinitely if the president was allowed to order the DOE and the NRC to terminate the Yucca Mountain Project and derail the entire nuclear waste program. If the technical review of the Yucca Mountain license application had been allowed to be completed as the law dictated, we would know once and for all whether the NRC considered it a safe and suitable site for nuclear waste disposal.

In the ruling of our case on August 13, 2013, the D.C. Court of Appeals Circuit Judge Brett Kavanaugh's statement thoroughly vindicated and supported our reasons for filing the lawsuit. Kavanaugh wrote:

> "This case raises significant questions about the scope of the Executive's authority to disregard federal statutes… Our [judicial]…task is to ensure…that agencies comply with the law as it has been set by Congress. Here, the Nuclear Regulatory Commission has continued to violate the law governing the Yucca Mountain licensing process…As things stand, therefore, the Commission is simply flouting the law. In light of the constitutional respect owed to Congress…we now grant the petition for writ of mandamus against the Nuclear Regulatory Commission."

> "Our analysis begins with settled, bedrock principles of constitutional law… the President may not decline to follow a statutory mandate or prohibition simply because of policy objections… Those basic constitutional principles apply to the President and subordinate executive agencies… [including] agencies such as the Nuclear Regulatory Commission…This case has serious implications for our constitutional structure. It is no overstatement to say that our constitutional system of separation of powers would be significantly altered if we were to allow executive and independent agencies to disregard federal law in the manner asserted in this case by the Nuclear Regulatory Commission. Our decision today

rests on the constitutional authority of Congress, and the respect that the Executive and the Judiciary properly owe to Congress in the circumstances here."[5]

How We Got Here: The National Plan to Deal with Nuclear Waste

My involvement with nuclear waste policy began in February 1982, when I was invited to attend a meeting at the White House along with other energy utility and industry leaders. The meeting was organized by President Ronald Reagan's Science Advisor, George Keyworth, to gather our ideas for revitalizing the nuclear industry.[6] The meeting was a follow-up to President Reagan's policy statement on October 8, 1981, in which he attempted to revitalize the nuclear industry. Former President Carter had profoundly damaged the industry when he stopped all reprocessing of spent nuclear fuel due to his proliferation concerns. Reagan directed his Secretary of Energy to cooperate with industry and state governments to proceed swiftly to determine a method of retrievably storing spent nuclear fuel, in case it later became economically feasible to reprocess it, and permanently disposing of defense high-level radioactive waste. There was general consensus in our discussions that the three major problems facing the nuclear industry were financing and financial investment risk, regulatory and licensing reform, and nuclear waste disposal—problems that remain today. In that meeting, we urged President Reagan to act rather than make pronouncements.

Based in part on our meeting, Keyworth drafted a presidential message to Congress encouraging it to pass the pending legislation of the NWPA.[7] Reagan's message, which the nuclear industry leaders supported, favored a bill that provided relief for the backlog of spent fuel stored at operating reactors by designating a place for temporary storage while siting a permanent disposal repository, and afforded states the opportunity to participate in siting the repository.

In late 1982, the Congress passed the NWPA, establishing a national policy for managing, storing, and disposing of the byproducts of the nuclear fuel cycle—high-level radioactive waste and spent nuclear fuel.[8] These materials are highly radioactive and need to be kept isolated from the public and the environment. Since 1957, when the first commercial nuclear power reactor began operating at Shippingport, Pennsylvania, the highly radioactive waste from these plants has been stored on the sites where it was generated.[9] By the early 1980s, Congress, representing the majority opinion of Americans, believed that safer, centralized repositories should be designed and built to store spent nuclear fuel and dispose of high-level nuclear wastes and byproducts. The repositories, and some interim retrievable storage sites, would be paid for by imposing a tax on ratepayers who used electricity generated by nuclear plants. The tax was small—$0.001 per kilowatt hour (kWh)—but it was significant because it was the *first* time in our country's history that consumers had been taxed to manage the wastes and byproducts generated by a specific energy source. In other words, the coal and oil industries are not taxed to manage their waste streams, nor are the consumers who burn their products. Yet, waste from burning these fossil fuels is freely discharged to the atmosphere, causing immeasurable harm.

President Reagan, in signing the NWPA into law on January 1983, succinctly summarized its purpose:

> "The Nuclear Waste Policy Act...provides the long overdue assurance that we now have a safe and effective solution to the nuclear waste problem. It's an important step in the pursuit of the peaceful uses of atomic energy...This act—the culmination of 25 years of legislative effort—clears the barrier that has stood in the way of development of this vital energy resource. It allows the Federal Government to fulfill its responsibilities concerning nuclear waste in a timely

and responsible manner… The step we're taking today
should demonstrate to the public that the challenge of
coping with nuclear waste can and will be met."[10]

The NWPA directed the DOE to select several potential sites for geologic repositories to place the waste, and then determine the most suitable three sites for further study. Already, $1.1 billion had been spent studying nine potential sites.[11] With study costs rising, and the official preliminary DOE studies showing Yucca Mountain in Nevada to be the most promising site,[12] Congress amended the law in 1987, designating Yucca Mountain to be studied exclusively for licensing as the national repository.[13] Most members of Congress were satisfied with this amendment, except the freshman Democrat Senator Harry Reid of Nevada. Senator Reid, a former chairman of the Nevada Gaming Commission and two-term representative from urban Las Vegas, evidently was worried that a nuclear waste repository would dampen Nevada's vital tourist and gaming industries. He dubbed the 1987 amendment of the NWPA as the "Screw Nevada Bill," and portrayed the federal government as forcing the repository on an unwilling state. This position was untruthful, however, since Nye County (home to the Nevada Test Site and Yucca Mountain) had supported locating the repository there in 1974 when the federal government conducted its first environmental impact statement (EIS) on managing high-level nuclear waste, and in 1975, the Nevada legislature passed a resolution supporting the same.[14] Since that time, support and opposition regarding siting nuclear waste facilities in Nevada have waxed and waned, often dominated by other political agendas and alliances. But Reid has made it his life's work to "kill" the Yucca Mountain Repository Project.

By 2000, the Yucca Mountain Project had been established and was charging ahead with more than 900 employees and an annual budget of approximately $350 million. The science and the geology looked sound, and Senator Reid, despite having three successful Senatorial elections behind him, was worried that he might lose over the repository war, an issue on which he had staked much of his reputation. In the view of much of the public, a massive nuclear accident at Chernobyl in Ukraine in 1986, and a vastly smaller earlier accident at Three-Mile Island, Pennsylvania, in 1979, had increased public fears of nuclear power, but also increased the need and demand for a safe national repository.

In the presidential election year of 2000, Reid worried that if Republican George Bush was elected, he would likely push ahead with repository construction as well as new nuclear plants. Reid sought an ally who could fight with him against the Yucca Mountain Project. He needed a Nevada outsider, so the fight wouldn't look parochial, and he needed someone with the scientific credentials that he did not possess. A fateful meeting that year with Gregory Jaczko, a newly minted Ph.D. in theoretical particle physics, resulted in Jaczko going to work on Reid's staff the same month George Bush was sworn into office in January 2001.

The Yucca Mountain Project Undone

Jaczko and Reid mounted an aggressive effort to discredit the Yucca Mountain Project through scientific objections.[15] The story of the actions they took, Reid's strategic appointment of Jaczko to the NRC in 2006, Jaczko's ascent to NRC chairmanship in 2009, and his subsequent resignation in disgrace in 2012 is told in later chapters of this book. In 2008, Barack Obama was elected president of the United States in a stunning victory notable for, among other reasons, his freshman status in the Senate. His victory was a long-shot, the run of an outsider against the much more senior and well-connected potential candidates. To get elected, he had to ally himself with powerful Washington insiders— among them Senate Minority Whip Harry Reid. It's clear to me and others that Obama and Reid cut a deal to provide political support for each other. The media had widely reported that Obama vowed to help Reid kill the Yucca Mountain Project. Soon after his election, President Obama began doing just that. The project was defunded and the technical license review by the NRC was cancelled.

Our Lawsuits and Why They Matter

Soon after the president terminated the Yucca Mountain Project, I sent a letter through my attorney to the president urging him to reconsider his decision. We pointed to the long years of effort, compromise, expense, and consensus-building that had already been devoted to the project. We emphasized the need for nuclear power as part of the nation's diversified energy portfolio in an era of unreliable foreign energy sources—issues that the president had stressed in his campaign. Most important, we told him that the law did not allow him to terminate the project.

In February 2010, when it became clear that the president was not going to honor us with a reply, we filed suit against him and Energy Secretary Steven Chu for violating the NWPA.

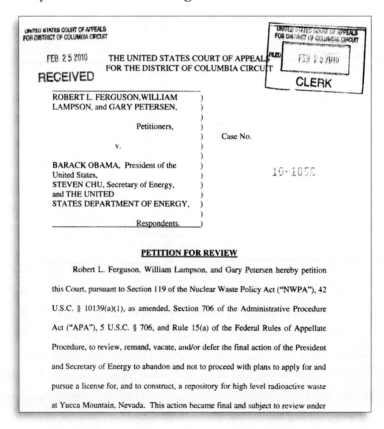

UNITED STATES COURT OF APPEALS
FOR DISTRICT OF COLUMBIA CIRCUIT

UNITED STATES COURT OF APPEALS
FOR DISTRICT OF COLUMBIA CIRCUIT

FEB 2 5 2010   THE UNITED STATES COURT OF APPEALS
FOR THE DISTRICT OF COLUMBIA CIRCUIT

RECEIVED

FILED

FEB 2 5 2010

CLERK

ROBERT L. FERGUSON, WILLIAM   )
LAMPSON, and GARY PETERSEN,   )
)
                 Petitioners,   )
)   Case No.
            v.   )
)
BARACK OBAMA, President of the   )
United States,   )
STEVEN CHU, Secretary of Energy,   )   10-1052
and THE UNITED   )
STATES DEPARTMENT OF ENERGY,   )
)
_____Respondents._____)

PETITION FOR REVIEW

Robert L. Ferguson, William Lampson, and Gary Petersen hereby petition

this Court, pursuant to Section 119 of the Nuclear Waste Policy Act ("NWPA"), 42

U.S.C. § 10139(a)(1), as amended, Section 706 of the Administrative Procedure

Act ("APA"), 5 U.S.C. § 706, and Rule 15(a) of the Federal Rules of Appellate

Procedure, to review, remand, vacate, and/or defer the final action of the President

and Secretary of Energy to abandon and not to proceed with plans to apply for and

pursue a license for, and to construct, a repository for high level radioactive waste

at Yucca Mountain, Nevada. This action became final and subject to review under

At nearly the same time, Aiken County, South Carolina, and the state of South Carolina filed a similar suit against the president, the DOE, and the NRC. Aiken County is home to the second largest collection of nuclear waste in the U.S., at the Savannah River Site, a nuclear defense production facility that has been generating waste for 60 years. Washington State also filed, as it stores the largest collection of nuclear waste in the western hemisphere at the 70-year old Hanford Site. The U.S. Court of Appeals for the District of Columbia Circuit combined our lawsuits, and the National Association of Regulatory Utility Commissioners (NARUC) joined the combined suit as an intervener. We began oral arguments in March 2011.

Case: 10-1050   Document: 1295518   Filed: 02/28/2011   Page: 1

SCHEDULED FOR ORAL ARGUMENT ON MARCH 22, 2011

NO. 10-1050, 10-1052, 10-1069, 10-1082 *Consolidated*

**UNITED STATES COURT OF APPEALS
FOR THE DISTRICT OF COLUMBIA CIRCUIT**

No. 10-1050

IN RE AIKEN COUNTY, Petitioner

No. 10-1052

ROBERT L. FERGUSON, *et al.*, Petitioners,

v.

BARACK OBAMA, President of the United States, *et al.*, Respondents.

No. 10-1069

STATE OF SOUTH CAROLINA, Petitioner,

v.

UNITED STATES DEPARTMENT OF ENERGY, *et al.*, Respondents.

No. 10-1082

STATE OF WASHINGTON, Petitioner,

v.

UNITED STATES DEPARTMENT OF ENERGY, *et al.*, Respondents.

On Petitions for Review and for Other Relief With Respect to Decisions of the President, the Secretary of Energy, the Deparment of Energy, and the Nuclear Regulatory Commission

---

**Amended Motion of Petitioners, Aiken County, Robert L. Ferguson,
William Lampson, Gary Petersen, State of South Carolina,
State of Washington, and Intervenor-Petitioner,
National Association of Regulatory Utility Commissioners
for Consideration of Format for Oral Argument**

This story is relevant because it shows how private citizens and states can make a difference. Details of our lawsuit, the arguments, the obstacles, and our eventual victory are covered in this book. The themes of this story are four-fold. Foremost, it is about the importance of upholding the constitutional principle of the separation of powers, the heart of our democracy, which I believe has been threatened by President Obama and Senator Reid's determined disregard for the NWPA. I felt a great responsibility to act when our country's founding principles were threatened. Moreover, that threat involved nuclear waste issues, in which I have been deeply involved during my career in nuclear energy spanning more than 50 years.

Many times, presidents have been sued by coalitions and groups, but rarely by private citizens. Rarer still are the times that private citizens have prevailed against a president. The last time was when Paula Jones, an Arkansas state employee, sued President Bill Clinton for sexual harassment in 1994. Jones won her case, and then won an out-of-court settlement.[16] President Clinton first claimed he was immune from prosecution because he was the president, and fighting a lawsuit would interfere with his duties. That argument was struck down and the case was allowed to go forward, because the court ruled that *no one*—not even the president—can break the law with impunity,[17] which is where the similarity with this case and mine begins and ends.

Second, our lawsuit spoke to not only constitutional principles, but to my belief in the value of nuclear energy and nuclear safety to our national security and the global transition to generating carbon-free energy.

Third, much of the rest of the developed and developing world is leaving the United States behind in essentially every aspect of nuclear technology—building new reactors, testing advanced reactor concepts, and managing and disposing of nuclear waste. The United States is not doing so, and in fact the number of operating nuclear energy plants is decreasing. The decline of nuclear energy in this country is dangerous to U.S. energy security and an incredible shame for this nation that ushered in the nuclear age 70 years ago and astounded the world with the brilliance and speed of its scientific breakthroughs.

Fourth, I intend to point out that President Obama has, and continues to, violate or change laws, practices, and procedures in ways that suit his political agenda without following the accepted processes of government.

As a private citizen, my purpose in suing the president was to defend the rule of law as it impacts the future of nuclear energy in the United States. That principle also is a common thread that runs throughout this book.

What You Will Learn in This Book

Today, extremely large collections of nuclear high-level waste and spent nuclear fuel sit at reactor sites next to large, densely populated American cities such as Chicago, New York, Boston, Washington, D.C., Baltimore, Philadelphia, and others, and along major national waterways including the Mississippi and Columbia Rivers, the Chesapeake Bay, the Great Lakes, and the Atlantic and Pacific Coasts. These collections are not imminently unsafe today, but the point is that they could be stored and/or disposed of in much safer, more cost-effective, and efficient ways in one or more centralized national repositories.

Chapter 1 discusses the nuclear waste collections state-by-state, not to scare people, but to inform and make them aware of the existence of these collections, where they are located, and why they are still there. The collections don't immediately endanger us today, but they can't be left in place forever because nuclear waste storage conditions degrade over time.

Chapter 2 describes the powerful renaissance in nuclear development that is happening in much of the rest of the developed and developing world, especially among nations who are and will be America's competitors in the foreseeable future. China, India, and Russia, as well as many smaller nations, are building new nuclear reactors at a breathtaking pace, and expanding their usable, base load energy production at profound rates. Worse yet for America, in terms of safe practices and safety assurances for their populations, competitors of the United States are finding ways to either store their spent fuel or dispose of the final waste products in temporary or permanent consolidated storage facilities. These nations are mustering the political will and the technology to dispose of their wastes, or store them for long periods at consolidated centers, away from their cities, rivers, and people.

Chapter 3 details the shoddy practices and blatant (though backdoor) deals made by President Obama and Senator Reid in casting aside the NWPA and blocking the Yucca Mountain Project.

Chapter 4 discusses the cost that our nation and the world is paying for our failure to come to grips with high-level waste and spent nuclear fuel and a transition toward an all-electric economy. The costs are enormous and threaten our nation's national and energy security.

Chapter 5 informs the interested public about the issues at stake while our national nuclear waste program is in political stalemate. In this chapter, I recommend a plan to move our nation forward to an energy-secure future that can make us all feel safe. I suggest several steps of a path forward that this nation can take almost immediately by making a few simple amendments to the existing law, the NWPA, that will re-energize plans to deal with our nuclear high-level waste and spent nuclear fuel. Chapter 5 also provides an outline of the nation's nuclear waste dilemma and how we reached this point, showing the proposals before Congress in 2014 that may work in conjunction with NWPA amendments.

This book is offered as a sequel to my 2012 book entitled *The Cost of Deceit and Delay: Obama and Reid's Scheme to Kill Yucca Mountain Wastes $Billions*.

## Chapter 1

The Nuclear Waste in Our Own Backyards

It is unlikely that we can meet our aggressive climate goals if we eliminate nuclear power from the table. However, there is no future for expanded nuclear without first addressing four key issues: public right-to-know, security of nuclear fuel and waste, waste storage, and proliferation.—President Barack Obama, *Campaign '08 Plan to Make America a Global Energy Leader*[18]

National Interest Harmed by Allowing Nuclear Power to Languish

In this quotation, President Obama demonstrated that he clearly understood the essential role of nuclear energy in mitigating global climate change and that the expansion of nuclear energy in the United States depended on a solution to the nuclear waste issue. Regardless, one of his first actions as president was to terminate the

Yucca Mountain nuclear waste repository and disband the existing nuclear waste program. He later ignored the warning from his own Blue Ribbon Commission on America's Nuclear Future (BRC) that "this nation's failure to come to grips with the nuclear waste issue has already proved damaging and costly. It will be even more damaging and more costly the longer it continues: *damaging for prospects to maintaining a potentially important energy supply option for the future, damaging to state-federal relations and public confidence in the federal government's competence, and damaging to America's standing in the world—not only as a source of nuclear technology and policy expertise but as a leader on global issues of nuclear safety, non-proliferation, and security.*"[19]

New nuclear power plants are needed in the United States to maintain the nation's most robust, non-carbon base load energy supply, but new plants won't be built in any significant numbers until the nuclear waste issue is resolved. There are 100 operating nuclear reactors in the United States as of December 2013; together, they generate approximately 19 percent of the total electricity used in this country. More important, that amount represents 69–70 percent of our nation's carbon-free energy.[20]

Extent of the U.S. Burden

The United States holds *the largest collection of spent nuclear fuel in the world*—approximately 69,700 metric tons (MT).[21] This fuel is from commercial nuclear power plants and does not include the small amounts of additional fuel used in government research reactors, which have been returned to government-owned sites. The U.S. nuclear industry adds to the total amount of commercial spent fuel at the rate of about 2,000 to 2,400 MT annually. As of December 2013, the fuel is stored at 122 different nuclear power plants in 38 states, including several plants within 50 miles of large population centers and major rivers.[22]

The total amount of spent nuclear fuel includes nearly 3,000 MT stored at 11 decommissioned power plants in nine states.[23] The BRC, empaneled by President Obama in 2010, calls the waste at these 11 decommissioned sites "high-priority waste…[because] the continued presence of spent fuel at shutdown reactor sites is problematic and costly. Most obviously, it prevents these shutdown sites from being reclaimed for economically productive or otherwise desirable uses that would benefit the surrounding communities…the cost attributable to storing spent fuel at plant sites increases dramatically once the reactor is shut down. Since the cost of loading fuel into dry storage casks has generally already been incurred at this point, continued storage involves little activity other than site security and monitoring. At an operating nuclear plant, security is already in place and only incremental effort is required to include the…[spent nuclear fuel storage facility] within the plant's security umbrella. The same is true for the personnel needed to monitor the status of the fuel and perform any routine maintenance. When the rest of the site is shut down, however, these structures, systems, equipment, and people are still needed to tend the spent fuel, and the cost is substantial. Recent studies find that the operation and maintenance costs for spent fuel storage at shutdown sites range from $4.5 million to $8 million per year, compared to an incremental $1 million per year or less when the reactor is still in operation… [Additionally], most of these shutdown reactor sites no longer have the capability to remove spent fuel from storage canisters for inspection if long-term degradation problems emerge that might affect the ability to transport the canisters."[24]

A Nuclear Energy Institute (NEI) map shows the location and amount of spent nuclear fuel stored by state.[25] Table 1 lists all of the individual U.S. nuclear power plants, operating and shutdown, that store spent nuclear fuel.[26]

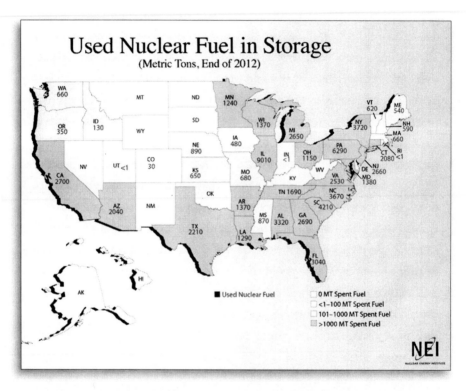

Spent Nuclear Fuel (also referred to as Used Nuclear Fuel) in Storage in the United States (Nuclear Energy Institute, December 2013)

Table 1. Spent Nuclear Fuel Stored at Operating and Shutdown Commercial U.S. Power Plants and Research Reactors, July 2013 (information derived from the Nuclear Energy Institute)

#	States	Nuclear Power Plants and Research Reactors in Operation	Shutdown Nuclear Power Plants	Spent Nuclear Fuel Stored in metric tons uranium (MTU)
1	Alabama	Browns Ferry 1 Browns Ferry 2 Browns Ferry 3 Joseph M. Farley 1 Joseph M. Farley 2		3320
2	Arizona	Palo Verde 1 Palo Verde 2 Palo Verde 3		2040
3	Arkansas	Arkansas Nuclear One Unit 1 Arkansas Nuclear One Unit 2		1370
4	California	Diablo Canyon 1 Diablo Canyon 2	Humboldt Bay Rancho Seco San Onofre 1 San Onofre 2 San Onofre 3	2970
5	Colorado		Fort St. Vrain	30

#	States	Nuclear Power Plants and Research Reactors in Operation	Shutdown Nuclear Power Plants	Spent Nuclear Fuel Stored in metric tons uranium (MTU)
6	**Connecticut**	Millstone 2 Millstone 3	Haddam Neck Millstone 1	2080
7	**Florida**	St. Lucie 1 St. Lucie 2 Turkey Point 3 Turkey Point 4	Crystal River 3	3040
8	**Georgia**	Edwin I. Hatch 1 Edwin I. Hatch 2 Vogtle 1 Vogtle 2		2690
9	**Idaho***			130
10	**Illinois**	Braidwood 1 Braidwood 2 Byron 1 Byron 2 Clinton Dresden 2 Dresden 3 La Salle 1 La Salle 2 Quad Cities 1 Quad Cities 2	Dresden 1 Zion 1 Zion 2	9010
11	**Indiana**	Research reactor at Purdue University		<1
12	**Iowa**	Duane Arnold		480

#	States	Nuclear Power Plants and Research Reactors in Operation	Shutdown Nuclear Power Plants	Spent Nuclear Fuel Stored in metric tons uranium (MTU)
13	**Kansas**	Wolf Creek 1		650
14	**Louisiana**	River Bend 1 Waterford 3		1290
15	**Maine**		Maine Yankee	540
16	**Maryland**	Calvert Cliffs 1 Calvert Cliffs 2		1380
17	**Massachusetts**	Pilgrim 1	Yankee Rowe	660
18	**Michigan**	Cook 1 Cook 2 Fermi 2 Palisades	Big Rock Point Fermi 1	2650
19	**Minnesota**	Monticello Prairie Island 1 Prairie Island 2		1240
20	**Mississippi**	Grand Gulf 1		870
21	**Missouri**	Callaway		680
22	**Nebraska**	Cooper Fort Calhoun		890
23	**New Hampshire**	Seabrook 1		590

#	States	Nuclear Power Plants and Research Reactors in Operation	Shutdown Nuclear Power Plants	Spent Nuclear Fuel Stored in metric tons uranium (MTU)
24	**New Jersey**	Hope Creek 1 Oyster Creek 1 Salem 1 Salem 2		2660
25	**New York**	Ginna Indian Point 2 Indian Point 3 J.A. Fitzpatrick Nine Mile Point 1 Nine Mile Point 2	Indian Point 1	3720
26	**North Carolina**	Brunswick 1 Brunswick 2 McGuire 1 McGuire 2 Shearon Harris 1		3670
27	**Ohio**	Davis Besse Perry 1		1150
28	**Oregon**		Trojan	350

#	States	Nuclear Power Plants and Research Reactors in Operation	Shutdown Nuclear Power Plants	Spent Nuclear Fuel Stored in metric tons uranium (MTU)
29	**Pennsylvania**	Beaver Valley 1 Beaver Valley 2 Limerick 1 Limerick 2 Peach Bottom 2 Peach Bottom 3 Susquehanna 1 Susquehanna 2 Three-Mile Island 1	Peach Bottom 1 Three-Mile Island 2	6290
30	**Rhode Island**	Research reactor at the University of Rhode Island		<1
31	**South Carolina**	Catawba 1 Catawba 2 H.B. Robinson 2 Oconee 1 Oconee 2 Oconee 3 V.C. Summer		4210
32	**Tennessee**	Sequoyah 1 Sequoyah 2 Watts Bar 1		1690

#	States	Nuclear Power Plants and Research Reactors in Operation	Shutdown Nuclear Power Plants	Spent Nuclear Fuel Stored in metric tons uranium (MTU)
33	**Texas**	Comanche Peak 1 Comanche Peak 2 South Texas Project 1 South Texas Project 2		2210
34	**Utah**	Research reactor at the University of Utah		<1
35	**Vermont**	Vermont Yankee 1		620
36	**Virginia**	North Anna 1 North Anna 2 Surry 1 Surry 2		2530
37	**Washington**	Columbia Generating Station		660
38	**Wisconsin**	Point Beach 1 Point Beach 2	Kewaunee LaCrosse	1370
	Total	**103**	**22****	**69,723*****

*Idaho National Laboratory stores 130 MTU of spent nuclear fuel and nuclear waste from the shutdown Three-Mile Island 2 plant.

**Spent nuclear fuel is stored at 19 of the 22 shutdown plants (see Table 2).

***Total MTUs include spent fuel stored at both operating and shutdown commercial nuclear power plants and university research reactors.

Table 2 shows the quantities and locations of stranded spent fuel. The last column in the table lists the senators who should be concerned about this spent fuel indefinitely stored and stranded in their states as a result of President Obama's legacy of political stalemate in the U.S. nuclear waste program.

Table 2. Stranded Spent Nuclear Fuel in Storage at Shutdown Commercial U.S. Reactor Sites

#	State	Shutdown Reactor	Shutdown Date	Storage Type	Spent Fuel Stored Onsite (MTUs)	Contact Senators www.senate.gov/general/ contact_information/ senators_cfm.cfm
1	CA	Humboldt Bay Rancho Seco	1976 1989	Dry Cask Dry Cask	31 228	Barbara Boxer (D) Diane Feinstein (D)
2	CO	Fort St. Vrain	1989	Dry Cask	25	Michael F. Bennet (D) Mark Udall (D)
3	CT	Haddam Neck	1996	Dry Cask	456	Richard Blumenthal (D) Christopher Murphy (D)
4	IL	Zion 1 Zion 2	1997 1996	Pool Pool	Combined pools - 1,019	Richard J. Durbin (D) Mark Kirk (R)
5	MA	Yankee Rowe	1991	Dry Cask	122	Susan M. Collins (R) Angus S. King, Jr. (I)
6	ME	Maine Yankee	1997	Dry Cask	542	Edward J. Markey (D) Elizabeth Warren (D)

#	State	Shutdown Reactor	Shutdown Date	Storage Type	Spent Fuel Stored Onsite (MTUs)	Contact Senators www.senate.gov/general/ contact_information/ senators_cfm.cfm
7	MI	Big Rock Point	1997	Dry Cask	70	Carl Levin (D) Debbie Stabenow (D)
8	OR	Trojan	1992	Dry Cask	345	Ron Wyden (D) Jeff Merkley (D)
9	WI	LaCrosse	1987	Pool	38	Tammy Baldwin (D) Ron Johnson (R)
Total Sites	11		Total MTUs		2,876	

Our U.S. Nuclear Power Plants Are Aging

Our nuclear power plants are getting old. As of 2013, the two oldest were 44 years old, and the average age of the rest of the U.S. reactors was 32.[27] To put that into the perspective of world events, 32 years ago in 1981, the U.S. space shuttle *Columbia* took its maiden voyage, Harrison Ford was introduced to the big screen as Indiana Jones in the *Raiders of the Lost Ark*, and Prince Charles of England married Lady Diana Spencer. Today, the space shuttle program is retired, Harrison Ford can collect Social Security, and Prince Charles is a grandpa. The median age of the U.S. population is 37 years, meaning that more than half of Americans alive today are younger than our average reactors. So is it any wonder that there is little public understanding of the nuclear waste issue?

Most U.S. nuclear plants originally were licensed for a 40-year period, and 73 of them have received 20-year license extensions. Fourteen more have filed for license extensions, and 15 more are expected to file through 2018. Even the newest U.S. reactor, Watts Bar Unit 1 in Tennessee, will need to file for a license extension by 2035. In 2014, only five nuclear reactors are under active construction in the United States[28]—Vogtle Units 3 and 4 in Georgia, Summer Station Units 2 and 3 in South Carolina, and Watts Bar Unit 2 in Tennessee.[29] Construction of Watts Bar Unit 2 was suspended in 1985 by its owner, the Tennessee Valley Authority, but it was reactivated in 2007.[30]

Waste Confidence Rulings

Aside from the inefficiency inherent in any aging machine and its instruments, and the loss of national prestige as a leader in new nuclear technology development, older nuclear plants are a problem for the United States because we can't keep re-licensing them forever. The Nuclear Regulatory Commission's (NRC's) official policy—the "Waste Confidence Decision" (10 CFR 51.23)—pertains to the safety of storing spent nuclear fuel in water pools or dry casks at nuclear plant sites until a repository is licensed and ready to receive it.[31] To license new nuclear power plants or relicense existing plants, the federal government is required to demonstrate that it can fulfill its waste disposal obligations under the Nuclear Waste Policy Act (NWPA). In 2010, in response to U.S. Department of Energy's (DOE's) shutdown of the Yucca Mountain Project, the NRC revised the Nuclear Waste Confidence Decision to reflect the uncertainty about "when" a nuclear waste repository might become available. The revision also contained a Temporary Storage Rule stating that spent nuclear fuel could be stored at power plants during the life of the plant and for up to 60 years after the plants were shut down. The rule also contended that a permanent repository would be ready to handle such wastes "when necessary."

The 2010 revision was challenged in federal court, and in June 2012, the U.S. Court of Appeals for the District of Columbia Circuit vacated both the Waste Confidence Decision and the Temporary Storage Rule, finding that "the NRC had acted hastily in concluding that spent fuel can be stored safely at nuclear plants for the next century or so in the absence of a permanent repository, and it must consider what will happen if no repository is ever established."[32] The court stated that the possibility that spent fuel could be stored at reactor sites "on a permanent basis" was unacceptable.[33] As a result of this ruling, the NRC now must study and document the implications of not having a repository.

The NRC's stated policy is that it "would not continue to license reactors if it did not have reasonable confidence that the wastes can and will in due course be disposed of safely."[34] In August 2012, the NRC issued a Memorandum and Order directing its staff not to "issue licenses dependent upon the Waste Confidence Decision or Temporary Storage Rule until the court's remand is appropriately addressed." This determination extends specifically to issuing final licenses and is not intended to stop licensing reviews or proceedings.[35]

The NRC has a "timely renewal doctrine" that will allow the power plants to operate while the commission deliberates.[36] Therefore, if the United States is to maintain—let alone grow—its supply of carbon-free energy from nuclear power, it must site an interim consolidated storage facility and/or or a permanent repository for spent nuclear fuel and high-level nuclear waste.

Wet Versus Dry Spent Fuel Storage

All nuclear power plants must cool freshly discharged spent nuclear fuel in "pools" for several years before the fuel rods can be moved to "dry cask" storage. The pools are made of reinforced concrete several feet thick, with steel liners. The water is typically about 40 feet deep and serves to shield the radiation and cool the rods. Fuel is usually cooled at least five years in the pool before it can be transferred to cask storage, although the NRC has authorized transfer as early as three years. The industry norm is about 10 years; but in many cases, spent fuel has been held in pool storage for several decades.

Most expert studies, as well as common sense analyses, find that dry storage of spent nuclear fuel inside heavy casks filled with inert gas is preferable to long-term storage in water pools. Pools, while not unsafe, have the obvious disadvantage of potential water leaks that could expose the fuel to air (where it could spontaneously burn, giving off toxic fumes) or could leak contaminated water into the environment. Pools, even when rigorously inspected and reinforced, could fail in natural disasters such as extreme weather events.

In addition to these risks, most nuclear power plants in the United States are located near waterways—many of which are major national assets such as the Mississippi and Columbia Rivers, the Great Lakes, the Chesapeake Bay, and the Atlantic, Pacific, and Gulf Coasts. It's just common sense that we shouldn't indefinitely store spent nuclear fuel alongside these major waterways. Only one nuclear power station in America, the huge Palo Verde Nuclear Generating Station in Arizona, is not located adjacent to a large body of above-ground water. The Palo Verde power plants evaporate water from the treated sewage of several nearby cities to meet their cooling needs.[37]

The National Academy of Sciences (NAS) studied the question of wet versus dry storage and concluded that "spent fuel pools are necessary at all operating nuclear power plants to store recently discharged fuel...dry cask storage has inherent security advantages over spent fuel pool storage, but it can only be used to store older spent fuel... There are no large security differences among different storage-cask designs."[38] Likewise, the U.S. Government Accountability Office (GAO), an investigative arm of Congress, found that transfers of spent nuclear fuel from wet to dry storage offer "several key benefits, including safely storing spent fuel for decades after nuclear reactors retire...and reducing the potential consequences of a pool fire."[39] One study by the Electric Power Research Institute (EPRI) pointed out that transferring spent nuclear fuel from wet to dry storage could expose workers to more radiation and increase risks of accidents during fuel transfers.[40]

Aside from the mechanics of fuel transfers, it is abundantly clear that long-term dry storage is preferable. Today, nearly 60 of the 66 reactor sites in the United States have some dry cask storage. *However, of the U.S. total of 69,700 MT of spent nuclear fuel, approximately 50,000 MT—or about 74 percent—are in pools. Only about 19,000 MT—or about 26 percent—are stored in dry casks.* Of the 11 decommissioned reactors, eight have dry cask storage, and three retired sites hold approximately 1,050 MT of spent nuclear fuel remaining in pool storage. If 2013 projections hold, about half of the spent nuclear fuel in the United States will be in dry storage by 2025, but essentially all except freshly ejected spent nuclear fuel will not be in dry storage until 2060.[41]

As of July 2013, there were 54 operating general licensed independent spent fuel storage installations (ISFSIs) and 15 specific licensed ISFSIs in 34 states, according to the NRC.[42] The ISFSIs store spent nuclear fuel in dry casks, after it has cooled in pools for at least three years (often five to ten years). Dry cask storage allows spent nuclear fuel to be surrounded by inert gases that contain and protect the fuel and prevent the buildup of other gases that could be flammable. The casks are typically steel cylinders that are either welded or bolted closed. Each cylinder is surrounded by additional steel, concrete, or other material to provide radiation shielding to workers and members of the public. The ISFSIs are licensed by the NRC separately from a nuclear power plant and are considered independent even though they may be (and usually are) located on the site of a power plant. Licensees must show the NRC that it is safe to store spent nuclear fuel in dry casks at their sites by creating an emergency plan and by analyzing earthquake and tornado intensity, and potential attack by missiles or other security events.[43]

Safety, Efficiency, and Cost of Spent Nuclear Fuel Storage—Why Move the Fuel?

If nuclear power plants are safe—and the record shows they have incomparably better safety and environmental stewardship statistics than any other energy source—why would anyone be concerned about living near one or having them located alongside important bodies of water? The issue is not the safety of nuclear power plants, but whether the spent nuclear fuel stored onsite represents a *potential* vulnerability. There are better ways of storing spent fuel than by leaving it sitting at multiple locations near population centers and national assets.

One potential vulnerability is terrorism. Most experts agree that a successful terrorist attack that could breach spent fuel pools would be difficult, but possible. A terrorist with enough technical knowledge and means could drain a spent fuel pool, triggering a fire that could release large amounts of radioactive material. An attack that breached the multiple containment barriers of dry cask storage facilities could also release radioactive material. In addition, lacking a centralized national storage facility for spent fuel, nuclear power plants often maintain their spent fuel pool inventories in amounts beyond the original design limits of the pool. Strategies for pool life extension include controversial techniques such as storage rack expansion and transshipment between neighboring units. Such strategies inherently increase vulnerability both to terrorism and accidents. In addition to terrorism, the issues of efficiency and cost make multiple-site storage of spent nuclear fuel undesirable.

Spent nuclear fuel is being kept safe at America's nuclear plants, but at higher costs, lower efficiency, and lower potential margins for safety than would be offered by a consolidated storage facility or a permanent repository. Even when the costs of building a consolidated storage facility or repository and transporting the fuel to them are factored in, the costs are still less than that of storing the fuel at the many locations, where it sits now. The Nuclear Waste Fund (NWF) contains money collected by the government from energy utilities that operate nuclear power plants—a cost passed on to ratepayers who receive energy from nuclear plants to pay for spent nuclear fuel storage and high-level waste disposal. The government has already collected about $36 billion in the NWF, including fees plus interest. Of that amount, nearly $30 billion remains available to be spent immediately on a repository.[44]

The cost savings and efficiencies gained by building a nuclear waste repository or centralized spent fuel storage facilities would be huge—not having to train and maintain security guard forces for every nuclear storage pool or cask site, or hire experts to monitor storage pools and casks, not providing expensive cyber-security, and not having to physically reinforce the storage areas to standards capable of withstanding terrorist attacks (including airborne attacks). The savings in security costs would be especially great at the nation's shutdown and decommissioned nuclear plants, where, in some cases, security guards, expensive physical security enhancements, and monitoring capabilities must be maintained for storage of the spent nuclear fuel alone.

The GAO has studied the spent fuel storage issue three times in the last four years and reached the conclusion April 2013 that "...centralized interim storage could allow DOE to consolidate the nation's nuclear waste after reactors are decommissioned, thereby decreasing the complexity of securing and overseeing the waste located at reactor sites around the nation and increasing the efficiency of waste storage operations."[45]

Since the terrorist attacks of September 11, 2001, the NRC has twice tightened security requirements for America's nuclear plants in major rulings. Plant areas that store spent nuclear fuel must be able to withstand the impact of a wide-body commercial aircraft.[46]

Another compelling reason for moving the U.S. burden of spent nuclear fuel to a permanent disposal site is because it's mandated by law for all of the reasons discussed here. The NWPA, which was passed by Congress in 1982, amended in 1987, and signed into law by the president, made a promise to the American people to build a safe, robust, permanent disposal site to dispose of high-level nuclear waste left over from production of nuclear weapons, and to store the spent nuclear fuel from nuclear power plants. This promise became law before nearly half of the Americans alive today were even born, but it remains the right of Americans to see the law implemented and the government is obligated to do so.

Already in Our Own Backyards: State-by-State Analysis

Illinois is the state that ought to be most concerned about accumulations of spent nuclear fuel and high-level waste from power reactors and the lack of a place for central interim storage or final disposal. Illinois has nearly 9,000 MT of spent nuclear fuel—the largest collection in the nation. The state has 14 nuclear plants, three of which are shutdown but still store their spent nuclear fuel. Illinois is nearly 50 percent dependent on nuclear energy for its electric power and its nuclear plants can generate 11.441 gigawatts[47] of energy. To date, Illinois' electricity ratepayers have paid nearly $2 billion into the NWF.[48]

The **Chicago** area is ringed by 11 nuclear reactors within a 100-mile radius, three of which are shutdown. Chicago itself is home to 2.7 million people, but the Chicago Combined Statistical Area (CSA)—the metropolitan area and surrounding suburbs—contains nearly 10 million residents. The Zion Station Units 1 and 2, opened in 1973 and 1974, respectively, are just 40 miles from Chicago on the shore of Lake Michigan. These power plants have been shut down since 1997. Two operating plants, Dresden Generating Station Units 2 and 3, are just 62 miles from Chicago at the head of the Illinois River near Morris, Illinois. At 42 and 43 years old, the Dresden plants are among the oldest operating nuclear power plants in the nation. Dresden Unit 1, which has been designated a Nuclear Historic Landmark, was shut down in 1978.[49] The giant Braidwood Units 1 and 2 are just 60 miles southwest of Chicago. At 25 years old, these plants are among America's newest. The LaSalle Units 1 and 2 are 75 miles southwest of Chicago, and hold the nation's record for the longest operating period between refueling—739 days. Among America's nuclear plants, the 30-year-old LaSalle plants are also relatively new. The Donald Cook Units 1 and 2 are located in Bridgman, **Michigan**, only 84 miles northeast of Chicago.[50]

The eight plants that operate near Chicago can generate nearly 9,000 megawatts electric (MWe) (*nine billion watts*) at any one moment in time, an amount the Chicago area would find it almost impossible to replace.[51] These eight plants store a staggering quantity of nearly 6,700 MT of spent nuclear fuel—the largest collection in proximity to a major CSA in the United States.[52] The Dresden Units 2 and 3 have had some of their spent nuclear fuel in dry cask storage since 2001 and 2003, respectively. The inventory of curies[53] in Dresden's spent nuclear fuel is among the highest in the nation.[54] The Braidwood and LaSalle plants just began "partial" dry cask storage (using both pool storage and dry cask storage) in 2011, and the Cook plants only opened their first dry cask storage facility in 2012, after twice expanding the spent nuclear fuel pools. Spent fuel at the Zion Station is stored in pools but the station is beginning preparation to transfer the fuel to a dry storage facility.[55] Among the operating plants near Chicago, the equivalent tonnage of 4 to 14 "core-loads" (the amount of nuclear fuel needed to run the reactor) *each* is stored in some pools.[56] The inability to move forward with sensible storage alternatives away from the plant sites is doubly ironic given the locations so close to the University of Chicago, home of the famed Metallurgical Laboratory where the world's first practical nuclear technology was developed more than 70 years ago.

Illinois contains five other nuclear power plants. The large Byron Units 1 and 2 are 110 miles from Chicago in northern Illinois, and the Quad Cities Units 1 and 2 are located on Illinois' western border along the Mississippi River—the nation's largest river and most significant in terms of commerce. The Clinton Power Station is 160 miles south of Chicago in central Illinois, next to the Clinton Lake State Recreation Area.[57] In total, these five plants store more than 3,200 MT of spent nuclear fuel at their sites. The Quad Cities plants have used some dry cask storage since 2006, Byron just began dry cask storage in 2011, and Clinton broke ground for its first dry storage facility in 2012.[58]

Pennsylvania, where ratepayers have paid nearly $1.7 billion into the NWF, has almost as much spent nuclear fuel in temporary storage at plant sites as Illinois. Pennsylvania is home to 11 nuclear power plants, two of which are shut down. The operating units generate nearly 10 gigawatts of power. Nearly 6,300 MT of spent nuclear fuel reside at these sites, most of it in pool storage. (The damaged spent nuclear fuel from the 1979 accident at the Three-Mile Island Nuclear Plant 2, and the fuel from the experimental Peach Bottom Unit 1, has been packaged and removed to the DOE's Idaho National Laboratory [INL].)[59]

All of Pennsylvania's nuclear plants are located along major rivers. The Susquehanna River is home to the large Susquehanna Units 1 and 2 near Allentown, as well as the Three-Mile Island Generating Station near Harrisburg, and the three Peach Bottom units (one of which is shut down). Susquehanna Unit 1 is now the largest boiling water reactor (BWR) in the United States.[60] The Beaver Valley Units 1 and 2 are located along the Ohio River, and the Limerick Units 1 and 2 reside along the Schuylkill River just 20 miles from **Philadelphia**.[61] Both Beaver Valley and Three-Mile Island Unit 1 (still operating) store their spent nuclear fuel exclusively in pools. The Susquehanna site has had partial dry cask storage for about 15 years, Peach Bottom for 12–13 years, and Limerick for about five years.[62]

South Carolina ranks third in the nation for quantities of spent nuclear fuel, with slightly more than 4,200 MT. South Carolina is the state that is second-most dependent on nuclear energy in the nation, deriving 53 percent of its electricity from nuclear power. Ratepayers there have paid more than $1.3 billion into the NWF.[63]

South Carolina has seven nuclear power plants and one small research reactor, the Carolina-Virginia Tube Reactor (CVTR), which has been decommissioned since 2009. South Carolina went into the nuclear business early. H.B. Robinson Nuclear Plant is among the oldest in the nation at 42 years old, and the three Oconee nuclear plants are 39 and 40 years old. Catawba Units 1 and 2 are among the newest, at 29 and 27 years old, while V.C. Summer is relatively new at age 31. Construction began just this year at Summer Station on two of the five new nuclear plants being built in the United States. The Robinson and Oconee plants have had partial dry storage of their spent nuclear fuel for nearly 25 years, but Catawba Units 1 and 2 have had partial dry storage for only four to five years. The operating Summer Plant uses only pool storage.[64]

Metropolitan areas in addition to Chicago that should be concerned about the lack of interim storage or final disposal of spent nuclear fuel and high-level nuclear waste are in **New York State** and the **Newark, New Jersey-Philadelphia—Wilmington, Delaware** corridor. The state of New York is home to the fourth largest burden of spent nuclear fuel and high-level waste in the nation, storing just over 3,700 MT. Nearby New Jersey, a relatively small state, ranks tenth in quantity, at nearly

2,700 MT. About a third of this total of 6,400 MT clusters near New York City and Newark—cities only 10 miles apart across the Hudson River and essentially part of the same CSA. This CSA is the largest and most densely populated in the United States, with nearly 19 million residents. Another third of the spent nuclear fuel clusters in southern New Jersey, where the Salem Units 1 and 2 and the Hope Creek Plant sit less than 40 miles from Philadelphia, and less than 25 miles from Wilmington, Delaware, along the Delaware River. The Oyster Creek Nuclear Station, the oldest operating plant in the nation, is almost equally distant from Philadelphia and Newark (58 and 65 miles away, respectively) and 86 miles from Wilmington, on an inlet of the Atlantic Ocean. The other third of the spent nuclear fuel in the New York-New Jersey area lies on the shores of Lake Ontario, at the James Fitzpatrick, Ginna, and Nine-Mile Point nuclear stations near **Rochester** and **Syracuse,** New York.[65]

New York and New Jersey have paid a combined total of slightly more than $1.5 billion to the NWF. New Jersey is nearly 52-percent dependent on nuclear energy for its electricity.[66] Of the 13 nuclear power plants in New York and New Jersey, two—Indian Point Unit 1 and Shoreham—are shut down. Indian Point Unit 1 was a small plant (at only 275 MWe) and operated for just 14 years from 1962 to 1974. Shoreham plant was built but never operated, and thus has no spent nuclear fuel. However, the Salem Units 1 and 2, with a combined 2,332 MWe of power, the Hope Creek Plant, the Indian Point Units 2 and 3, and the Nine-Mile Point Unit 2 plants are quite large. Indian Point Units 2 and 3 alone supply about 30 percent of the electricity to New York City. The Ginna Station and Nine-Mile Point Unit 1 are almost as old as the Oyster Creek Plant at 44 years, and Indian Point Unit 2 is 42 years old. Later this year, it will become the first nuclear plant in the nation to operate with an expired license. (The NRC won't review its license renewal application for another year, but the plant can keep operating because its owner filed for renewal more than five years before the expiration date.)[67]

The Oyster Creek Plant and the James Fitzpatrick Station have had partial dry storage since 2000 and 2002, respectively. However, most of the other nuclear plants in New York and New Jersey have used partial dry storage for only one to seven years, and Salem Unit 2 and Nine-Mile Point Unit 2 still store their spent nuclear fuel in pools.[68]

North Carolina ranks fifth in the nation for quantities of spent nuclear fuel, with nearly 3,700 MT stored in that state. North Carolina has paid approximately $900 million into the NWF, a disproportionately high amount considering that the state holds only three percent of the nation's population. The five nuclear plants in the North Carolina have operated for many years, and four have transitioned to partial dry cask storage—the McGuire Units 1 and 2 about 11 years ago, and the Brunswick Units 1 and 2 approximately five and six years ago, respectively. However, the Shearon Harris plant, 22 miles southwest of **Raleigh**, still relies exclusively on pool storage.[69]

The trio of **Alabama, Florida,** and **Georgia**, clustered in the southeastern corner of the nation, rank sixth, seventh, and ninth in the nation in amounts of spent nuclear fuel. Together, they store more than 9,000 MT of spent nuclear fuel, generated by 13 operating nuclear power plants and one plant that is shut down at Crystal River, Florida. In total, these three states have paid nearly $2.4 billion into the NWF for access to a permanent repository.[70]

Alabama was another early adopter of the nuclear business, opening its five nuclear power plants in the years from 1973–1980. Alabama's five plants generate just over 5,000 MWe, with the largest grouping of three reactors at Browns Ferry in the northern part of the state on the Tennessee River. Browns Ferry Station was the largest nuclear plant in the world when it came on line in 1974, and was the first nuclear plant in the nation to generate more than one billion watts of power. The two smaller plants of the Joseph Farley Nuclear Station are located near Dothan, Alabama, in the southern part of the state near the Florida Panhandle.[71]

Florida also embraced nuclear energy in the 1970s, opening its five plants along its two coasts in 11 years between 1972 and 1983. The Turkey Point Units 1 and 2, on the Atlantic side just 36 miles from populous **Miami,** are among the oldest in the nation at 40 and 41 years old, respectively. The two St. Lucie plants are also on the Atlantic Ocean about 125 miles north of Miami. In February 2013, Duke Energy Corp. announced that it would not reopen the Crystal River Plant that had supplied the **Tampa Bay** area along the Gulf of Mexico. The 36-year-old plant had been closed since 2009 for upgrades and repairs that proved too difficult and costly.[72]

The two Edwin Hatch nuclear power plants and the Vogtle Plant Units 1 and 2 in Georgia generate a total of slightly more than 4,000 MWe of power. The Vogtle Plants, Georgia's largest, and the Crystal River Station, Florida's largest, store their spent nuclear fuel exclusively in pools. Georgia's Hatch Plant has stored part of its fuel in dry casks for nearly 15 years, but the other nuclear plants in Alabama, Florida, and Georgia have used partial dry storage for only one to eight years.[73]

California ranks eighth in the nation in the amount of spent nuclear fuel stored. This state has seven nuclear power plants and additional small research reactors. Although five of the power plants and two of the research reactors have shut down, none of the 2,700 MT of spent nuclear fuel has left the state. Ratepayers in California have paid nearly $875 million into the NWF.[74] At present, only the two large Diablo Canyon Units 1 and 2 on the Pacific Coast in central California still operate. The two other large reactors—San Onofre Units 2 and 3 between **Los Angeles** and **San Diego**—with a combined generating power of 2,150 MWe--shut down in January 2012. Southern California Edison announced in June 2013 that they would not reopen. San Onofre Unit 1 has been closed since 1992 and the Rancho Seco Plant since 1989. The Humboldt Bay Plant has been shut down since 1976. The spent nuclear fuel at the two research reactors as well as the Rancho Seco and

Humboldt Bay plants has been placed in dry casks. San Onofre Station has stored partial amounts of the spent nuclear fuel in dry casks since 2007, and Diablo Canyon has used partial dry storage since 2010.[75]

Michigan ranks eleventh in the nation with 2,650 MT of spent nuclear fuel. Michigan ratepayers have paid nearly $575 million into the NWF. The large Donald Cook Units 1 and 2 on the shore of Lake Michigan were discussed earlier in this chapter in relation to the Chicago area. Michigan's Palisades Nuclear Station also has provided much of its power to Chicago, but it has been shut down since May 2013 due to a cracked pipe. Michigan's largest nuclear power plant is Fermi Unit 2, just 40 miles from **Detroit** on Lake Erie. The much smaller Fermi Unit 1 was a prototype fast breeder reactor (not a standard type for power plants, at least at present), and was shut down many years ago in 1972. In 2008, Detroit Edison Company (now known as DTE Energy), filed an application with the NRC to build a new BWR at the Fermi site, to be known as Fermi Unit 3.[76]

The Big Rock Point nuclear power plant on Michigan's Upper Peninsula on Lake Michigan was shut down in 1997, after becoming the longest-running nuclear plant in the United States at that time. Big Rock Point opened in 1962 as the fifth commercial nuclear plant in the nation, and is now a Nuclear Historic Landmark. The spent nuclear fuel at the shutdown Big Rock Point Nuclear Station is all stored in dry casks. The Palisades plant has had partial dry storage for about 20 years, but the Fermi Unit 2 only began partial dry storage in 2010 and, as previously noted, the Cook Plants began partial dry storage in 2012.[77]

Virginia ranks twelfth in the nation, storing 2,530 MT of spent nuclear fuel, and paying nearly $740 million into the NWF. Virginia is nearly 41-percent dependent on nuclear power for its electricity. The Surry Units 1 and 2 are located on the James River approximately 60 miles from **Richmond.** At 40 and 41 years old, they are among the oldest in the nation, but were also among the first in the United States to use partial dry storage for their spent nuclear fuel. The slightly larger

North Anna Units 1 and 2, located on the North Anna River about 50 miles from Richmond, are newer at 33 and 35 years old. They have placed part of their spent nuclear fuel in dry casks for about 15 years.[78]

Texas and **Arizona** rank thirteenth and fifteenth in the nation, respectively, in amounts of stored spent nuclear fuel. Texas, with 2,210 MT of spent nuclear fuel has paid nearly $680 million into the NWF, and Arizona, with 2,040 MT of spent nuclear fuel has paid $580 million.[79] The four nuclear plants in Texas are among the newest in the nation. At 20 and 23 years old, the Comanche Peak Units 1 and 2, 60 miles west of **Dallas**, are the newest anywhere in the country except for the Watts Bar Unit 1 in **Tennessee.** The large South Texas Project Units 1 and 2 on the Gulf of Mexico approximately 105 miles from **Houston** are only 24 and 25 years old. The South Texas units hold the national record for the most electricity generated in a year at 11.8 billion kilowatt hours (KWh) in 2007.[80]

The Comanche Peak and South Texas Project filed with the NRC for permission to build two more nuclear plants each in 2008 and 2007, respectively. The Comanche Peak license application is still pending, but the South Texas Project license application was rejected in April 2013 because too large a portion of the new plants would be foreign owned.

Texas enthusiasm for more nuclear energy ought to be coupled with demand for a consolidated storage facility or national repository, considering that almost all of the spent nuclear fuel in Texas is stored in pools. Partial dry storage of spent nuclear fuel was introduced to Comanche Peak in 2014. South Texas Project still exclusively uses pool storage.[81]

Arizona is home to the largest nuclear power plant complex in the nation. The three reactors of the Palo Verde Generating Station, 45 miles west of **Phoenix**, can produce a total of nearly 4,000 MWe of power at any given instant, making Palo Verde the largest nuclear power producer in the nation. Some of the power goes to nearby Southern

California and New Mexico. The Palo Verde Station has used partial dry cask storage of spent nuclear fuel for approximately 10 years.[82]

No region of the country is as reliant on nuclear power as **New England**. In 2013, **Vermont** was the most nuclear-dependent state in the nation at nearly 75 percent. However, Vermont's energy challenges are about to change dramatically when the Vermont Yankee nuclear plant shuts down in the last quarter of 2014.[83] **Connecticut** is nearly 49-percent dependent on nuclear energy, and **New Hampshire** nearly 43 percent. In New England, only tiny Rhode Island has no commercial nuclear plants.[84] The five states of New England that have nuclear power plants have paid almost $900 million into the NWF, and store nearly 5,000 MT of spent nuclear fuel. Both of these figures represent disproportionately high totals for a region with less than two percent of the square mileage of the United States and only four and a half percent of the national population.[85]

Five nuclear power plants operate in New England, and four other plants are shut down. The operating plants range from among the oldest in the nation to among the newest. Pilgrim Unit 1 on the Atlantic Ocean on Cape Cod, **Massachusetts,** and Vermont Yankee on the Connecticut River in Vermont opened in 1972, while Seabrook Unit 1 on the Atlantic Coast in New Hampshire opened in 1990. The other two operating nuclear plants, Millstone Units 2 and 3 located in Connecticut on the Atlantic Ocean along the north side of Long Island Sound, opened in 1975 and 1986, respectively. Collectively, the five plants generate nearly 4,000 MWe of power. The Seabrook Unit 1 is the largest single nuclear plant in New England, at 1,246 MWe, but the Millstone Station, with two operating plants, generates the most power at nearly 2,100 MWe. The spent nuclear fuel in New England's shut down plants has been placed in dry storage. However, most of the spent nuclear fuel at the operating plants is stored in pools. The Pilgrim Station and Millstone Unit 3 rely exclusively on pool storage, whereas Millstone Unit 2, Vermont Yankee, and Seabrook have had partial dry storage for the past 6–10 years.

Of the remaining U.S. states, seven store burdens of spent nuclear fuel between 1,000–2,000 MT each, and nine more store burdens below 1,000 MT.[86] The majority of the spent nuclear fuel in most of these states is stored in pools, and at three locations—Wolf Creek, **Kansas**; Callaway, **Missouri**; and Watts Bar, **Tennessee**—it is stored exclusively in pools.[87] In most cases, the nuclear plants and their fuel are unremarkable, with the possible exception of the Calvert Cliffs Units 1 and 2, located on the western shore of the Chesapeake Bay just 45 miles from downtown **Washington, D.C.**, and 77 miles from **Baltimore.** The CSA for Washington, D.C., much of which draws power from Calvert Cliffs Station, contains nearly 10 million people. The ratepayers of **Maryland**, where the plants are actually located, have paid $387 million into the NWF, an amount that seems disproportionately high considering that Maryland's population is only 1.8 percent of the nation and Maryland is the ninth smallest U.S. state with a land mass of only one-third of one percent of the country. The Calvert Cliffs Units 1 and 2 are 38 and 36 years old, respectively. In 2013, the NRC rejected an application to build a third nuclear plant at Calvert Cliffs because too much of the ownership would be foreign. To their credit, Calvert Cliffs Units 1 and 2 have used partial dry storage of spent nuclear fuel for nearly 20 years, but much of their inventory of 1,380 MT of spent nuclear fuel is still stored in pools.[88]

Shutdown or Decommissioned Nuclear Power Plants and Stranded Spent Nuclear Fuel

Nuclear power plants that have been shut down or decommissioned and the residents who live nearby them are the demographic most in need of a sensible national energy policy that includes an interim consolidated storage facility and a permanent repository for disposal of spent nuclear fuel. "Stranded" is the term applied to the spent nuclear fuel left behind at decommissioned nuclear plants. The term is apt because, after decommissioning ends, staff and site security could go to near zero were it not for the need to monitor and safeguard the spent nuclear fuel.

With the June 2013 announcement that the large San Onofre Station Units 2 and 3 in California would not re-open, San Onofre has become the nuclear plant site with the most stranded spent nuclear fuel in the nation. San Onofre Unit 1, which shut down in 1992, still stores the spent nuclear fuel from its operation at the station. The San Onofre site now joins many other sites that need to devise plans to store stranded spent nuclear fuel for an indefinite period. The Crystal River Station in Florida announced its shut down in February 2013 and still stores its spent nuclear fuel exclusively in pools, and the Kewaunee Plant near Green Bay, **Wisconsin**, announced its shut down in late 2012. Spent nuclear fuel is still stored in pools at Zion Units 1 and 2 in Illinois, which closed in 1998, and at the Millstone Unit 1 in Connecticut, shut down in 1995.[89]

Eleven other shutdown nuclear power plants in the United States continue to store their spent nuclear fuel on site, even though, in many cases, their decommissioning is otherwise complete or nearly complete. These 11 plants, in nine states, store approximately 3,000 MT of spent nuclear fuel. Pennsylvania and Minnesota stand alone as the only states to have had the spent nuclear fuel from their closed nuclear reactors removed from the reactor sites. As noted earlier, the fuel from the Peach Bottom Unit 1 and the Three-Mile Island Unit 2, both near Harrisburg, Pennsylvania, was removed. The fuel from the Three-Mile Island Unit 2 was damaged in the 1979 accident, so the condition of its fuel was of interest to researchers at the DOE's INL. The Peach Bottom Unit 1 was a small (200MWe) demonstration reactor cooled by high-temperature gas, a technology that has not yet been adopted for commercial power reactors. As such, its fuel was also of interest to researchers at the INL. Spent fuel has also been removed from the site of the tiny Elk River reactor near **Minneapolis, Minnesota**.[90]

In some cases, the amount of spent nuclear fuel stored at closed power reactor sites is quite small, but all NRC requirements for safe storage still must be met, making the costs especially burdensome and wasteful. Some of the decommissioned plants were small and constructed as part of the Atomic Energy Commission's technology demonstration program. Like the Peach Bottom Unit 1 in Pennsylvania, the Fort St. Vrain power plant in **Colorado**, which only operated for 10 years from 1979–1989, was cooled by high-temperature gas.[91]

The decommissioned Fort St. Vrain reactor site stores just approximately 15 MT, the Humboldt Bay reactor site in northern California stores only about 29 MT, and the Genoa reactor site near LaCrosse, Wisconsin, stores approximately 38 MT. The Genoa plant, shut down in 1987, waited 25 years until 2012, to see its spent nuclear fuel moved out of a pool and into dry storage nearby. The cost of moving the fuel into dry storage was $45 million. Dry storage will cost about $3 million annually to maintain, but will save the utility approximately $3 million per year in costs previously spent on pool storage.[92] However, utility officers of the plants and elected officials from the states and cities storing spent nuclear fuel at closed sites are becoming more vocal in demanding a solution to the storage issue. One way in which utilities have expressed their displeasure with the spent fuel storage stalemate is by filing lawsuits against the federal government, charging breach of contract for failure to take the spent nuclear fuel as promised by 1998—the year the DOE was supposed to open the deep geologic nuclear waste repository at Yucca Mountain, Nevada. The nuclear energy utility companies are suing for damages; that is, the extra costs accruing to them for having to store the waste at power plant sites in pools and the costs to move the spent fuel into dry casks. Thus far, all judgments in these cases have been won by the utilities.

In 2011, DOE estimated that total damage awards to utilities managing both closed and operating nuclear plants could amount to $20.8 billion if the federal government begins accepting spent fuel by

2020. However, the fact that the Yucca Mountain Project has been illegally terminated by President Obama and former Energy Secretary Chu makes it impossible for DOE to estimate when a repository or an interim storage facility will be available to take the spent fuel. The Department of Justice (DOJ) pays the liability judgments from the Department of the Treasury's Judgment Fund, which is funded by U.S. taxpayers. Thus far, the DOJ has paid out slightly more than $2 billion in utilities' claims. Many more claims are pending and there is little doubt these claims are valid and will be settled in the utilities' favor. According to the DOJ, the government's liability increases by $500 million each year. This fact means that taxpayers will be burdened indefinitely with a literally boundless liability for the future.

Moreover, the funds in the NWF are being spent to buy U.S. savings bonds, which means they are being used to partially underwrite the federal debt—a purpose for which those funds were never intended by the NWPA.[93]

Utilities and elected officials also have been expressing their displeasure by speaking directly to the public. In late 2012, Maine Yankee Company, owner of the decommissioned Maine Yankee nuclear plant near Wiscasset, **Maine**, where nearly 550 MT of spent nuclear fuel are stored, issued a public statement urging the federal government to "fulfill its obligation to remove the spent nuclear fuel." The plant's community advisory panel, which still functions even though the plant has been closed for 17 years, likewise advocates for the "prompt removal" of the spent nuclear fuel.[94]

In May 2013, Senator Chris Murphy (D-CT) stated: "These spent fuel rods…were never intended to remain here in Connecticut for decades to come…For states like Connecticut, with both active and deactivated nuclear plants, it's a problem our nation needs to solve, and solve now."[95]

Connecticut stores more than 2,100 MT of spent nuclear fuel, much of it at the Millstone site on Long Island Sound. More than 400 MT are still stored at the Haddam Neck Nuclear Station, along the Connecticut River 43 miles from **New Haven**. Like Maine Yankee, Haddam Neck station has been closed for 17 years.

These calls are just the latest. In a hearing of the House Subcommittee on Energy and Air Quality, titled "Next Steps Toward Permanent Nuclear Waste Disposal," held in July 2008, Representative Fred Upton (R-MI) stated that "after an allocation of these resources [decades of payments into the NWF], one would think that we have something to show for it. We do NOT...Properly dealing with the spent nuclear fuel is the key to [our future energy supply]."[96]

Michigan is home to closed reactors Fermi Nuclear Unit 1 and Big Rock Point Plant. Since the 2008 hearing, Upton has repeatedly called for siting a repository.

At the same "Next Steps" hearing in 2008, Anne George, Commissioner of the Connecticut Department of Public Utility Control and Chair of the National Association of Regulatory Utility Commissioners' Committee on Electricity, told the subcommittee: "Simply put, the Federal Government needs to meet its obligation under the Nuclear Waste Policy Act to accept spent nuclear fuel from utilities and other nuclear generators in a timely manner for safe disposal."[97]

Some who live near Zion Nuclear Units 1 and 2, closed since 1997, are speaking out in newspapers. Roger Whitmore, past president of the Zion, Illinois, Chamber of Commerce, expressed his concern about the spent nuclear fuel still stored in pools near Lake Michigan. "If we had a big earthquake or seiche," referring to a large wave from Lake Michigan, "what's (the waste) going to do, sweep into the lake?"[98]

Decommissioning of Zion Station began in 2010 as a 10-year, $1-billion project, the largest commercial nuclear dismantling project yet undertaken in the United States. The decommissioning plan does not include removing the spent nuclear fuel from the site.

Also in Illinois, home to the shutdown Dresden Station, Representative John Shimkus (R) authored a guest commentary in the

Chicago Tribune in which he stated: "We are all frustrated by the failure to dispose of nuclear waste on a timetable provided in current law."[99] Shimkus has spoken many times on the same point.

In 2012, Lee Hamilton, former Democrat Representative from Indiana and most recently co-chair of the BRC, told a House Energy and Commerce subcommittee hearing: "We cannot really claim to be a leader in nuclear power if we can't solve one of the fundamental problems with nuclear power: what to do with nuclear waste." He called the decades-long quest to establish a permanent nuclear waste repository a "serious failure of the American government."[100] In June 2013, Hamilton and Brent Scowcroft, the other co-chair of the BRC, spoke directly to the citizens of **Oregon**, where the decommissioned Trojan Nuclear Plant still stores more than 350 MT of spent nuclear fuel, to galvanize their elected officials. "Efforts to implement a lasting disposal solution for spent nuclear fuel and high-level radioactive waste remain at a standstill… a breakthrough is long overdue… continued paralysis serves no one's interests and will only grow more costly over time."[101]

In spring 2013, the attorneys general of Vermont, New York, Massachusetts, and Connecticut announced they were petitioning the NRC for a more thorough review of spent nuclear fuel storage at reactor sites. "Federal law requires that the NRC analyze the environmental dangers of storing spent nuclear fuel at reactors that were not designed for long-term storage," said Vermont Attorney General William Sorrell. "NRC staff is continuing to ignore serious public health, safety and environmental risks related to long-term, on-site storage…The communities that serve as de facto long-term radioactive waste repositories deserve a full and detailed accounting," said New York Attorney General Eric Schneiderman.[102] New York, Massachusetts, and Connecticut are all home to closed nuclear plants. In Vermont, the most nuclear-dependent state in the nation, public meetings to expand the fuel storage facilities at the operating Vermont Yankee Plant have been contentious.[103]

In many other jurisdictions, town councils, Boards of Commissioners, and others have called for the federal government to follow the law and remove spent nuclear fuel from their areas. These actions have occurred near shut down and decommissioned nuclear plants, as well as near operating ones. Strong opinions advocating federal nuclear waste storage have even been heard in areas, and from spokespersons, where no nuclear waste is stored. Representative Ed Whitfield (R) represents western **Kentucky,** and has consistently labelled the cancellation of the Yucca Mountain Project an "error in judgment by the Obama Administration."[104] Kentucky has no nuclear power plants, but Whitfield's district borders Tennessee near the Watts Bar Station, where one nuclear plant stores its fuel exclusively in pools and another nuclear plant is under construction.

Legacy Defense Spent Nuclear Fuel and High-Level Waste

In addition to spent nuclear fuel and high-level waste from commercial nuclear power plants, other forms of spent nuclear fuel and high-level nuclear waste and byproducts await disposal in a national repository. These materials were generated by the government in the nation's nuclear defense (weapons) effort.

The "fuel cycle" as practiced in commercial nuclear power plants in the United States is quite simple. Uranium-based fuel is irradiated in a power reactor, heat is generated and harnessed to make electric power (usually through generating steam), and then the fuel is transferred into a water pool and considered "used" or "spent." However, the fuel cycle in the nuclear weapons program operated quite differently. This cycle is described in the past tense because no weapons-grade plutonium is purposely being produced in the country today. The plutonium in commercial reactors is not used for nuclear weapons.

Production of weapons-grade plutonium—the core material in most U.S. nuclear weapons—required irradiating uranium-based fuel in reactor time periods that were very short—days to months—compared to those practiced today in modern commercial nuclear power plants. For this reason, the plutonium in commercial reactors is not usable for nuclear weapons. It's also for this reason that reprocessing commercial spent nuclear fuel produces less waste for each fuel cycle.

The defense reactors were located at Hanford, **Washington**, and Savannah River, **South Carolina**. After the fuel was discharged from the reactors, it was stored for varying periods of time and then taken to chemical plants on the defense sites and dissolved in acid. The fuel thus changed from a solid into a liquid mixture. The liquid mixture was chemically processed in a series of reactions that separated the components, such as uranium and plutonium, into different fractions. The recovered plutonium was removed and fabricated into the form that is used in nuclear weapons. The chemical processes were called "separations" or "reprocessing," since the uranium was being processed a second time—the first time in the reactors and the second time in the chemical plants.[105]

The chemical reprocessing of irradiated nuclear fuel to make plutonium produced vast quantities of liquid wastes. High-level waste is the term applied by statute to "radioactive material resulting from the reprocessing of spent nuclear fuel."[106] However, within the legal definition of high-level waste, there are physical categories based on intensity of radioactivity. High-activity waste is the most radioactive fraction, and low-activity waste is less radioactive, although both activity levels are highly radioactive and are defined as high-level waste. Through legally binding agreements, the DOE and states that store spent nuclear fuel and high-level waste from defense reprocessing have agreed as to which portions of the waste will go to a national repository for disposal.[107]

In addition to Washington and South Carolina, **Idaho** has an agreement with DOE to remove the spent nuclear fuel as well as certain wastes and nuclear materials, partly because the U.S. Navy has stored the spent nuclear fuel from its nuclear-powered ships at the INL near

Idaho Falls for many years. Other spent nuclear fuel is stored at the INL from the decommissioned Three-Mile Island Unit 2 and Fort St. Vrain reactor, the West Valley Site in New York State, and some other test reactors. Some spent nuclear fuel is generated at the INL by operations of the Advanced Test Reactor.[108]

Colorado and New York also have agreements with DOE to remove government spent nuclear fuel and high-level nuclear waste stored in those states. Colorado's 1996 agreement commits the DOE to removing the small amount of spent nuclear fuel remaining at the Fort St. Vrain site. The 15 MT of spent nuclear fuel was to have been shipped to the INL along with other Fort St. Vrain fuel that was shipped there gradually between 1980 and 1986. However, political and tribal opposition and lawsuits stopped the shipments in 1991, stranding the tiny fraction of spent nuclear fuel in Colorado. The Idaho agreement permits the DOE to send the Colorado fuel to INL for further treatment only if a permanent repository or consolidated storage facility outside of Idaho is opened and begins accepting spent nuclear fuel.[109]

New York's 1980 agreement commits the DOE to removing 275 canisters of vitrified high-level waste (waste that has been converted to a solid glass form) from the West Valley Demonstration Project (WVDP) site near Buffalo. The WVDP was a government project in which spent nuclear fuel from commercial power plants was reprocessed as a demonstration of feasibility and technology. It operated from 1966–1972, reprocessing 640 MT and producing 640,000 gallons of high-level waste. This waste was vitrified between 1996–2002 and stored on site. In 2001, remaining spent nuclear fuel was removed from storage pools at the WVDP and placed into dry casks. The fuel was shipped away from the site to the INL in 2003.[110]

The Idaho Settlement Agreement and Consent Order commits the DOE to remove spent nuclear fuel from the state by January 1, 2035, and to have high-level waste prepared for shipment, but not actually removed, by that same date. The **Colorado** agreement commits the DOE to remove the spent nuclear fuel from the state by the same date. The **Idaho** agreement was modified in 2008 to allow the Navy to continue sending a limited volume of spent nuclear fuel to the INL after 2035, provided that all Navy spent nuclear fuel that arrived in Idaho prior to 2026 has been removed. In 2011, the GAO found that cancellation of the Yucca Mountain Repository threatened these agreements and their deadlines. The DOE disagreed, but the GAO maintained its position, stating that "DOE's comments provide no basis for revising our findings." The **Washington**, **South Carolina**, and **New York** agreements do not contain specific deadlines for removal at this time.[111]

The total amount of spent nuclear fuel at the nation's defense sites is very small compared to the total amounts stored at commercial nuclear power plant sites. The roughly 2,465 MT at the defense sites is only about 3.6 percent of the 69,700 MT stored at power plant sites. However, high-level waste from reprocessing exists only at the defense sites, and most of it is still in liquid form being stored in aging, underground tanks, some of which are leaking.[112] Three government sites—Hanford, the Savannah River Site, and the INL—store approximately 90 million gallons of high-level waste in liquid form. The Savannah River Site and the WVDP also store nearly 3,000 canisters of vitrified high-level waste, and the INL stores high-level waste that has been solidified by methods other than vitrification.[113]

The majority of defense spent nuclear fuel and high-level waste for which the government is directly responsible lies at the Hanford Site in southeast Washington State. Hanford contains 87 percent of the defense spent nuclear fuel in the nation, and about 45 percent of the high-level waste canisters projected to be produced by defense waste vitrification. Hanford's total is even higher—61 percent—if we consider only the high-level waste that exists in liquid form, because none of Hanford's high-level waste has been vitrified, whereas vitrification has started at the Savannah River Site and cementation of waste has begun at the INL. The Hanford Waste Treatment Plant, which is being built to perform the vitrification process, is designed to produce high-activity waste canisters that conform to the Yucca Mountain repository acceptance criteria. The defense waste resulting from reprocessing at Hanford now sits in underground tanks about eight miles from the Columbia River. Headlines during 2012–2013 about leaks from these tanks, as well as attention from the Washington State Governor and senior Senator Patty Murray (D-WA), have galvanized state, local, and citizen concerns that Washington may become the largest de facto repository in the nation.[114] Hanford's spent nuclear fuel was dried and placed in massive canisters designed specifically to meet Yucca Mountain acceptance criteria, in a large project between 2000–2004.

Washington State has already agreed to retain the largest fraction of vitrified high-level waste—the low-activity portion—in a landfill on the Hanford Site, but is adamant that DOE get on with vitrification and take possession of the high-activity portion, as well as Hanford's 2,130 MT of spent nuclear fuel, in a permanent repository.[115] A consent-based approach to siting a repository of a consolidated storage facility, as recommended by the BRC, seems especially ironic to Washington's residents since the Hanford Site was founded during World War II in total secrecy. Hanford produced the plutonium for the world's first and third atomic explosions—the Trinity test bomb and the Nagasaki weapon—without informing state or local officials, or its own workers, of its purpose because of national security. Hanford then went on to produce approximately two-thirds of all the weapons-grade plutonium ever produced by the United States, again in isolation, classifying its documents and not allowing state officials to inspect the site until court-ordered to do so when the Cold War was almost over.[116]

Washington's citizens may harbor the most anger in the nation at the DOE's broken promises. For more than two decades, as deadlines for waste vitrification have passed, they've elected governors pledged to hold DOE accountable, and put teeth into their Department of Ecology (one of the signatories to Hanford's historic cleanup agreement). The state has twice sued the DOE and come away with legally binding Consent Orders setting timetables for high-level waste treatment. Washington's Governor Jay Inslee stated in June 2013 that he will insist on an accelerated cleanup plan for Hanford's high-level waste, and "if we do not receive satisfaction... we have several legal options available to us. And we'll act accordingly."[117]

Unfortunately, Washington State and the courts do not have the power to accelerate cleanup because the DOE appropriations and internal decisions constrain and confound enforcement actions. Washington's and Oregon's officials and residents participate eagerly in a citizen action group called the Hanford Advisory Board (HAB) and have joined with neighbors of other contaminated defense sites in the Energy Communities Alliance (ECA). Oregon is concerned about Hanford's high-level waste because its lies downstream from Hanford along the Columbia River, and because waste that is transported in or out of Hanford often travels through Oregon. The ECA "supports geologic disposal pursuant to the Nuclear Waste Policy Act (NWPA). Much of the HLW [high-level wastes] and spent nuclear fuel across the DOE complex must be removed from sites such as Idaho National Laboratory, Hanford, and the Savannah River Site (SRS) under stated commitments and/or binding legal agreements...Without a geologic repository, these wastes could remain orphaned in communities that never planned to be permanent or long-term storage sites. A final geologic repository...is essential to the final disposition of HLW and integral to the success of DOE's Environmental Cleanup programs."[118]

The ECA speaks not just for the region surrounding Hanford, but also for the communities surrounding the Savannah River Site and the INL (as well as Oak Ridge, Los Alamos, Paducah, Rocky Flats, Yucca, and other sites in DOE's "cleanup" program). These sites also have citizen advisory boards similar to the HAB. At the Savannah River Site, which stores the second largest collection of defense high-level waste in the nation, the Citizens Advisory Board (CAB) stated in 2012: "There is no evidence that Yucca Mountain is not scientifically sound or safe for the repository mission. Meanwhile, taxpayer liabilities under the NWPA are increasing…and the lack of a nuclear waste management policy ultimately threatens the future of the nuclear energy industry to help meet America's growing energy demands and the world's need for clean, safe and cheap power… it is within DOE's Environmental Management (EM) responsibility to assure that the EM program is on a path to decommissioning…facilities housing radioactive wastes, including the Savannah River Site."

The CAB went on to suggest that the Yucca Mountain site be designated as a consolidated storage facility if, indeed, the president and Energy Secretary succeeded in terminating it as a national repository.[119] The Savannah River Site's vitrification facility—the Defense Waste Processing Facility—has been operating since 1996, and has already produced about 3,000 canisters of high-level waste, all of which conform to, and were designed for, Yucca Mountain repository acceptance criteria.

South Carolina has reacted powerfully in recent years against becoming a de facto repository for nuclear wastes, byproducts, and surplus materials. In 2001 and 2002, Governor Jim Hodges stared down the federal government and refused to allow shipments of excess plutonium from the decommissioned Rocky Flats Nuclear Weapons Plant in Colorado to be shipped into South Carolina. He threatened to block the roads with state troopers and sued the federal government for trying to make South Carolina a de facto storage site. He demanded an enforceable agreement to make sure the plutonium would not remain in the state indefinitely.[120] South Carolina lost its legal challenge, and the plutonium was shipped, along with much more plutonium over the ensuing years. However, the DOE did agree to fund a new facility to convert much of the stored plutonium into mixed oxide (MOX) fuel as part of a non-proliferation agreement with Russia.[121]

Nevertheless, opposition to storing nuclear materials indefinitely continues to be strong in South Carolina. Construction of the MOX plant is far behind schedule and far over budget, making it vulnerable. During Energy Secretary Ernest Moniz's confirmation process in early 2013, both South Carolina Senators Lindsey Graham (R) and Tim Scott (R) threatened to block the nominee unless funding was restored to speed the MOX plant.[122]

Granted, plutonium is not nuclear waste, and the Yucca Mountain Repository was not designed nor intended to store plutonium. However, the principle of opposing de facto "decisions" about nuclear materials is the same. South Carolina's citizens and elected officials are outspoken in their desire to see a consolidated storage facility or preferably a national repository sited. Senator Graham has often expressed his support for the Yucca Mountain Project, and has twice introduced national legislation to force the federal government to rebate funds in the NWF to nuclear utility customers and to the utilities to upgrade their spent nuclear fuel storage facilities.[123]

Idaho is no pushover either, when it comes to voicing its opposition to being a de facto repository. Idaho's 1995 Settlement Agreement is often called the "Batt Agreement" after Governor Phil Batt who achieved major concessions concerning nuclear waste shipments from the federal government. Back in 1988, Governor Cecil Andrus banned nuclear waste shipments into Idaho, saying he acted, in part, to spur the federal government into acting on "long-neglected promises to start removing nuclear waste" from the INL. Idaho state attorneys filed for an emergency stay when the government wanted to resume shipments in 1991, and won a total block from a federal judge in 1993.[124] In 1994, Batt was elected governor and hammered out a tough agreement in which the federal government must place all spent nuclear fuel in Idaho in dry storage by 2023, remove all spent nuclear fuel from Idaho by 2035, and include Navy spent nuclear fuel in the early shipments to the Yucca Mountain Repository. Idaho will receive penalty payments of $60,000 per day if the federal government fails to remove all the spent nuclear fuel by January 1, 2035. In the same agreement, Idaho agreed to accept

1,133 new waste shipments—about 110 tons—by 2035. Shipments did resume in 1995, despite vigorous opposition in Idaho that included a blockade of a major shipping road by the Shoshone-Bannock tribe of Native Americans. Sixty percent of state voters said they backed the Batt Agreement.[125]

The agreement was revised slightly in 2008, but faced its first real test in 2012 when Governor Butch Otter created the Leadership in Nuclear Energy (LINE) Commission to look at the economic benefits of pursuing more nuclear research and business at the INL. The tradeoff was obvious—allow more nuclear waste and spent nuclear fuel into Idaho or possibly truncate lucrative growth at the INL. Andrus and Batt both spoke strongly against any major revisions to the Batt Agreement, newspapers throughout the state editorialized, and the LINE Commission itself refused to recommend changes. In 2013, Governor Otter announced that he wouldn't propose any changes to the Batt Agreement.[126]

Likewise, New York State is vocal in demanding aggressive cleanup and waste disposition schedules for the WVDP high-level waste. Senior Senator Charles Schumer (D) has called it "critical that we effectively contain and dispose of the nuclear waste at West Valley." The state has also shown its teeth by joining, with the full backing of Governor Andrew Cuomo, three other states in petitioning the NRC to more thoroughly scrutinize spent nuclear fuel storage around "communities that serve as de facto long-term radioactive waste repositories."[127]

Chapter 2

America Left Behind

It would be a mistake...to let Fukushima cause governments to abandon nuclear power and its benefits. Electricity gener-ation [through coal] emits more carbon dioxide in the United States than does transportation or industry, and nuclear power is the largest source of carbon-free electricity in the country.—Ernest Moniz, U.S. Secretary of Energy, re-ferring to the 2011 accident at the Fukushima Daiichi nuclear plant.[128]

America's competitors are moving ahead with secure energy sources. In much of the rest of the developed and developing world, especially among nations who are and will be America's com-petitors in the foreseeable future, the nuclear industry is robust and growing exponentially. These nations realize that having safe, reliable base load energy supplies will be the key to their economic futures and their independence. After all, almost all wars in modern history, aside from those fought over religious differences, have been struggles over energy supplies. Very recently, we have witnessed struggles in Crimea and other parts of Ukraine where power over energy sources and supplies played a significant role in international tensions and decisions.

China is actively working to increase nuclear energy production for peaceful (industrial and consumer) purposes by *20-fold* by the year 2030.[129] India is building to produce half of its energy from nuclear power by 2050. Since it now produces only about one percent from nuclear energy, this statistic means that India's nuclear output will increase by *50-fold* in the next 37 years.[130] Russia is actively building now to increase its peaceful nuclear energy production by 50 percent by 2020—just seven years from now. Another doubling of Russia's nuclear energy production—beyond the 2020 figures—is expected by 2030.[131] These nations are building nuclear plants rapidly with the intention that nuclear energy will become their main base load power source. Base load is the minimum amount of power that a utility or distribution company must have available to meet minimum customer demands based on reasonable expectations of customer requirements. In other words, nuclear energy is the steady, reliable power that will always be there, not subject to whims of weather, rivers, winds, clouds, or other disrupting forces. It is "old faithful," and a modern society cannot function without it.

Additionally, many of the nations who are and will be competing with America in the global economy in the coming decades are re-using the fuel in their nuclear power plants many times over before they discard it.[132] This practice, called "reprocessing," allows them to stretch nuclear fuel supplies to almost limitless capacity.

By contrast, America uses its nuclear fuel only once, and then removes and discards it in 66 locations scattered around the country at power plant sites that were never intended for long-term storage.[133] These sites are necessarily near cities and rivers, because the power plants were located there to serve population centers. Using the fuel only once is extraordinarily expensive and wasteful, and it's expensive and far less than ideal to store it where it sits. Also, the United States isn't planning any major expansions in nuclear energy production in the coming decades, staying level at about 19–20 percent of its energy supply coming from nuclear power.[134]

In addition, our nuclear infrastructure—that is, the companies who supply specialized parts, materials, welding, and fabrication techniques and other services specifically geared to the nuclear industry—is shrinking and has nearly collapsed. At the same time, nuclear suppliers are growing rapidly in other nations, as are nuclear business and marketing companies. They are responding to the law of supply and demand—they are expanding because they are in demand and being called upon to do business and make profits.

Finally, in terms of safe and sensible nuclear waste disposal practices, competitors of the United States are siting centralized places to either store temporarily or dispose permanently their spent nuclear fuel and high-level waste.[135] It takes political will, consensus-building, money, and technology development to site a consolidated storage facility or a deep geologic repository. However, these nations have decided that those investments are better than storing spent nuclear fuel and high-level waste near their cities, rivers, and people.

Other Nations Moving Ahead With Nuclear Growth

Today, 70 new reactors are actively under construction in 14 countries. The World Nuclear Association (WNA), based in the United Kingdom (UK), projects that 298 new nuclear reactors will be operating by 2030, and that 60 to 158 reactors may retire by 2030 (at least 60 of them small ones). These statistics mean that, depending on the number of reactor retirements, *world nuclear power will increase by 32 to 54 percent in the next 17 years.*[136]

China is now building toward the greatest growth in nuclear power in the world. In 2013, it had 15 nuclear power reactors, supplying no more than two percent of its power. Mainland China has 28 more reactors under construction, with *120 additional reactors* planned by 2030. Taiwan had six nuclear power plants and is building two additional reactors. China is expected to generate as much as 40 percent of its domestic energy from nuclear power plants by 2030.[137] Taiwan supplies 20 percent of its energy from nuclear power.[138]

India today has 20 nuclear power plants, with seven more under construction, and 39 additional plants planned by 2030. India has more than doubled its output of nuclear power in just three years. The newest nuclear power plant in the world, the 1,000-MW Kudankulam Nuclear Power Project (KNNP), began operating in late 2013.[139]

Russia hosts 33 nuclear reactors, is constructing 10 more, and planning 24 additional reactors by 2030. Nuclear energy provides about 17 percent of civilian energy in Russia, with an ambitious program to increase to 25 to 26 percent by 2020.[140] In Europe, the UK has 16 reactors, and is planning nine more by 2030. That nation today generates about 16 percent of its power from nuclear energy. Official UK policy is to proceed with constructing more replacement plants through private sector investment, and many of the world's major nuclear investors/companies are presently in engaged in negotiations to permit and construct such plants.[141]

France has 58 reactors, is constructing one more, and planning an additional reactor by 2030. Approximately 77 percent of its power comes from nuclear energy, *making it the most nuclear-dependent nation in the world*. The Électricité de France (EDF) Group, the principal French utility, is the leading electricity producer in Europe, and is actively reaching into markets in greater Europe, Asia, Russia, and North America.[142]

Also in Europe, Armenia, Belgium, Bulgaria, the Czech Republic, Finland, Hungary, Lithuania, The Netherlands, Poland, Romania, Slovakia, Slovenia, Spain, Sweden, Switzerland, and Ukraine have or are planning nuclear programs that total 70 operating reactors, with three actively under construction, and 25 additional ones planned by

2030. Belgium and Ukraine each supply nearly 50 percent of their power from nuclear energy, placing them among the most nuclear-dependent nations in the world.

Much of the nuclear fuel used by power reactors in the nations that were part of the former Soviet Union is supplied by Russia, giving Russia inordinate influence over many of them. This situation, coupled with Russia's vast gas supplies to these nations, allows Russia to hold their economies hostage if it chooses. As we have seen in the 2014 case of Russia annexing the Crimean peninsula away from Ukraine, economic power can range from persuasive to decisive. Even territorial independence cannot be guaranteed or maintained if a nation's energy supplies are not in its own control.

Germany, Italy, Switzerland, and Belgium are phasing out nuclear power generation, although Belgium's shut down (voted in 2003) will not occur until 2025, and Switzerland's (voted in 2011) until 2034. Italy halted the use of its last reactor in the 1980s, and voted in 2011 not to return to nuclear power.[143]

Japan has 50 operable reactors, but as of early 2014, it still is not operating most of them due to safety inspections following the accident at the Fukushima Dai-ichi power station in March 2011. Japan was actively constructing three more reactors, with five more actively planned for operation by 2030. Japan was generating nearly 30 percent of its energy from nuclear power in early 2011, and was planning to increase to 40 percent by 2020, and to 60 percent by 2100. However, policy issues and debates in Japan, resulting from the Fukushima Dai-ichi accident, may or may not alter the course of its nuclear future. National elections in Japan in December 2012 favored the pro-nuclear stance of the Liberal Democratic Party.[144]

South Korea has 23 reactors, with four more under construction, and five more planned by 2030. Nuclear energy supplies 33 percent of the power in South Korea, and the nation plans to supply 59 percent from nuclear energy by 2030, making it very nuclear-dependent. South

Korea is also building a large industry and marketing aggressively in reactor design and sales abroad.[145]

In the rest of Asia, Bangladesh, Indonesia, Malaysia, North Korea, Thailand, and Vietnam have no reactors, but are actively planning a total of 20 reactors by 2030.[146]

In South America, Argentina, Brazil, and Mexico already operate two nuclear power plants each, and are proposing to double their numbers. Some planning scenarios under consideration in Mexico would build 10 more plants by 2028. Chile also has active proposals underway to build four reactors.[147] In 2014, Argentina became the first nation in the world to begin construction on a small modular reactor (SMR) power generating plant. The SMR represents an inherently safe, state-of-the-art nuclear technology.[148]

Ten African countries are pursuing nuclear power including South Africa, which has two nuclear power plants.[149]

Even portions of the oil-rich Middle East are planning, building, or operating nuclear power plants. Jordan and the United Arab Emirates (UAE) are pursuing plans and license applications, Saudi Arabia has plans to build 16 reactors by 2030, Egypt has plans to build one, and Iran already has a 1,000-megawatt (MW) plant at Bushehr. Pakistan has three operating nuclear power plants, two under construction, and plans for two more by 2030.[150]

In addition to the countries listed above, Turkey is planning to build four nuclear power plants by 2030, and Israel and North Korea are each planning to build one.[151]

Among large, developed nations, only Canada and the United States are slow to expand their nuclear power supplies. Canada has 18 nuclear power reactors today, has two more under construction, and is planning three more by 2030. Nuclear energy supplies about 15 percent of the power in Canada today, and will move to nearly 20 percent by 2030 if the five new reactors planned are constructed and commissioned.[152]

As of the end of 2013, the United States has 100 commercial nuclear power plants—more than any other nation in the world. It is constructing five new plants and planning to build 13 more by 2030. By that time, some of the existing reactors are expected to retire, leaving the percentage of American energy production from nuclear energy flat or decreasing if the number of retired plants exceeds the number of new plants. The 100 nuclear power plants operating today generate approximately 19 percent of the electricity used in the United States, an amount representing nearly 69–70 percent of the nation's carbon-free energy.[153]

The Fuel Cycle

Understanding the basic principles of the nuclear fuel cycle is essential to understanding why reprocessing the fuel is so important. Uranium nuclear fuel is irradiated in most commercial reactors for approximately two to six years to generate electric power. Fuel lifetime is limited by the structural integrity of the fuel cladding and the amount of uranium-235 that has been consumed in the fuel. Once the fuel is discharged from the reactor, it is called spent nuclear fuel. It is often said to be "burned up," but in fact only a small portion of its energy potential has been used. Substantial amounts of unconsumed uranium and newly created plutonium remain.

Mature technology has existed for many years to reprocess spent nuclear fuel, and then fabricate major portions of it into new fuel elements that can be irradiated again. Fuel that is fabricated from reprocessed spent nuclear fuel is called mixed oxide (MOX), because reprocessed uranium oxide is blended with small amounts of recovered plutonium oxide. The fuel cycle—use, reprocessing, fabrication, and re-use—can be repeated in several iterations before the fuel is totally "spent."

Spent nuclear fuel handling can be addressed in one of two ways. It can be reprocessed, fabricated into MOX fuel, and reused sequentially; or it can be irradiated just once and disposed. This latter option is called "direct disposal." Reprocessing and re-use of nuclear fuel is practiced on an everyday basis today in France, Russia, India, and the UK.[154] Many other nations, including Japan and China, have been moving toward reprocessing.[155] Reprocessing is not practiced by the United States at this time.[156]

Reprocessing creates liquid/sludge high-level waste that must be stabilized and disposed. For this reason, and due to proliferation concerns, the technology has been somewhat controversial for non-nuclear weapon states. Generally speaking, reprocessing is not economically justified unless for security of supply or for waste management. Techniques and methods exist to contain and safeguard the plutonium separated in reprocessing, and to dispose of the waste.

Reprocessing/Recycling

Many nuclear nations either reprocess their spent nuclear fuel, or send it to other countries for reprocessing. Some do so to ensure the security of their fuel supply. Some other nations do not reprocess because they have access to, and can afford, a plentiful supply of fresh uranium. Of the major nuclear nations, only the United States, Canada, South Korea, Sweden, and Germany have policies of direct disposal. (In none of these nations has direct disposal actually occurred yet, as all are still storing their spent fuel.) The United States has maintained the option to reprocess at some future date by designing the Yucca Mountain repository to retrievably store spent nuclear fuel. Sweden and Germany have reprocessed their fuel outside of their own borders in the past. South Korea wants to reprocess, but is prohibited by treaty with the United States.[157]

Among major nuclear nations, France, Russia, China, India, the UK, and Japan have decided on reprocessing, although China's program is more conjecture than reality at this point and Japan's policy may change. The International Atomic Energy Agency (IAEA) estimates that nearly 350,000 metric tons (MT) of spent nuclear fuel has been discharged from civilian power reactors throughout the more than

50 years of the commercial nuclear power era. Of that roughly one-third (115,000 MT) has been reprocessed, and about two-thirds (235,000 MT) is being stored.[158]

In 2011, China announced it had mastered the technology for reprocessing nuclear fuel. In early 2012, China boasted that its technology could "boost the utilization of uranium 60-fold." Some projections from the known nuclear fuel supplies available to China indicate that reprocessing could yield enough extra fuel to extend China's nuclear fuel supply to 3,000 years. No timeframe was given as to when China will begin reprocessing on an industrial scale, although some estimates place the start of operations between 2020 and 2025.

In late 2010, the China National Nuclear Corporation (CNNC) and French fuel manufacturer Areva signed a contract to build a large (800 MT/year) reprocessing plant in Gansu Province in remote northwestern China. Areva made clear its expectation that the plant would become a reprocessing center for all of Asia. However, the project is not on a fast track for many reasons, among them caution over the accident at Fukushima, Japan in 2011, and the fact that Areva's existing reprocessing plants presently have excess capacity. Construction on the "Gansu Project" has not yet begun.[159]

India has actively reprocessed since the beginning of its nuclear industry. It considers spent nuclear fuel to be a resource, not a "waste." There are several reprocessing plants in India, all operated by the government's Department of Atomic Research via its Bhabha Atomic Research Centre (BARC). India's newest reprocessing plant came on line at Tarapur in 2011. India has recently signed reprocessing contracts with state-owned French and Russian nuclear companies.[160]

Russia has actively reprocessed civilian spent nuclear fuel for many years at a plant at Mayak, one of the "secret cities" of the former Union of Soviet Socialist Republics (USSR). Today, Russia's official policy is to have a completely "closed" fuel cycle—that is, one that practices reprocessing. This policy is embodied in the Concept of Spent Nuclear

Fuel Management, adopted in 2008. The Concept states that "SNF is not radioactive waste... SNF is a valuable secondary feed for producing nuclear fuel components and a number of radioactive isotopes used in medicine, agriculture and industry." Russia's spent nuclear fuel management strategy is directed toward establishing a reliable system for long-term, controlled storage, development of spent nuclear fuel reprocessing, and "balanced involvement of the SNF recovery products" into the nuclear fuel cycle.[161]

Reprocessing has been practiced in the United Kingdom for many years, both for UK-generated spent nuclear fuel, and spent fuel from Japan and many other customer nations. The government-affiliated company British Nuclear Fuels Limited (BNFL) performed the reprocessing at the Sellafield nuclear site until 2008. Today, a government contractor company reprocesses fuel removed from the UK's "Magnox" reactors and encapsulates it at Sellafield. The company also reprocesses commercial oxide fuel from British and overseas reactors in its Thermal Oxide Reprocessing Plant (THORP) facility at Sellafield. No decision has yet been made as to whether spent nuclear fuel from newly built reactors in the UK will be reprocessed or sent for direct disposal.[162]

France has the world's largest spent nuclear fuel reprocessing facility at La Hague, operated by Areva. It has operated since 1976, and previous to that a smaller reprocessing plant operated at Marcoule. The La Hague facility also reprocesses spent nuclear fuel from other nations, including several European nations, Australia (research reactor fuel), and, in the past, from Japan. About 850–1,000 MT of spent nuclear fuel per year was reprocessed at La Hague in recent years, but the operator is pursuing plans to increase the rate to about 1,500 MT per year by 2015. Contracts require that the high-level waste resulting from reprocessing be shipped back to the countries where the spent nuclear fuel originated.[163]

Germany does not have reprocessing facilities. However, previous to 2005, German spent nuclear fuel was sent to the Areva plant at La

Hague and the BNFL plant at Sellafield for reprocessing. Shipments of spent nuclear fuel for reprocessing were banned by government policy in 2005. The last shipment from France was completed in November 2011, following Germany's decision to abandon nuclear power.[164]

Many other European nations, including Belgium, The Netherlands, Spain, Sweden, and Switzerland formerly sent their spent nuclear fuel to La Hague in France or BNFL in the UK for reprocessing. They have suspended these practices while they develop their own facilities either for reprocessing or waste disposal.[165] In the Soviet era, satellite states affiliated in or with the USSR received their nuclear fuel from the USSR, and sent their spent nuclear fuel back to the USSR for reprocessing.[166] Today, Ukraine is trying to develop its own reprocessing capabilities. Poland and the Czech Republic are also planning to develop full fuel-cycle capabilities. Nuclear power is expanding rapidly in those nations, and some private companies are developed enough to consider entering the fuel cycle market. Russia still allows the import of Russian-originated spent nuclear fuel from other nations for reprocessing (i.e., originally exported from Russia).[167]

Beginning in 1969, Japan sent its spent nuclear fuel to Britain or France, where it was reprocessed by BNFL or Areva (then known as Compagnie Générale des Matières Nucléaires [COGEMA]). A total of approximately 7,000 MT of spent nuclear fuel was shipped from Japan, about 60 percent to the UK, and about 40 percent to France. Reprocessing of Japanese spent nuclear fuel finished in France in 2004 and in the UK in 2007. Between 1977 and 2006, Japan Atomic Energy Agency (JAEA) operated a pilot-scale reprocessing facility at Tokai.[168]

In 1985, agreement was reached between the Japanese Federation of Electric Power Companies, Aomori Prefecture, and Rokkasho-mura Village to locate a spent fuel reprocessing plant, uranium-enrichment facility, and vitrified waste storage center there.

The Rokkasho Reprocessing Plant (RRP) was supposed to start full operations in 2008, but technical and financial issues postponed the opening. The debate over nuclear power that has occurred in Japan since the March 2011 earthquake has further delayed the opening. As of today, the RRP has processed only test amounts of spent nuclear fuel. Plant capacity is projected at 800 MT per year.[169]

South Korea does not reprocess because it is prohibited from doing so by a 1970s non-proliferation agreement with the United States. Approximately 80 percent of the storage facilities for spent nuclear fuel in South Korea are filled, and with the agreement with the United States set to expire in 2014, many South Korean leaders are advocating reprocessing.[170]

Canada does not reprocess, and has no active plans to build reprocessing facilities because it uses natural uranium, not enriched, and as long as there is an abundance of uranium at competitive cost, reprocessing is not economical. Another reason is that the Canada Deuterium Uranium (CANDU) reactors used in Canada yield considerably less recoverable materials than do the pressurized water reactors (PWRs) or boiling water reactors (BWRs) used in much of the rest of the world. However, in 2007, Canada stated that it might eventually enter the reprocessing market since it is a major producer and exporter of uranium. Thus far, reprocessing plans have not materialized.[171]

The United States is virtually alone among large nuclear nations because it does not reprocess its fuel nor has it sent any nuclear fuel to be reprocessed abroad. The United States built two small, prototype reprocessing plants in the 1960s and 1970s, but stopped pursuing reprocessing technology because of a policy decision made by President Jimmy Carter in 1977, due to his proliferation concerns. President Ronald Reagan reversed Carter's decision in the 1980s, but did not implement reprocessing due to other pressing work in nuclear defense production.[172] The administration of President George W. Bush began investigating reprocessing in the Global Nuclear Energy Partnership (GNEP) initiative, and sponsored a successful, small-scale reprocessing experiment at the Oak Ridge National Laboratory during 2007–2008.

At the same time, the Nuclear Regulatory Commission (NRC) gathered information about how it might license commercial reprocessing facilities, perhaps at federal energy sites.[173]

At the present time, the United States has no plans to reprocess commercial spent nuclear fuel. In trade agreements with nations developing new nuclear programs, the United States actively tries to discourage reprocessing. For example, the United States signed a trade agreement with the UAE in 2009, in which the UAE pledged that it would not reprocess spent nuclear fuel in its newly developing nuclear program. At the present time, the United States is pressuring South Korea and Taiwan to sign or update similar trade agreements with similar provisions.[174]

MOX Fuel Manufacture and Use

France is the only nation in the world that manufactures MOX fuel on a commercial production scale, but many other nations are planning or building MOX plants. In Europe, MOX fuel is used fairly widely in civilian reactors, where 40 are licensed to burn MOX and 35 are doing so, mostly in France. France derives about 17 percent of its power from burning MOX fuel.

The MOX fuel is fabricated in France at the large Melex Plant near Marcoule, which was built in 1990 with a 40-year design life, but is expected to operate until 2040 with life-extension improvements. In 2006, contracts for MOX fuel supply were signed with Japanese utilities. France is aggressively marketing MOX services across the world, and was reported to have about 30 MT/year in contracts outside of France, with strong demand.[175]

The UK no longer has an operating MOX plant. However, in 2011, Britain's Department of Energy and Climate Change (DECC) announced that its preferred option for disposing civilian plutonium that has resulted from reprocessing spent nuclear fuel was to burn it as MOX in civilian reactors. The British government then requested proposals for how to dispose of the UK's 112-MT stockpile of civilian plutonium—the largest such stockpile in the world. The government is now evaluating options from the proposals received, as well as an option to burn its plutonium in MOX fuel in CANDU reactors in Canada, and another option to convert the stored plutonium powders into ceramic blocks and bury them in a repository.[176]

China is rapidly pursuing reprocessing and MOX technology, and plans to burn MOX when it is able. In 2010, China and Belgium signed an agreement to build a MOX plant in China.[177]

India has the Advanced Fuel Fabrication Facility (AFFF) at Tarapur, producing small quantities of MOX fuel for the civilian reactors at Tarapur Atomic Power Station. India is preoccupied with aggressively building new nuclear power plants, and does not now have enough accumulated spent nuclear fuel to begin manufacturing MOX on a large scale.[178]

Russia has a small MOX fabrication line at the Russian Institute at Obninsk, producing experimental MOX fuel pins for the Obninsk Atomic Power Station. Russia is actively pursuing fast reactor development and plans to fuel these reactors with MOX.[179]

Along with the United States, and in conformance with an arms destruction agreement, Russia is building a plant to manufacture MOX from a small amount of military plutonium.[180]

For many years, Japan received MOX fuel from overseas and planned to "burn" it in reactors, beginning in 2009 with the Monju fast breeder reactor in Fukui Prefecture. In the meanwhile, in 1994, nine member utilities in the Japanese Federation of Electric Power Companies formed the "pluthermal" program to use MOX fuel in commercial reactors. By January 2010, the Ministry of Economy, Trade, and Industry (METI) had approved burning MOX in 10 commercial reactors, although implementation had not occurred by the time the Fukushima accident in March 2011 closed all Japanese reactors for safety evaluations. Japan was planning to use MOX in one-third of its reactors before recent policy fluctuations.[181]

In 2005, Aomari prefecture approved construction of Japanese Nuclear Fuel Limited's (JNFL's) J-MOX plant at Rokkasho, adjacent to the reprocessing plant. Construction began in October 2010, and is now expected to be completed in 2016. In the meantime, several Japanese utilities have sought MOX fuel supplies from Areva in France.[182]

Canada and the United States do not manufacture MOX fuel for commercial purposes. Along with Russia, and in conformance with an arms destruction agreement, the United States has agreed to build a plant to manufacture MOX from a small amount of military plutonium.[183]

The Nuclear Supply Chain

Most of us recognize the truth in the phrase—*"use it or lose it."* This phrase can apply to physical fitness, mental skills, the humming of a finely tuned motor, or components of the economy. For example, if we don't practice speaking a foreign language we've taken pains to learn, we'll eventually forget much of it and sound awkward and slow when we speak it. Likewise in business, if customers stop buying a particular product, the companies that make that product will go out of business. Then, when we need that product again, the factories and expertise to produce it will no longer be available. The same is true for the nuclear supply chain. As the United States virtually stopped building new nuclear reactors between the mid-1980s and recently, most of our onshore nuclear businesses have shut down or concentrated their efforts and growth overseas. A good example is Westinghouse Electric Co., which built the nuclear reactor for the USS Nautilus, the world's first nuclear-powered submarine in 1954, and the reactors for the USS Enterprise, the world's first nuclear-powered aircraft carrier in 1960. Westinghouse built the first nuclear power plant in the United States at Shippingport, Pennsylvania, during 1957–1958. France acquired the Westinghouse technology and then upgraded and replicated the design for all of its reactors. Westinghouse also provided most of the PWRs in the United

States and their design was used in about half of the reactors in heavily nuclear-dependent Japan. Westinghouse is now foreign-owned, sold to BNFL in 1999, and then to an investment group led by Toshiba (of Japan) in 2006.[184]

In 1986, Exxon, the world's largest oil company at the time, sold its nuclear division to Kraftwerk Union A.G., a wholly owned subsidiary of Siemens A.G., based in Muelheim, Germany.[185] Siemens divested its nuclear business as German politics halted Germany's nuclear program. Siemens Nuclear, located in Richland, Washington, was sold to the French company Areva.

Exxon Nuclear was responsible for providing the first fuel loading for Washington State's only operating nuclear plant, the Columbia Generating Station, originally called WNP-2 in the early 1980s. I was responsible for building this plant as one of five that were under construction when I signed on as Chief Executive Officer for the Washington Public Power Supply System (WPPSS). WNP-2 was the only plant completed after we determined that the demand for electric power in the region had been grossly overestimated. Combustion Engineering, Inc., was providing nuclear reactors for two of the five discontinued plants and Babcock & Wilcox (B&W) Company provided the other two reactors. Areva now owns B&W, and Combustion Engineering was bought by Westinghouse, now owned by Toshiba of Japan. Combustion Engineering transferred its nuclear design to South Korea, and South Korea now is competing worldwide with this customized design. All of the U.S. reactors and reactor systems were developed by U.S. companies that are now owned outright or are in joint ventures with other countries.

The Shaw Group, a Fortune 500 company with approximately 25,000 employees and $6 billion in revenue in 2012 has provided engineering, construction, maintenance, technology, fabrication, remediation, and support services for clients in the energy field, including nuclear energy, since the mid-1980s. In 2013, it was acquired by the Chicago Bridge & Iron Company (CB&I), based in La Hague, Netherlands.[186] In 2007, General Electric, perhaps the manufacturer of more nuclear power reactors still in use in the United States than any other company, announced a global nuclear alliance with Hitachi of Japan to provide advanced reactors and other nuclear services. The company is now known in the United States as GE Hitachi Nuclear Energy (GEH), and in Japan as Hitachi-GE Nuclear Energy, Ltd.[187]

At two of the five new nuclear plants being built in the United States now, Vogtle Units 3 and 4 in Georgia, the two reactors were jointly designed by Westinghouse (which retains its American name) and Shaw (now CB&I). Likewise, Westinghouse has the contract to supply the reactors for the Summer Station Units 2 and 3 nuclear power plants now being built in South Carolina, and as it does for the reactor being placed in the Watts Bar 2 nuclear plant under construction in Tennessee. In another case, the NRC rejected a license application to build two new reactors at the South Texas Project in the Houston area in April 2013, because too large a portion of the ownership of the new plants would be foreign.[188] At nearly the same time, the NRC also rejected an application to build a third reactor at the Calvert Cliffs Nuclear Power Station in Maryland, for the same reason.[189]

The contract for another large nuclear building project in the United States, the government's MOX Plant in South Carolina, is held by a partnership of Shaw and French-owned Areva. The United States and Russia are each building a MOX plant to use up some of their weapons-grade plutonium left from Cold War weapons production. They have each agreed to blend in, and eventually burn up, 34 metric tons of plutonium. However, in 2006, with both plants behind schedule and Russian technology deemed too immature to proceed, the U.S. Department of Energy (DOE) awarded a contract to COGEMA—now Areva—to transfer design information for a modern MOX fabrication facility to Russia.[190]

Areva is owned by the French government primarily, and is one of the largest nuclear companies in the world with tentacles into all sectors of nuclear energy production including reactor design, construction, reprocessing, manufacture of MOX fuel, and vitrification of high-level wastes. Areva dominates the French fuel-making and reactor design/ construction market, and bids for nuclear contracts around the world. It is recognized as the world leader in reprocessing, and has reprocessed more spent nuclear fuel than any other company/facility in the world. In late 2010, Areva and the CNNC signed a contract to build a large reprocessing plant in China. Areva made clear its expectation that the plant would become a reprocessing center for all of Asia. A partnership of Areva and Mitsubishi Heavy Industries (MHI) of Japan has been discussing building a dedicated nuclear fuel fabrication facility in the United States. In 2011, Areva proposed building a U.S. reprocessing plant, and has stated that one of its goals is to build a reprocessing plant in the United States.[191]

At the largest federal construction project in the nation, the Waste Treatment Plant (WTP) at the Hanford Site in Washington State, the lack of qualified nuclear suppliers has been given as one of the reasons for delays and cost overruns in the facility's construction. Many parts of the equipment must meet the highest nuclear quality assurance standard in the nation—the ASME NQA-1 2000 standards, promulgated by the American Society of Mechanical Engineers—to stand up to the highly radioactive mixtures that will process through the plant. Soon after construction began in 2000, the WTP's contractor found that the number of firms that were "NQA-1-qualified" had dwindled remarkably since the mid-1980s. Such qualifications are expensive to maintain, and there was simply not enough market for them for the suppliers to invest.[192]

Across the world, there are plenty of companies that want to dominate the nuclear market, which is booming in many nations outside of the United States.[193] In 2007, the Russian government ordered more than 30 nuclear-related companies to amalgamate into a state-owned giant called AtomEnergoProm, which today bills itself as "the company of state corporation Rosatom." Rosatom is Russia's state-owned nuclear energy corporation. The AtomEnergoProm conglomerate is ambitiously selling nuclear plants and nuclear services in Asia, Africa, the Middle East (including Iran), Turkey, and South America. Russia also has agreements with uranium-rich Ukraine to mine, enrich, and fabricate uranium, and cooperate on fuel-cycle research.[194] Rosatom has an overseas subsidiary called ZAO Rosatom, and in 2012, applied for a license to try to enter the Horizon Project building nuclear power plants in North Wales and Gloucestershire. Further, Rosatom is fabricating nuclear fuel for PWRs in western countries. Russia already supplies nuclear fuel, produced in association with Areva, to some reactors in the UK. NUKEM Technologies, although headquartered in Germany, is a Rosatom subsidiary that has long provided international nuclear decontamination and decommissioning (D&D) services.[195]

In Japan, as has been shown, major companies such as Hitachi and Toshiba are buying or forming partnerships with U.S. firms. Before an accident at the Fukushima Power Station in 2011, Japan was heading towards a complete nuclear fuel cycle, building a major reprocessing facility, and developing fast breeder reactors to burn MOX fuel. In 2007, the Japanese government selected MHI as the core company to develop fast reactors. Advanced thermal reactors, also capable of burning MOX, were being built by GE-Hitachi and Toshiba. A Japanese manufacturing company, Ishikawajima-Harima Heavy Industries Co., Ltd. (IHI), has also been a major player in nuclear construction. Since the accident, Japan has been engaged in a debate over its nuclear future, making its leading nuclear companies all the more anxious to seek business across the world.[196]

In South Korea, the Korea Electric Power Co. (KEPCO) is an aggressive company seeking to build reactors throughout the world. A South Korean consortium led by KEPCO and involving Samsung,

Hyundai, and Doosan, as well as Westinghouse recently beat leading United States and French firms to win a $20-billion contract to build nuclear reactors in the UAE.[197] KEPCO also recently signed a contract to supply a research reactor to Jordan. South Korea aims to capture 20 percent of the world market in building nuclear reactors by 2030.[198]

Chinese firms are either synonymous, or entwined, with the Chinese government. In addition to CNNC planning a reprocessing facility in Gansu Province with Areva, the Nuclear Power Institute of China is partnering with Atomic Energy Limited of Canada (AECL) in developing techniques to dispose of spent nuclear fuel by burning it directly in CANDU reactors. The technique is called Direct Use of Pressurized Water Reactor Spent Fuel in CANDU. In 2010, AECL announced the first re-use of nuclear fuel in a CANDU reactor in China's Qinsham nuclear power station. Chinese atomic energy corporations are also rumored to be trying to buy into the Horizon Project in the UK.[199]

Clearly CANDU Energy Inc. is marketing broadly and expanding into alternative fuels and international partnerships. It has operations in Canada, Argentina, Romania, China, Pakistan, India, and South Korea. In 2012, CANDU Energy signed an expanded agreement with three CNNC subsidiary companies, to continue co-operation in the development of reprocessed uranium and thorium as alternative fuels for new CANDU reactors in China. The 24-month agreement is expected to result in a detailed conceptual design of the Advanced Fuel CANDU Reactor that is optimized to use reprocessed uranium and thorium fuel. The agreement marks the third phase of cooperation between Canada and China that began in 2008.[200]

In 2012, China and Saudi Arabia signed an agreement for the peaceful use of nuclear technology. The agreement covers the maintenance and development of nuclear power plants and research reactors as well as the manufacturing and supply of nuclear fuel elements. The sharp rise in the export of nuclear technology and nuclear business agreements between China and the rest of the world, as well as South Korea and the rest of the world, has coined the new phrase "Nuclear Silk Road." The phrase is a comparison to the original Silk Road, which was a network of early trade routes established between China, Europe, and the Middle East. The comparison is apt because the original Silk Road linked cultural interactions across civilizations that might not otherwise have met, and fostered not just trade but ties, understandings, and mutually beneficial relationships.[201]

The giant GDF (Gaz de France)-Suez Corp., headquartered in London, UK, but with offices all over Europe, and the French utility EDF also are aggressively marketing themselves throughout the world. In 2011, GDF-Suez combined with International Power and now calls itself the leading utility company in the world.[202] In 2009, EDF (London) bought British Energy, and now calls itself "one of the three largest energy companies in Europe." It has eight nuclear reactors in Britain, and also does business in Germany, Italy, and France.[203]

In addition to the GDF-Suez and EDF offices in the UK, Babcock International, a leading British engineering firm, services the Royal Navy's nuclear submarine fleet, and also services nuclear power plants in South Africa among its many other endeavors.[204] Four major energy companies that have been operating in Germany, E.ON, EnBW (Energie Baden-Württemberg AG), RWE (Rheinisch-Westfälisches Elektrizitätswerk AG), and Swedish government-owned Vattenfall, are now expanding their international divisions to pursue markets in Russia, southeastern Europe, Sweden, and other areas. They need to expand and find new markets to survive, because Germany has recently made a decision to suspend nuclear power.[205] The RWE and E.ON. have formed a joint venture called the Horizon Project to build new nuclear plants in North Wales and Gloucestreshire.[206] Vattenfall already does business in Denmark, Finland, France, Germany, The Netherlands, Norway, Sweden, and the United Kingdom.[207]

The CEZ (České Energetické Závody) Group is an ambitious multinational headquartered in Praha, Czech Republic. It is largely state-owned (70 percent) and is aggressively marketing and expanding in southeastern Europe and Turkey, building various types of electricity-producing plants. Separate bids to perform nuclear work in the Czech Republic have been received from Westinghouse, Areva, and a joint Russian-Czech venture (Skoda JS [Czech] and AtomStroyExport and Gidropress [Russian]). In all cases, local partnerships with CEZ are a necessary part of the bids.[208]

Even small European countries are marketing themselves in the world-wide nuclear business. In October 2010, China and Belgium signed a framework for construction of a pilot MOX fabrication plant in China. Partners were Belgonucleaire, SCK-CEN (Studiecentrum Voor Kerkenerge—Centre L'Etude de L'Energie Nucleaire [Belgian Nuclear Research Center]), and Tractebel Engineering (a GDF-Suez Belgian subsidiary headquartered in Brussels).[209] Posiva Oy, the company constructing Finland's geologic repository for spent nuclear fuel and high-level nuclear waste at Olkiluoto, is a large company working with international partners Swedish Nuclear Fuel and Waste Management Company, National Agency for Management of Nuclear Waste (ANDRA, in France), National Cooperative for the Disposal of Radioactive Waste (NAGRA in Switzerland), Ontario Power Generation in Canada, Radioactive Waste Repository Authority (RAWRA in the Czech Republic), the Nuclear Waste Management Organization (NUMO), and the Radioactive Waste Management Funding and Research Center (RWMC), both in Japan.[210]

Deep Geologic Repositories and Consolidated Storage Facilities

Whether spent nuclear fuel results from just one use in a reactor or from sequential reprocessing, it will eventually need to be disposed. Nearly all nuclear nations have made policy decisions to pursue deep-geologic disposal. Some, notably Finland, Sweden, and France, are acting quickly to site and build deep-geologic repositories. These three nations expect to open deep-geologic repositories in the next 12 years.[211] In the meantime, many other nations are establishing interim consolidated storage facilities that will at least isolate their spent nuclear fuel and high-level wastes away from population centers and rivers, and cut the expense of storing and guarding these byproducts in multiple locations. These nations have begun the immense preparatory work, including public involvement with potential host communities, license preparations, and transportation planning and permitting.

All of China's reactors went online after 1990, so there is presently very little need for spent nuclear fuel and high-level waste storage capacity. By contrast, three-fourths of the reactors built to date in the world went online before 1990. Only two power plants in China are presently known to be accumulating more spent fuel than they can store. China's inventory of spent nuclear fuel was estimated to be only 3,800 MT in 2005, and may be as high as 12,300 MT by 2020. Taiwan presently has only about 3,350 MT of spent nuclear fuel. Projections of China's inventory of spent fuel by 2035 could range from 13,670 MT to 21,645 MT, depending on realization of low- or high-growth in nuclear energy.[212]

Nevertheless, despite not having a pressing need for a deep-geologic repository, China announced in 1985 a state policy aimed at siting a repository, and in 2006 set specific timetables for the plan. Laboratory studies and site selection would take place 2006–2020, followed by underground in-situ tests 2021–2040, and construction 2041–2050. Since China plans to reprocess its fuel, the deep-geologic repository would contain the end products of the fuel cycle after sequential reprocessing, and therefore could be relatively small and still accommodate the waste from robust nuclear production. Since that time, siting studies have focused on granite deposits in the Beishan area in Gansu province in northwestern China, a remote area of the Gobi Desert. China already has a small consolidated storage facility at Lanzhou in the same area, with capacity to double in size.[213]

India has reprocessed fuel since 1964, and presently has a very small nuclear industry. Therefore, its inventory of spent nuclear fuel is very small. Nevertheless, India has an active consolidated storage facility for high-level waste at Tarapur, and is developing another facility at Kalpakkan, the site of a power reactor and reprocessing plant. Like China, and despite having a very low near-term need, India announced in 2012 that it is actively seeking to site a deep-geologic repository for high-level waste and end-cycle spent nuclear fuel over the next five years. In situ boreholes and other preliminary characterization work have been ongoing in northwest and central India since the early 2000s.[214]

Because Russia has reprocessed heavily, it has only about 15,000 MT of spent nuclear fuel. It does not have an actual consolidated storage facility, and civilian power plant waste is stored at several reactor sites across the country. However, Russia's dry storage facility Zheleznogorsk in Siberia is the largest such facility in the world.[215]

Russia passed a new Radioactive Waste Management Law in June 2011, placing time limits on interim storage and quantities in storage for waste generators, and defining how generators must bring wastes into condition suitable for transfer and disposal. A special fund, paid by waste generators, was established in Rosatom, Russia's state corporation for nuclear energy, to provide for future disposal. Russia is actively searching for a deep-geologic repository site. The massive Nizhnekansky granite deposits in Krasnoyarsk territory are being investigated most intensely, with an underground rock laboratory planned in the Yeniseysky area by 2017. A decision on construction of a repository is due by 2025, with completion of the facility by 2035.[216]

In 2006, the United Kingdom announced a decision to site a deep-geologic repository for products of the end of the fuel cycle after sequential reprocessing. A siting council began the search for a volunteer host community. West Cumbria expressed interest, and a 2012 poll showed more than half of residents in favor of hosting the repository in exchange for several financial and industrial benefits. The affected units of local government are presently considering a report released in July 2012 on a potential repository. Much of the spent nuclear fuel and high-level nuclear waste in the UK is stored at the Sellafield site in Cumbria. However, Sellafield is not an official interim consolidated storage facility.[217]

In 2006, France decided to pursue building a deep-geologic repository for high-level waste—defined in that country as the products of the end of the fuel cycle after sequential reprocessing. A subcontractor to the French government is managing the conceptual and front-end phases of the CIGEO (Centre Industrial de Stockage Geologique) repository.[218] Officials from the U.S. DOE have visited the CIGEO facility many times, as well as the nearby Underground Research Laboratory where the French are fine-tuning disposal technologies.[219]

Germany has investigated the Gorleben salt dome as a final repository for high-level waste that has resulted from fuel reprocessing outside the country. It has built and begun operating a pilot conditioning (drying) plant at Gorleben. Timetables have shown such a repository opening between 2030 and 2035. However, after the Fukushima accident in Japan in March 2011, Germany decided to forego nuclear power. The new direction in nuclear policy has slowed its deep-geologic repository effort and there are no reliable predictions at this time about a timetable.[220] In the meantime, Germany has found it necessary to buy power generated by nuclear plants in the Czech Republic, Ukraine, and France. The practice of buying nuclear energy from other countries is called "greenwashing."

In Europe, Finland chose the Olkiluoto site in Eurajoki in northwest Finland and is actively constructing a repository scheduled to open perhaps as early as 2020. Sweden has selected the Forsmark site north of Stockholm in 2009, and submitted license applications to the Swedish government for a deep-geologic repository in 2011. As of 2014, the site is undergoing public review, and timelines call for operations to commence in 2023.[221]

Switzerland began planning for high-level waste disposal many years ago. In 2008, the Swiss government agency NAGRA proposed six potential siting regions and all were approved for further study in 2011. Phase II of the siting process (current through about 2015) will conduct site-specific studies and narrow the choice of regions. Phase III will conduct further in-depth studies and prepare a license. The Swiss Federal Council is expected to decide on a final location in about 2020, with the high-level waste repository opening about 2045.

Likewise, Belgium is researching a deep-geologic repository for high-level waste and spent nuclear waste, focused on deep clay beds at Mol. No timetable is given. The Czech Republic is also planning for a repository. The Czech Nuclear Act calls for a national deep-geologic repository to be chosen by 2015 and open in 2065.[222]

Several smaller European nations, including several former Soviet-bloc countries and The Netherlands, have expressed interest in waiting for international (perhaps regional) repositories to be developed. The Association for Regional and International Underground Storage (ARIUS) (Baden, Switzerland), a non-commercial group, was established in 2002 to promote the concept of regional and international facilities for storage and disposal of various types of long-lived nuclear wastes. In 2006, the European Union (EU—formerly European Community [EC]) funded the Strategic Action Plan for Implementation of European Regional Repositories (SAPIERR), indicating EU/EC recognition that up to 25 individual national repositories in Europe would not be economical, safe, or secure. The first SAPIERR symposium in 2009 resulted in 14 countries preparing a consensus model to establish a European Repository Development Organisation (ERDO). Discussions among potential participants are underway. [223]

In 2000, Japan passed a law mandating deep geologic disposal of high-level waste, defined as vitrified waste from spent nuclear fuel reprocessing. Potential sites were short-listed and detailed investigation had begun. Final site selection was projected to occur in 2030, with operation beginning in 2035. In 2007, Japan passed a supplementary law stating that "final disposal is the most important issue in steadily carrying out nuclear policy." It mandated the government to take a more active role in promoting the need for, and benefits of, a deep-geologic repository to the general public.[224] However, due to the re-evaluation of nuclear policy following the Fukushima accident, the Japanese government in August 2012 announced it would begin to study direct disposal of spent nuclear fuel. The nation is evaluating three scenarios for the use of nuclear power—0, 15, and 20 to 25 percent. If the zero option was selected, all spent nuclear fuel would be buried in direct disposal and not reprocessed. In the 15 percent and 20 to 25 percent options, both reprocessing and direct burial would be considered. In all of the options, a repository would be sited. Due to the political turmoil surrounding nuclear energy in Japan, no timetable for a repository can be considered realistic at this time.[225]

South Korea has built the Korea Underground Research Tunnel (KURT) in a mountainous area in Yusung Gu, Deajeon, as a research laboratory to develop a Korean technical strategy for a potential deep-geologic repository. Groundwater flow and rock mass characteristics are being investigated, but there is no timetable for siting and constructing a repository.[226]

In 2010, Canada began the search for a deep-geologic repository for high-level waste and spent nuclear fuel. Community-based acceptance and both rail and road transportation were stipulated. Thus far, eight Canadian communities have expressed interest in being studied as potential host communities—three in northern Saskatchewan and five in Ontario. It is estimated that a deep-geologic repository site will be chosen by 2020, and the repository would open in 2035.[227]

The United States has an inventory of approximately 69,700 MT of spent nuclear fuel from civilian nuclear power plants—*the largest collection in the world.* The U.S. nuclear industry adds to this total at the rate of about 2,000 to 2,400 MT annually. The fuel is stored at 122 different reactor plants in 38 states, including several plants within 50 miles of large population centers and major rivers. The majority (approximately three-quarters) of the fuel is stored in indoor water pools, and about one-quarter has been dried and placed in casks. The total amount of spent nuclear fuel includes nearly 3,000 MT stored at 11 power plants that have been shut down in nine states.[228] No consolidated storage facility exists, and plans for a deep-geologic repository, in progress since the Nuclear Waste Policy Act (NWPA) was passed in 1982, were terminated by the DOE and President Obama in 2009.

In December 1987, Congress amended the NWPA to designate Yucca Mountain, Nevada, as the only repository site to be studied. The Act imposed a process wherein, if the site was found suitable, and was formally recommended as the final choice by Congress and the president, the DOE would need to prepare a license application for technical review by the NRC. Formal recommendation by the Congress and the president did come in the form of the Yucca Mountain Development Act of 2002.[229] The DOE's 8,600-page Yucca Mountain repository license application was submitted to the NRC in 2008. From that date, the NRC was allotted three years by the NWPA to complete the review and determine the Yucca Mountain site's acceptability.[230] However, in March 2009, President Obama proposed a federal budget for fiscal year 2010 that cut off almost all of the funding for the Yucca Mountain Project.

On January 29, 2010, Obama ordered Secretary of Energy Steven Chu to terminate the project. In subsequent federal budgets, the Yucca Mountain Project has received essentially no funding. In March 2010, Chu filed a motion asking the Atomic Safety and Licensing Board, the NRC's administrative panel, to dismiss the Yucca Mountain license application.[231] Lawsuits were filed challenging that action,[232] however, all work on the geologic repository stopped.

In the 16 years since the DOE missed the NWPA's original 1998 deadline to begin taking spent nuclear fuel from commercial nuclear power plants and placing it in a national repository, nuclear utility companies have filed claims for breach of contract and damages for the costs they have paid to the federal government for spent nuclear fuel storage and security. Thus far, approximately $2.2 billion has been paid by the federal government to the utilities in such claims, and many more claims are pending and likely to be settled in the utilities' favor.

In 2011, the DOE estimated that total damage awards to utilities could amount to $20.8 billion if the federal government begins accepting spent nuclear fuel by 2020. The Nuclear Energy Institute estimates that damage awards to utilities will reach $31.8 billion by 2042 if the federal government does not begin accepting spent nuclear fuel until that time. According to the Department of Justice (DOJ), DOE's liability increases by $500 million each year, with essentially boundless liability into the future if a deep-geologic repository or interim consolidated storage facility is not sited.[233]

The facts are plain and simple. The United States, despite having nearly five times as much spent nuclear fuel as France and Russia, approximately seven times as much as China, more than 10 times as much as the UK, and an amount that may approach 25 times as much as India, has no plans for a consolidated storage facility or deep-geologic repository. Finland, with only 1/40th the spent nuclear fuel of the United States, and Sweden with 1/12th the spent fuel of the United States, are on track to open repositories within the next 12 years. The United States has accumulated approximately $30.9 billion in its Nuclear Waste Fund (NWF) (collected from utility ratepayers, as mandated in the NWPA), and has spent more than $15 billion on the Yucca Mountain Project alone.

## Chapter 3

Obama's Lawless Legacy

The President "shall take Care that the Laws be faithfully executed."—Article II, Section 3, U.S. Constitution

How did we get into this situation where our nuclear high-level waste and spent nuclear fuel are stored indefinitely in our nation's back yards? While many countries in the developed and developing world are bypassing the United States in advancing nuclear technology and securing their own independent energy supplies, the United States is locked in a political stalemate on nuclear waste that has brought its tentative nuclear renaissance to a near standstill. The stalemate stems from President Barack Obama's decision to unlawfully terminate the Yucca Mountain Project and the Nuclear Regulatory Commission's (NRC's) former chairman Gregory Jaczko's action to illegally stop the review of the Department of Energy's (DOE's) license application to make Yucca Mountain America's first national geologic repository for high-level nuclear waste and spent nuclear fuel. We sued the president and the NRC for violating the Nuclear Waste Policy Act (NWPA)—the law that directed the U.S. nuclear waste program. The introduction to this book briefly explains the background of our nation's decisions and laws—particularly the NWPA—to deal with the highly radioactive byproducts of nuclear energy production.

When Mr. Obama was the presidential candidate in 2008, he needed the help of the much more senior and well-connected insider Senator Harry Reid (D-NV) to get elected. It's common knowledge that candidate Obama made a campaign promise to Senator Reid to shut down the Yucca Mountain Project in exchange for Nevada votes and Reid's assistance as a powerful senior Senator in working with Congress. Since he was first elected as a Democrat Representative from urban Las Vegas in 1982, Reid had opposed the Yucca Mountain Project.[234] He was elected Senator from Nevada in 1986, just a year before the NWPA was modified to designate the Yucca Mountain site in his state as the only location to be studied by the DOE for suitability as the nation's nuclear high-level waste repository. When the NWPA was amended in 1987, Reid dubbed it the "Screw Nevada Bill,"[235] even though the scientific and technical evaluations consistently ranked the tuff rock of the Yucca Mountain site as the safest and most geologically sound of all the sites considered.

Multi-year characterization efforts by more than 2,500 scientists from universities, the U.S. Geological Service (USGS), and the DOE and its contractors (including five national laboratories) resulted in a 1998 DOE study that found the Yucca Mountain site "well-suited," viable, and valid for high-level nuclear waste storage.[236] This report was peer-reviewed by the U.S. Nuclear Waste Technical Review Board, an independent federal agency whose purpose is to provide independent scientific and technical oversight of DOE's program for managing and disposing of high-level waste and spent nuclear fuel. However, before DOE finalized its recommendation for the Yucca Mountain site, it commissioned one more independent expert review, known as a Total System Performance Assessment (TSPA). A joint peer review panel composed of top international experts assembled by the International Atomic Energy Agency (IAEA) and the Organization for Economic

Cooperation and Development's (OECD's) Nuclear Energy Agency (NEA) completed the TSPA and concluded in November 2001, that the "performance assessment [undertaken by DOE]...provides an adequate basis for...the site recommendation decision."[237]

When Harry Met Gregory

By 2000, while the international team of experts was reviewing DOE's findings on the Yucca Mountain site, Senator Harry Reid had three successful Senatorial runs under his belt and had become Minority Whip—the second most powerful Democrat in the Senate. However, he was far from confident his party would prevail in the presidential election that November. Losing would mean Republican George W. Bush would become president and push the repository, along with expanded building of new nuclear power plants. The Yucca Mountain Project, by that time, had grown to be a huge project, employing thousands, and was aiming straight at becoming the nation's first geologic repository for high-level waste and spent nuclear fuel.

At the same time, Gregory Jaczko, a newly minted Ph.D. in theoretical particle physics, began a one-year tenure as a Congressional Science Fellow in the office of Democrat Representative Ed Markey of Massachusetts. Markey is well-known as one of the most anti-nuclear members in Congress. Congressional Science Fellow positions are generally considered to be jumping-off points for promising young graduates to gain exposure and become known around Washington so they can move on to more permanent, prominent positions. Jaczko, ambitious and young, was looking for his next position, and his association with Markey sparked Reid's interest. Jaczko's previous position was as adjunct professor under Dr. Francis Slakey, a physics and public policy Distinguished Lecturer at Georgetown University who advocates stricter nuclear security standards, a strategy commonly used by anti-nuclear activists to stop or delay nuclear activities, knowing that safety and nuclear security is always a public concern.

Evidently, Reid also was intrigued with Jaczko's eastern pedigree. Raised in Albany and educated as an undergraduate at Cornell University in rural New York State, Jaczko had never lived west of Madison, where he earned his Ph.D. from the University of Wisconsin.[238] Reid needed someone who wasn't from Nevada or any other western state—someone who wouldn't appear biased—to help him oppose the Yucca Mountain Project. He already had a bevy of Nevada state officials opposing the project based on its perceived potential harm to the gaming industry of Las Vegas. Officials from the host localities, Nye County and its cities and towns surrounding the Nevada Test Site (NTS), were not influenced by Nevada gaming interests and favored the Yucca Mountain Project for its economic benefits. Reid could see that an Easterner with an academic degree in physics would be the ideal addition to his arsenal of those opposing the project.

Reid and Jaczko clicked—Reid saw in Jaczko a smart and ambitious individual with the right background, education, and values to help him achieve his career-long goal to "kill" the Yucca Mountain Project, and Jaczko saw in Reid an established power base with infinite opportunities for advancing his career. Their relationship is a chilling example of political henchmanship. By January 2001, Jaczko was on Reid's payroll as science advisor. The visibility of a position with the Minority Whip and the implied advancement possibilities were ideal for him.

The same month that Jaczko went to work for Reid, George W. Bush was sworn in as President. Bush was ready to implement the NWPA, by then a nearly 20-year-old law whose realization was long overdue. The law directed DOE to begin taking possession of the nation's commercial spent fuel and legacy nuclear waste from weapons production by January 1998. The DOE already was in default by three years for not removing the commercial spent fuel from temporary storage sites at 104 nuclear power plants across America.

The NWPA also had created a Nuclear Waste Fund (NWF) to pay for the licensing and construction of a repository to collect and retrievably store the spent fuel and permanently dispose of the legacy waste. These monies had been collected from nuclear energy utilities and ratepayers since 1982. By the time Bush took office in 2001, the NWF had collected approximately $20 billion, growing at the rate of about $750 million per year. As long as no repository was opened, ratepayers and utilities were receiving no benefit from those funds.[239]

The House of Representatives was solidly Republican, and control of the Senate was split, but the Yucca Mountain Project had widespread bi-partisan support. Worse yet for Reid's hopes to stop the project, Bush appointed Spencer Abraham as his Secretary of Energy. Abraham was a former Republican Senator from Michigan, anxious to dispose of Michigan's spent fuel (the ninth largest collection in the United States). He had co-sponsored temporary waste repository legislation in the Senate. Even the Nevada Commission on Nuclear Projects warned that an affirmative recommendation for the Yucca Mountain Project in the coming summer was "overwhelmingly likely."[240] However, on May 24, 2001, Senator Jim Jeffords of Vermont left the Republican Party and became an independent, switching control of the Senate to the Democrats. Democrat Tom Daschle of South Dakota was solidly opposed to the Yucca Mountain Project. When Daschle became Majority Leader and Reid became Majority Whip, the situation appeared to become a bit brighter for Reid's ambition to kill the Yucca Mountain Project, although he still didn't have the votes to stop it. Secretary Abraham could still recommend the Yucca Mountain site and President Bush could approve it. Clearly, for Reid, the battle needed to swing into the realm of science to convince "on the fence" Senators and Representatives and give them defensible reasons for cancelling the repository and leaving spent nuclear fuel and nuclear high-level waste scattered in 38 states near cities and rivers. The battleground also needed to focus on regulation—the pivotal need to "prove" that the Yucca Mountain Project could not meet NRC licensing criteria, or at least to entangle the licensing process.

"I have some plans to surprise and confuse the Secretary of Energy," said Reid early in the summer of 2001.[241]

Reid and Jaczko Go to Work

That December, the U.S. Government Accountability Office (GAO), an investigative arm of Congress, issued a report raising questions about the Yucca Mountain Project. The report, which had been requested by Reid and received input from Jaczko, his new science advisor, concluded that "making a site recommendation at this time is premature," as the project had nearly 300 open, key technical issues.[242] Managing contractor Bechtel SAIC Co. had told investigators that some of the issues would not likely be settled until 2006. Although all of these technical issues were later resolved, Reid commented that the GAO's report was "a damning indictment of the whole process and it strikes at the heart of what they're trying to do scientifically."[243] Bechtel protested "factual and legal inaccuracies" in the report, and Abraham complained to the NRC that the document seemed to be "assembled to support a predetermined conclusion." He vowed that the Bush administration would push forward with plans to license and open the repository at the Yucca Mountain site.[244]

Republicans Push Fast and Hard for Yucca Mountain

Two months later, in February 2002, the DOE issued its huge Environmental Impact Statement (EIS), which was a prerequisite for the president and the Secretary of Energy to formally recommend the Yucca Mountain site to be the nation's spent nuclear fuel and nuclear high-level waste repository. The EIS found that "the specific impacts at the repository site would be very small… The transportation impacts would be associated mainly with nonradiological traffic fatalities and very low radiological doses to members of the public from the routine transportation of radioactive materials… As a result of this evaluation, DOE does not expect the repository to result in impacts to public health beyond those that could result from the prescribed radiation exposure and activity concentration limits in 40 CFR Part 197 and 10 CFR Part 63 during the 10,000-year period after closure." In other words, radiation exposure would be within limits deemed safe in federal regulations. On the other hand, the EIS said that if the "No-Action Alternative" was adopted and the nation's spent nuclear fuel and high-level waste were left where it currently sits, "there could be large public health and environmental consequences under the No-Action Alternative if there were no effective institutional control, causing storage facilities and containers to deteriorate and radioactive contaminants from the spent nuclear fuel and high-level radioactive waste to enter the environment. In such circumstances, there would be widespread contamination at the 72 commercial and five DOE sites across the United States, with resulting human health impacts."[245]

President Bush quickly approved the EIS.[246] In a letter to Nevada Governor Kenny Guinn, Secretary Abraham stated that "the science behind this project is sound."[247] However, the U.S. Nuclear Waste Technical Review Board soon reported technical questions about the repository's performance to Abraham. Corrosion of waste canisters was emerging as a key concern, and questions about transportation safety issues reached new heights in the spring. Reid and other Yucca Mountain Project critics pointed out that the NRC had tested only parts of the waste shipping containers, but relied on computer models to test their overall strength.[248] Reid's science advisor was sparking questions all over Washington.

The NWPA site selection guidance allowed the governor of a host state to veto the president's choice; however, a majority vote in the House and Senate could override that veto. Governor Guinn did veto the Yucca Mountain site's recommendation, and a majority vote by Congress overrode his veto. In May 2002, the House of Representatives voted 306–117, and in July, the Democrat-controlled Senate voted 60–39 to approve the Yucca Mountain Project.[249] President Bush quickly signed the Yucca Mountain Development Act into law.[250]

A majority of Nevada residents, living mostly in the urban Las Vegas area, have opposed the Yucca Mountain Project for many years; however, when President Carter cancelled atomic testing at the NTS in 1977, the Nevada Congressional delegation, as well as a statewide panel of citizens, recommended projects and programs to use all available resources at the site, including locating a repository for high-level wastes.[251]

The Yucca Mountain Project is located at the southeastern border of the former NTS, now re-named the Nevada National Security Site. In Nye County, home to the Yucca Mountain site, support for the project has never wavered. In March 2012, just after President Barack Obama's Blue Ribbon Commission on America's Nuclear Future (BRC) recommended a consent-based approach to siting a high-level waste repository, Nye County sent a letter to the Secretary of Energy stating that "we formally consent to host the proposed repository at Yucca Mountain, consistent with our previous resolutions that support the safe development of the Yucca Mountain repository."

In December 2002, Nevada filed suit in the U.S. Court of Appeals for the District of Columbia (D.C.) Circuit, arguing that DOE's plan to use engineered barriers (casks and other man-made barriers) to isolate the waste violated the NWPA's mandate that the site's geology "form the primary barrier" to keep waste away from people and the environment.[252]

Nevada's lawsuit was filed despite the fact that the NRC had always advocated a multi-layered system of barriers—including man-made containers and fill material—to isolate the waste.

Scientific Arena Key to Raising Doubts

Opponents of the Yucca Mountain Project, led by Reid, continued to launch a clever barrage of scientific questions at the project. They landed an appreciable blow in April 2004, when a new GAO report, again requested by Reid and prepared with information input from Jaczko, criticized DOE's quality assurance program at the Yucca Mountain Project. The report called quality assurance problems "persistent," and stated that "some data sets could not be traced back to their sources, some processes for software development and validation were inadequate or not followed, and model development and validation procedures were not followed."[253]

Nevertheless, in July 2004, a federal court rejected Nevada's claim that the 2002 Congressional resolution approving the Yucca Mountain Project was unconstitutional, providing a major victory for DOE. At the same time, the court rejected the radiation protection standards promulgated by the Environmental Protection Agency (EPA) for the site, saying that the standards needed to extend further than 10,000 years.[254]

The closing months of 2004 brought important changes to Reid's fight against the Yucca Mountain Project. Reid himself was re-elected for his fourth term in the Senate, and was soon chosen unanimously as Democrat Minority Leader. Daschle had lost his re-election bid that year. George W. Bush was re-elected with a Republican majority in the Senate and an even stronger Republican majority in the House. Soon after his election, he famously stated that he had "political capital" and intended to spend it.[255] The Yucca Mountain Project appeared to be on a fast track. When the 109th Congress convened in January 2005, Republicans initiated proposals to funnel even more money to Yucca Mountain Project development.

Reid Places Jaczko inside the Nuclear Regulatory Commission

Things might have looked bleak for Reid's battle, but there was one bright spot. He used his power in the Senate to hold up some of Bush's key nominees for high-level positions in order to place his science advisor Jaczko inside the NRC. By November 2004, Reid had blocked 175 of Bush's presidential nominations by filibuster, and refused to release them until he nominated Jaczko to a commissioner position within the NRC. Reid finally "persuaded" Bush to nominate Jaczko, but the Senate would not confirm him. Bush had to appoint him to a two-year term as a recess appointment in January 2005, which did not require Senate confirmation. The Senate later confirmed him in May 2006. However, Jaczko was required to recuse himself from any decisions regarding the Yucca Mountain Project during his first year at the NRC.[256]

Bush's Secretary of Energy during his second term was Samuel Bodman, a Ph.D. in chemical engineering with prestigious scientific credentials to bolster Bush's pro-nuclear, pro-Yucca Mountain Project programs. However, just weeks after his confirmation, Bodman was embarrassed when e mails came to light in which USGS hydrologists had discussed possible falsification of quality assurance documents concerning water infiltration at the Yucca Mountain site. In March 2006, Bodman told the House Energy and Water Appropriations Subcommittee that the process of managing the Yucca Mountain Project was "broken, and we are trying to fix it."[257]

Later, at the end of a thorough investigation, the USGS emails were shown to be nothing more than water-cooler banter, and the science and quality assurance associated with Yucca Mountain Project was deemed sound by the NRC.[258]

Money Talks

The national and world-wide recession that began in 2007 provided easy cover for any elected official who was willing to horse-trade for other favors—to cut program budgets. President Bush's requests for funding for the Yucca Mountain Project ran into even stiffer opposition after the 110th Congress convened in January 2007. With a Democrat majority in the House, an even split of 49 Democrats and 49 Republicans, plus two Independents in the Senate, Bush had very little leverage.

The budget shouldn't have been an issue because the money had already been collected and deposited in the NWF from nuclear utilities and their ratepayers specifically for nuclear waste disposition. By not authorizing the use of the special NWF, the funds remain in government bonds, allowing Congress to borrow money to support pet programs unrelated to the disposition of nuclear waste. However, Reid and his powerful Democrats used the recession as an excuse to further cut the Yucca Mountain Project's budget. President Bush requested $544.5 million for the Yucca Mountain Project for fiscal year (FY) 2007, but Congress appropriated $100 million less.[259] The budget cuts didn't really start to sting until FY 2008, when the President requested $494.5 million for the Yucca Mountain Project but received only $386.5 million from Democrats. Approximately 900 project employees were laid off.[260]

Meanwhile in December 2007, an NRC panel rejected Nevada's challenge to the DOE's Yucca Mountain Project database.[261] The state had argued that the federal database was incomplete. The ruling against Nevada angered Reid, but he was pleased when, at nearly the same time, the Nuclear Waste Technical Review Board refused to endorse a crucial water infiltration computer model that had been re-worked after earlier emails indicated it had been compromised.[262] There was even better news for Reid that December when both front-running Democrat presidential candidates, Hillary Clinton and Barack Obama, vowed they would block the Yucca Mountain Project if elected.[263]

In June 2008, DOE raced to submit its 8,646-page license application to the NRC to build and operate the Yucca Mountain repository while George W. Bush was still president.[264] The application was formally docketed on September 8, 2008, starting the countdown of a three-year clock to complete the review.[265] At about the same time, Jaczko's term as NRC commissioner was renewed.[266]

Changing Politics and the Yucca Mountain Project

Reid and the Yucca Mountain Project opponents in Nevada were in limbo as the November 2008 presidential election loomed. With the license application submitted, the NRC would be forced to follow the requirements in the NWPA to review it, and a Republican administration led by candidate John McCain would surely press for timely review and restore funding to the project. If candidate Barack Obama should win, he would need to keep his campaign promise to Reid to kill the Yucca Mountain Project in exchange for Nevada votes, but his actions would have to be seen as more than just raw-boned political dealing.

The NRC came to the aid of the anti-Yucca Mountain forces just before the election when it issued a Waste Confidence ruling in October 2008 stating that used nuclear fuel could be safely stored without adverse environmental impacts at reactor sites for at least 30 years beyond reactor operations.[267] The Waste Confidence ruling was later challenged in the U.S. Court of Appeals for D.C., which ruled that an EIS was needed before the NRC could change the Waste Confidence ruling.[268]

Obama's election came as a triumph for Yucca Mountain opponents. In November, the *Las Vegas Review-Journal* reported that president-elect Obama and Senator Reid had several discussions about the Yucca Mountain Project, after which Reid predicted the demise of the nuclear waste burial plan. He stated in an interview, "Yucca Mountain is history, OK? Just watch, we'll see what happens real soon, just watch. You will see it bleed real hard in the next year."[269]

Reid began to make good on his threat the following month when Nevada filed 229 challenges and objections to the DOE's license application.[270]

Kill Strategy—Flouting the Law

As soon as President Obama took office, the long knives came out against the Yucca Mountain Project. In March 2009, he proposed and Senator Reid supported a federal budget for FY 2010 that cut off almost all of the funding for the Yucca Mountain Project.[271] Reid, as Senate Majority Leader, held crucial power to block any attempts to amend the budget to fund the Project. He and the president may have thought they could simply starve the project of funds. When Congress, specifically the House of Representatives, wouldn't go along with defunding the Project, President Obama took a more direct route to keeping his campaign promise. In May 2009, he unilaterally decided to shut down the Yucca Mountain Project, and directed his Secretary of Energy, Steven Chu, to announce its termination.[272]

Secretary Chu went along with the president's decision and made the termination announcement, even though it seemed he was betraying his own convictions. Less than two years earlier, Chu, a Ph.D. physicist, had signed a white paper along with nine other national laboratory directors advocating the essential role of nuclear energy, and supporting and recommending that the Yucca Mountain Project be licensed and constructed as the nation's deep geologic nuclear waste disposal.[273]

Chu's announcement was short and simple, stating only that the Yucca Mountain site was now "off the table" and was "unworkable."[274] He was unable, or chose not, to give any scientific, technical, or safety reasons for the termination then or since. On almost the same day, at Reid's request, President Obama named Jaczko chairman of the NRC. Later, a report issued by the GAO[275] in 2011 confirmed that the administration's decision to terminate the Yucca Mountain Project was not based on any scientific or technical reasons, and "appeared to have been made based on policy"—in other words—the decision was entirely political.[276]

Project staff members were laid off by the hundreds as operations were buttoned up at the Yucca Mountain Project, where staff had already been reduced by half since 2004. Immediately, the Obama administration began closing down the $400-million-per-year effort with such speed and disorder that federal records management requirements weren't even followed. The president's budget request for FY 2010 allocated only $197 million to shut down the Office of Civilian Radioactive Waste Management (OCRWM), which was created by the NWPA to oversee the government's effort to build a waste repository.[277]

Hundreds of people were laid off, and a large new federal contract for Yucca Mountain Project licensing and construction, won through a competitive bidding process by a substantial American company, was defunded and rendered useless.[278] The regional economy around the Yucca Mountain Project was decimated, so much so that the unemployment levels in Nye County, Nevada—home to the Yucca Mountain Project—reached 17 percent in 2011.[279] Although Nevada as a whole had been experiencing a recession, economic times were getting better in other parts of the state by 2009–2010. Not so in Nye County, where home prices fell up to 6 percent between 2006 and 2011, school budgets were cut sharply, and other disastrous economic effects rippled through the area.[280] The Yucca Mountain Project had been estimated to cost $90 billion from start to finish—the largest public works project in U.S. history. Because the influx of workers, traffic, and specialized industry affected every aspect of roads, schools, hospital, water, police and fire services, and other public facilities and services, 10 counties around the Yucca Mountain Project had been receiving federal payments to compensate for these "spillover" effects and costs. That funding shrunk to zero within a year of Yucca Mountain Project termination, leaving high, dry, and often bankrupt the local businesses and developers that had taken out loans in anticipation of growth.[281]

Crossing the Line

During the first phase of the Yucca Mountain Project shutdown, the license application remained ongoing for the time being. The NRC had reportedly spent $58 million reviewing it by FY 2009. However, in March 2010, the DOE formally filed a motion asking the Atomic Safety and Licensing Board (ASLB), the NRC's administrative panel, to dismiss the Yucca Mountain Project license application "with prejudice."[282] An application that is withdrawn "with prejudice" is generally barred from being resubmitted in the future. The NRC gave the ASLB only 30 days to make its decision. On June 29, 2010, the ASLB rejected DOE's request, ruling that DOE lacked the authority to withdraw the license, according to the NWPA.[283]

The NRC, led by Chairman Jaczko, took the initiative to ask the DOE whether the ASLB decision should be reviewed by the full Commission—a highly unusual request that blurred the lines between the DOE and the NRC. These two agencies were formed in 1974 when the Atomic Energy Commission was abolished and its responsibilities were split into two completely separate agencies to avoid a conflict of interest between promotion and regulation of nuclear matters. The NRC was created as an independent regulatory agency to shield it from political influence by the president and Congress; however, the DOE, under Secretary Chu, took the not-so-subtle political cue from NRC Chairman Jaczko and agreed that the ASLB decision should be reviewed by the full Commission and put to a vote.[284]

Of the five NRC commissioners, only four were eligible to vote on this case. One of the newer commissioners had recused himself from voting on any matters pertaining to the Yucca Mountain Project because of his prior work related to the site. After the four votes were cast, Chairman Jaczko withdrew his vote without explanation and held up the proceeding for months. Conveniently, this hiatus occurred at just the right time to help Senator Reid win his tough re-election challenge in Nevada by continuing the belief that he had successfully killed the Yucca Mountain Project. When Jaczko resubmitted his vote months later, the vote was two to two and the stalemate continued until September 30, 2011, when Jaczko arbitrarily closed the proceeding.

In October 2010, while the appeal was still pending before the NRC, Jaczko directed NRC staff to use funds appropriated under the FY 2011 Continuing Appropriations Act rather than the enacted FY 2010 appropriations to close down the agency's review of the Yucca Mountain Project license application. Jaczko justified his action saying that the budget guidance was "consistent with NRC's obligation to spend funds prudently under a Continuing Resolution pending final budget by Congress."[285] However, officially, the ruling by the ASLB that the DOE license application cannot be withdrawn still stands.

Many members of Congress protested the Yucca Mountain Project's termination, especially those whose states store high-level waste from nuclear weapons production. In July 2010, Senator Patty Murray (D-WA) and Congressman Richard "Doc" Hastings (R-WA), sent a letter to Secretary Chu signed by 91 bipartisan members of Congress asking that DOE "halt all actions to dismantle operations at Yucca Mountain" until the NRC and the D.C. Circuit Court of Appeals resolved the license dispute.[286] The letter made clear the members' position that DOE had "overstepped its bounds" and "ignored congressional intent" in attempting to terminate the Yucca Mountain Project.[287]

How Low Can You Go?

If actions such as those taken by Chairman Jaczko and Secretary Chu had been committed by officials of a private corporation, the perpetrators might have landed in prison. Even so, Jaczko and Chu's flagrant disregard for the law continued. The FY 2011 budget requested by Jaczko for the NRC anticipated DOE's attempt to withdraw the license application and directed that "upon the withdrawal or suspension of the licensing review, the NRC would begin an orderly closure of the technical review and adjudicatory activities and would document the work and insights gained from the review." Accordingly, the NRC requested only $10 million for "work related to an orderly closure of the agency's Yucca Mountain licensing support activities."[288]

Jaczko continued to close down the license review. Two of his fellow commissioners protested. One argued that the NRC "should continue to follow the Commission's direction in the FY 2010 budget as authorized and appropriated by Congress," rather than using the suggested guidance in the Continuing Resolution memorandum to change course. The other commissioner called his actions "grossly premature," as the FY 2011 budget request had made clear that the NRC would only begin its orderly closure of the Yucca Mountain Project review "upon withdrawal or suspension of the licensing review."[289]

When Congress approved the NRC's FY 2011 budget proposal in passing the Full-Year Continuing Appropriations Act of 2011, Jaczko used this budget action as an implication that Congress had sanctioned his decision to terminate the license review, even though the Yucca Mountain Project license application had not been officially withdrawn by the ASLB.

The majority staff of the House Oversight and Government Reform Committee conducted an investigation into NRC's decision-making practices and found that "the Chairman's interpretation of his authority evolved to closely resemble that of a single administrator—his management style and aggressive behavior simultaneously eroded the collegial structure and values inherent in the NRC."[290]

Congressman Fred Upton (R-MI) and Congressman Ed Whitfield (R-KY) sent a letter to the Inspector General (IG) of the NRC, Hubert T. Bell, to "convene a formal investigation into the Chairman's recent actions to shut down the project."[291] The IG released his official report on June 6, 2011.[292] The scope of the investigation included a consideration of the chairman's decision to terminate all Yucca Mountain license review activities; the delay in the NRC's review of the Board's decision on DOE's authority to withdraw the Yucca Mountain license application. However, the IG does not comment on legal issues and his report did not find that the chairman had violated any laws or acted illegally. (For a detailed account of these investigations, see *The Cost of Deceit and Delay*.)[293]

Bullying at the NRC

The NRC commissioners were worried about their own reputations and professional credibility. The NRC is an independent agency, deliberately created to separate regulation of nuclear safety and licensing away from DOE, the government agency given responsibility for promoting the use of nuclear energy. As such, it is supposed to make decisions based on science and facts, and not be influenced by politics or the president. If the NRC commissioners bent to political pressure—if they even appeared to violate the spirit of scientific objectivity and fairness that has been a hallmark of the NRC's reputation—they would damage their integrity and credentials to qualify for future prestigious consulting jobs or other posts in Washington.

In October 2011, all four of Jaczko's fellow NRC commissioners sent a letter to the White House expressing "grave concern" about his actions and blatant prejudice in attempting to stop the Yucca Mountain Project.[294] In December, Commissioner William Ostendorff, a Republican, told a House oversight committee that Jaczko's "bullying and intimidation...should not and cannot be tolerated." Even worse, Commissioner William Magwood, a Democrat, testified that Jaczko had humiliated senior female staff in meetings and "reduced them to tears in front of colleagues and subordinates." The "most troubling" issue with Jaczko, Magwood said, was his propensity for "raging verbal assault" against agency staff.[295] Senator Reid's response in an interview concerning Magwood and his statements was to call Magwood "a shit stirrer...a liar and a first-class rat."[296]

In spite of the troubling allegations by his staff, Jaczko stated that he did not intend to resign. The NRC's IG had begun an investigation of six allegations against Jaczko and a report was underway. By spring 2012, the drift of the draft report was well known, and it was highly critical of Jaczko. "NRC senior executives and commissioners provided specific examples of what they perceived as intimidating and bullying tactics by Chairman Jaczko so that they would be influenced to side with the Chairman's opinion despite their own judgments," the report said. It added that the investigation found more than 15 examples of incidents "where the chairman's behavior was not supportive of an open and collaborative work environment." However, the report did not find Jaczko guilty of any legal violations.[297] This finding was not surprising because the IG does not comment on legal issues, and he was aware that there was an ongoing lawsuit naming Jaczko as one of the defendants.

In anticipation of the IG's report, Jaczko apparently changed his mind and announced his plans to resign as soon as a new NRC Chairman was chosen.[298] The report was issued in June, and Jaczko was officially replaced by Allison MacFarlane as Chairman on July 9, 2012.[299]

During the IG's investigation of his performance, Jaczko hired legal counsel to advise him. Staff members and former staff members of Senator Reid established a defense fund to help Jaczko raise money for his legal expenses. In July 2012, Reid's political action committee, the Searchlight Leadership Fund, donated $10,000 to Jaczko's defense fund. The fund's website states that "Dr. Jaczko spent 7½ years working for the American people at the Nuclear Regulatory Commission. Because of relentless, unfounded persecution from Congressional Republicans and industry insiders, Dr. Jaczko was forced to protect himself and incurred substantial debt standing up to the attacks. Your support can help set a precedent so other public servants won't be afraid to stand up for what is right."[300]

Both Jaczko and Energy Secretary Chu authorized activities and the expenditure of funds for illegal purposes. The use of such funds remains a matter for further Congressional investigation and possibly litigation because Nuclear Waste Funds can be used *only* for activities related to licensing the Yucca Mountain repository, not shutting it down.

Our Lawsuit

In February 2010, while efforts to terminate the Yucca Mountain Project were becoming obvious, I asked two of my colleagues[301] in Washington State to join me in filing a lawsuit against the president. When I made this decision, I didn't do it lightly. We believed that an important Constitutional principle was at stake and Congress had not reacted as it should have to stop the president from violating the

NWPA. The consequences of allowing a president to flaunt the law and get away with it, even once, is to say that the rule of law does not exist in our country. There also was much at stake for our state and at least 37 additional states left to store nuclear waste indefinitely if the president was allowed to terminate the Yucca Mountain Project and derail the entire nuclear waste program, as he has done anyway.

The initial intent of our lawsuit was to try to stop DOE from further dismantling the Yucca Mountain Project before the NRC could finish reviewing its license application. In late 2009, I received reports from friends at the Hanford Site and the Yucca Mountain Project concerning the rapid dismantling of the site. A report by the GAO, the audit and investigative arm of Congress, quoted several DOE officials who said that "they had never seen such a large program with so much pressure to close down so quickly."[302] That report also noted that the Obama administration had failed to take the time to plan or identify risks associated with its hasty closure. At the president's direction, DOE was destroying the site that had cost more than $15 billion to study and develop. It was obvious that this tactic was designed to make it difficult, if not impossible, ever to restart the program.

I wrote a white paper for the Washington State Attorney General describing my concerns about the cost and consequences to the country, and particularly to Washington State, if President Obama and Secretary Chu were allowed to abandon the Yucca Mountain Project. I hoped to motivate him to file a lawsuit to protect the interests of the state and the Tri-Cities—the communities located near the Hanford Site. However, the state had not decided whether it would file suit. We believed time was running out for Yucca so I contacted a respected attorney in Washington, D.C.,[303] who was familiar with the legislative and legal history surrounding the NWPA and had handled cases heard by the U.S. Court of Appeals for the D.C. Circuit. We began the long and expensive legal battle in February 2010. The county of Aiken, South Carolina, filed suit just before we did, but in the U.S. Court of Appeals for the Fourth Circuit, which includes South Carolina, and then the states of South Carolina and Washington filed. When our lawsuits were combined, the case was called Aiken County et al. vs. President Barack Obama, Secretary of Energy Steven Chu, and the DOE. When we filed a new petition for a writ of mandamus against the NRC, in July 2011, at the suggestion of the D.C. Circuit Court judges, two other petitioners joined the suit—Nye County, Nevada, and the National Association of Regulatory Utility Commissioners (NARUC).

The Blue Ribbon Commission

Amidst the controversy that erupted after President Obama and Secretary Chu announced the termination of the Yucca Mountain Project, Senator Reid suggested they empanel a new commission (which became the BRC), and give it two years to reevaluate the nation's nuclear waste program. Convening another Blue Ribbon Commission to study what other Blue Ribbon Commissions had already studied was an obvious diversionary tactic to draw attention away from the illegal abandonment of the Yucca Mountain Project. Reid congratulated himself for this idea on his web site: "The time is long overdue for America to find a new approach for solving the nation's nuclear waste problem. That is why I proposed the creation of a Blue Ribbon Commission of experts to make credible, scientifically sound recommendations for a new approach to nuclear waste. I am pleased that President Obama and Secretary Chu agreed with this approach, and on March 3, 2010, announced the creation of the Blue Ribbon Commission on America's Nuclear Future. ... The panel ... is scheduled to present their final report on the best alternatives to Yucca in January 2012. *While this commission prepares its report, I will ensure that Nevada's health and safety are never again threatened by nuclear waste.*"[304]

The italics in the last sentence are mine, added to highlight Reid's intent to use this delay to irretrievably demolish the Yucca Mountain Project without interference from Congress. The BRC's charter expressly excluded consideration of the Yucca Mountain site. "The Yucca Mountain project is dead and it is not coming back," Reid celebrated on his website while the BRC still deliberated.[305] When it finished its report, he crowed: "It's over with…the Yucca Mountain project failed and is now a relic of the past."[306]

In a presidential memorandum to Secretary Chu regarding the purpose of the new BRC, Mr. Obama said that its purpose was to investigate newer and better science and technology developed in recent years that had not been considered within the DOE's nuclear waste program. Secretary Chu said thereafter in an interview with *Technology Review* magazine: "We realize that we know a lot more today than we did 25 or 30 years ago. The NRC is saying that the dry cask storage at temporary sites would be safe for many decades,[307] so that gives us time to figure out what we should do for a long-term strategy. We will be assembling a blue ribbon panel to look at the issue."[308]

Fast forwarding to the release of the BRC's report in January 2012, the commissioners were quick to point out in the Executive Summary: "The elements of this strategy *will not be new* to those who have followed the U.S. nuclear waste program over the years."[309]

Regardless that President Obama and Senator Reid commissioned the BRC to distract and delay, the BRC team produced a report that provided achievable long- and short-term strategies for nuclear waste management, but no new technologies or "advanced knowledge" that had not already been considered by the DOE and others, including Secretary Chu and his former colleagues at the national laboratories.

The bipartisan BRC co-chairs, Representative Lee Hamilton and General Brent Scowcroft, urged the president to implement specific recommendations immediately to break the stalemate. However, more than two years after the BRC's final report was released, the president has ignored these urgent recommendations. His inaction was disappointing but not unexpected. Convening a commission and giving it two years to study all possible nuclear waste solutions except the Yucca

Mountain Project was a ruse invented by Senator Reid to buy time until the outrage over the president's unilateral decision to terminate the project died down.[310] When the BRC presented its report to the president and Secretary Chu, Obama and Reid created a further delay by directing the Energy Secretary to establish a DOE working group and gave the group another six months to conduct an in-depth review of the BRC's recommendations and to develop a nuclear waste strategy. Secretary Chu explained this internal process was necessary to consider the BRC's recommendations at a more detailed level.[311]

Tasking the DOE to "re-review" the BRC's work was unnecessary at best, and a glaring conflict of interest at its worst, especially in light of the fact that one of the recommendations was to remove the nuclear waste program from the DOE and transfer it to a new organization. No agency can be expected to analyze objectively a recommendation to dismantle a large part of itself.

In the meanwhile, even as the BRC worked, Senator Reid continued to flaunt his intention to kill the Yucca Mountain Project by using his position as Senate Majority Leader to cut funding and block budget bills that contained any funding for it.[312] Reid said as much in 2011 to the *Las Vegas Sun*: "Let me be clear. Any attempt to restart the Yucca Mountain project will not happen on my watch as Senate Majority Leader."[313]

As long as Reid remains Majority Leader in the Senate, I don't anticipate Congress will be allowed to allocate any funding to the NRC to complete the Yucca Mountain Project's license review.

Vindication for the Rule of Law

As recounted earlier, our decision to file the lawsuit and our request for a writ of mandamus were vindicated on August 13, 2013, when the D.C. Circuit Court of Appeals ruled in our favor and ordered the NRC to follow the law and resume the review of the Yucca Mountain Project license application. Two of the judges on the three-judge panel agreed that the NRC had violated the NWPA when former Chairman Jaczko stopped the review. In writing for the majority, Circuit Judge Brett M. Kavanaugh stated that "the President and federal agencies may not ignore statutory mandates or prohibitions merely because of policy disagreement with Congress." Judge Kavanaugh also wrote that the D.C. Court of Appeals decision was nominally about nuclear waste, but fundamentally about the Constitutional limits on presidential power.[314]

The act of terminating the Yucca Mountain Project was a direct violation of the NWPA, which requires, by law, that the DOE study the Yucca Mountain site and apply for a license to construct a nuclear waste repository. Our lawsuit has been a long and personally expensive endeavor, but we accomplished what we set out to do—establish that the president of the United States and his appointed officials are not above the law, nor are the federal agencies that are supposed to be independent.

When Senator Reid received the news that the D.C. Court of Appeals had ruled that stopping the Yucca Mountain Project license review violated the law and issued an order to the NRC to resume its review, he continued to defy the law and the judges: "As a result of a political compromise, we put some really bad judges on the D.C. circuit court and they produced a 2–1 decision requiring the Nuclear Regulatory Commission to license Yucca Mountain," Reid said during an appearance before the Las Vegas Metro Chamber of Commerce. "Their opinion means nothing. Yucca Mountain is dead. It's padlocked. There's nothing going on there."[315]

It may be partly the result of the court's ruling in our case that in November Reid used his clout in the Senate to end the filibuster rule for all executive and judicial appointments except for Supreme Court nominees. This move, dubbed the "nuclear option" because it is so destructive, represents a historic power grab and a huge blow to the procedural prerogatives of the minority party in the Senate.[316] Reid was well-known for using the filibuster to his advantage when Democrats were the minority party during the administration of President George W.

Bush. As mentioned earlier, Reid used the filibuster to hold up a great number of President Bush's nominees until he finally agreed to use a recess appointment to install Jaczko as a commissioner of the NRC.

Reid's determination to end the filibuster in late 2013 was designed to allow Democrats to pack the D.C. Circuit Court of Appeals by filling several vacancies with Reid's hand-picked "good" judges. The D.C. Circuit is the court that decides important regulatory cases such as ours, and has always had a balanced roster of four judges appointed by Democrats and four judges appointed by Republicans. Reid's purpose is to upset this balance in his favor.

The court's ruling in our case was a testament to the function of the judicial branch of government to uphold the law above politics; however, our victory was bittersweet. While we fought our battle in the courts, the president and his administration completely dismantled the offices and stopped all activities at the Yucca Mountain site. The equipment is gone, the engineers, scientists, and skilled workers are gone— scattered all over the world by now. Energy Secretary Chu abolished the NWPA's mandated nuclear waste management organization—the OCRWM—and the gates of the Yucca Mountain site are padlocked.

The one bright spot in the outcome of our lawsuit is that the NRC has been ordered to restart the license review. With only $11 million left in the budget, it won't be able to do much, but it could and should issue the full Yucca Mountain Safety Evaluation Report.

A redacted version of the Safety Evaluation Report was issued in response to a Freedom of Information Act (FOIA) request from the Heritage Foundation. This report is one that Senator Reid and Chairman Jaczko wanted to keep from public review.[317] However, any conclusions about whether the Yucca Mountain site would be safe for storing radioactive waste were omitted from the report, and the executive summary was not included. The NRC said the redactions were justified by a FOIA exemption that excludes material that could affect a legal process.

Even in late 2013, Senator Reid continues to ignore the court's ruling that President Obama violated the law when he terminated the Yucca Mountain Project. His website states: "Nevadans...can rest safely now that the Obama Administration has put this project [the Yucca Mountain Project] to rest."[318]

Jaczko Back in the News

Gregory Jaczko was named in the lawsuit we filed against the NRC. Since his departure from the NRC, his benefactor Reid has been busy job-shopping for him in Washington, D.C. April 2013 brought a double bonanza for Jaczko, beginning with an announcement on April 17 by publisher Simon and Schuster that it had signed a book deal with the former NRC chairman. According to the publisher, the book, tentatively titled "Splitting the Atom" will plumb Jaczko's thoughts about nuclear power, the aftermath of the 2011 Fukushima nuclear accident, and interactions he had with the nuclear industry. Simon and Schuster stated that "the book will also make palpable the impact of nuclear power by an examination of the science behind it."[319]

The same day the book deal was made public, the chair of the Congressional Advisory Panel on the Governance of the Nuclear Security Enterprise announced, on behalf of Majority Leader Reid, the appointment of Gregory B. Jaczko to be a member of the panel.[320] The panel is charged with making recommendations for the structure and mission of weapons work under the National Nuclear Security Administration, a part of DOE.

Jaczko's appointment prompted Senator Jim Inhofe (R-OK), ranking member of the Senate Armed Services Committee, to wonder "how much damage he [Jaczko] can do" in this new position.[321] Jaczko put his reputation on the line for Reid during his tenure as the NRC chairman and fairly ruined his future in politics, if he had aspirations in that area. He is now known in Washington, D.C., as a contentious manager, bully, and opportunist who will ignore the law for political gain.

President's Lawlessness Not Confined to Terminating the Yucca Mountain Project

A growing number of articles in the *Wall Street Journal*, the *New York Times*, and other publications have noted President Obama's penchant for ignoring laws that interfere with his political agenda. In one article entitled "Obama Suspends the Law," Michael McConnell, Director of the Constitutional Law Center at Stanford, writes: "Taking care that laws are faithfully executed is the President's duty, not a discretionary power. While the President does have substantial discretion about how to enforce a law, he has no discretion not to do so."[322]

McConnell's concern was the president's recent unilateral decision to suspend the employer mandate portion of the Patient Protection and Affordable Care Act (also known as "ObamaCare"). However, that instance is not the first time the president has chosen to ignore the law when it interfered with his political agenda. He has broken his promise to individuals who already owned insurance policies that they would be able to keep those policies and keep the doctors they depend on by failing to provide safeguards within the Affordable Care Act to prevent insurance companies from canceling existing policies.[323] Yet, in autumn 2013, while defending implementation of (other parts) of the Patient Protection and Affordable Care Act, the President Obama said: "It [the Affordable Care Act] passed the House of Representatives. It passed the Senate. The Supreme Court ruled it Constitutional ... It's the Law of the Land. It's here to stay."[324] The same can be said for the NWPA and other laws that the president has chosen to violate or ignore since he pledged his oath to uphold U.S. laws.

In quick succession in early 2013, multiple other offenses of the Obama administration came to light, some of them outright illegal. In May, a senior official at the Internal Revenue Service (IRS) division that deals with tax-exempt organizations, admitted that the agency had targeted taxpayers due to their political beliefs. Organizations that advocated conservative positions received lengthier and more difficult scrutiny in their applications for tax-exempt, non-profit status than did organizations whose more liberal beliefs coincided with those of the president. Although the president at first condemned the practice, it soon became clear that the illegal actions within the IRS were not the result of some rogue individuals, but had been known at the highest levels of the agency and even within the president's closest associates.[325]

In June, Edward Snowden, former employee of a contractor to the National Security Administration (NSA) revealed that the agency had been conducting domestic electronic surveillance on the private conversations of millions of Americans, in direct violation of privacy laws. Although Snowden himself violated laws by making his disclosures, the impact of his disclosures was stunning. By August, the House of Representatives nearly voted to strip the NSA of some of its most vital powers and tools, all due to the disintegration of public trust that the highest levels of government would properly supervise the agency.[326] At almost the same time, Americans learned that the DOJ had secretly seized the phone records of several Associated Press[327] reporters. Usually, a news organization or any private entity is notified if its records are going to be subpoenaed, so that it has the opportunity to challenge the subpoena in court. However, in this case, the subpoena was issued and executed in secret, in clear violation of the First Amendment to the Constitution. That Amendment states in part that the government can't make any laws "abridging the freedom of speech [or] infringing on the freedom of the press."[328] In October 2011, the Committee to Protect Journalists, a New York-based non-profit that seeks to point out infringements on press freedom worldwide, criticized the Obama administration for its chilling effect on journalists. "The administration's war on leaks and other efforts to control information are the most aggressive" seen in the United States since the Nixon administration tried to cover up its involvement in the Watergate scandals, stated the report.[329]

Additionally in June, an EPA warehouse in Maryland was found to contain extremely expensive furniture, gymnasium equipment, microwaves, couches, chairs, and other luxury accoutrements in spaces hidden from security cameras and seemingly having no useful purpose in the business of government. At the same time, it was revealed that the EPA had released the personal information of farmers and ranchers in unauthorized ways, and that former EPA Director Lisa Johnson had masqueraded as a fake employee named Richard Windsor, possibly to avoid complying with FOIA requests.[330]

In July 2013, President Obama announced the unilateral suspension of key provisions of the Patient Protection and Affordable Care Act, prompting McConnell's *WSJ* editorial. The president suspended the mandate for employers of more than 50 full time employees to provide health coverage, along with certain eligibility requirements and out-of-pocket costs. In fact, according to the Congressional Research Service, the Obama administration has missed or waived more than one-third of the requirements and provisions of this historic legislation, passed as a signature Obama initiative in 2010. These changes have prompted protests from the American Cancer Society and the Multiple Sclerosis Society among others.[331] Yet the point is not whether the law and its provisions are good or bad. The point is that it was passed by the duly elected U.S. Congress and then partially negated or ignored by President Obama on a solitary basis.

In October, the world learned that the NSA had eavesdropped electronically on officials in at least 35 foreign governments, including heads of state. President Obama said he didn't know about the practice, but many sources, including the prominent German newspaper *Der Spiegel*, alleged that he did. The revelations caused angry push-back from several world leaders, including Chancellor Angela Merkel of Germany and President Felipe Calderon of Mexico.[332]

The list of other instances in which President Obama has bypassed, circumvented, trampled protocol, and/or outright ignored laws and established procedures in the government is growing, and the media (even those media outlets generally supportive of Mr. Obama) and many other elected officials and citizens are taking notice. He has issued health-care mandates that undermine the Religious Freedom Restoration Act, made unconstitutional appointments to the National Labor Relations Board and the Consumer Financial Protection Bureau while the Congress was in recess (to avoid the messy process of Congressional consensus), failed to enforce existing immigration laws against illegal aliens who were brought to the United States as children, and waived certain welfare work requirements.[333] He continued sending military aid to Egypt after that nation's July 2013 military coup, although he did takes steps to curtail the much smaller amount of economic aid going to Egypt in late August.[334] By law, the United States must stop sending military aid to any nation whose democratically elected government is overthrown by a coup.[335]

Obama's Responses: Does He Understand the Gravity?

Beginning on July 24, 2013, President Obama began referring to the growing criticisms of his actions in bypassing laws as "Phony Scandals." He used that term publicly at least seven times in two weeks, and his Press Secretary mimicked the term in briefings to reporters.[336] In his obvious attempts to re-define events in his own terms, perhaps the president should take a look at history. On January 30, 1974, one year after his landslide re-election, President Richard Nixon told the Congress and the American people: "One year of Watergate is enough...I believe the time has come to bring that investigation and the other investigations of this matter to an end... I was elected to the office that I hold...for the purpose of doing a job and doing it as well as I possibly can. And I want you to know that I have no intention whatever of ever walking away from the job that the people elected me to do for the people of the United States."[337] Less than seven months later, the president resigned in disgrace, as the probes of credible people into his lies and actions revealed indefensible acts. In 1977, he told interviewer David Frost that "when the President does it [takes any action], that means that it is not illegal." This quote stands as one of the most infamous, discredited statements in modern U.S. history.[338]

President Lyndon Johnson labeled protesters against the Vietnam War as "cut and run people," yet his Presidency was brought down by his repeated lies to Congress and the American people about the basis for the war, the war's progress, and his own covert, unauthorized bombings.[339] President Clinton was impeached in 1998 by the House of Representatives (but not removed from office) for perjury and obstruction of justice for lying about an improper relationship with White House intern Monica Lewinsky.[340] His impeachment came not because of the act that occurred between him and Lewinsky, but because, once again, the American system of laws asserted that *no one*—not even a president—can break the law. His famous flouting of our system of laws by evading direct answers to questions in a Grand Jury proceeding stood as a "last straw" moment. When he said that his answer to a question about his conduct with Lewinsky depended "on what the definition of 'is' is," people were offended and impeachment followed.[341] In the United States, we don't ordain kings—we elect civilian citizen presidents who are not free to flout laws that apply to the rest of us.

More than 75 years ago, President Franklin Roosevelt attempted to "pack" the Supreme Court with new justices who would uphold his reforms, embodied in a political agenda known as the New Deal. His idea to appoint extra judges to "assist" those justices who were 70 years of age or older, would have allowed him to appoint up to six new justices favorable to his political strategy. When Congress and even members of his own administration learned of the plan in 1936, they soundly rejected it. The proposal was seen as a blatant attempt to undermine separation of powers, a fundamental pillar of our democracy. Defeated, the plan stands as a blight on the record of a man generally regarded as a heroic war president.[342] Nearly 240 years ago, the British King mistakenly underestimated the determination of a "rag-tag band of volunteers" in colonial America. "Taxation without representation is tyranny," they cried. In other words, paying taxes without being able to elect a legislature to set tax rates was unfair, the American colonists said. The British King ignored and dismissed the principles of the Americans and the rest is history. The most powerful nation on earth—the United States of America—was born because its founders believed so strongly in fairness and the rule of law. The American people are slow to anger, and don't generally bear grudges. However, when it comes to someone ignoring laws and the basic tenets of fairness, it's a different story.

Michael McConnell concluded his *Wall Street Journal* article by saying: "Of all the stretches of executive power Americans have seen in the past few years, the president's unilateral suspension of statutes may have the most disturbing long-term effects."[343] The ruling of the D.C. Court of Appeals in our lawsuit on August 13, 2013, which upheld the NWPA, is a reassuring reminder that our nation does have laws, and that these laws cannot be ignored with impunity.

## Chapter 4

The Road Ahead—
Why We Can't Wait

The world will need greatly increased energy supply in the next 20 years, especially cleanly generated electricity. Electricity demand is increasing twice as fast as overall energy use and is likely to rise at least 73% to 2035...Nuclear power is the most environmentally benign way of producing electricity on a large scale.—World Nuclear Association, 2013[344]

If the United States does not break the current political stalemate that blocks all progress in managing the nuclear high-level waste and spent nuclear fuel stored across the country, the consequences will be enormous and far-reaching. The immediate financial costs can be calculated some years ahead, but the total financial costs cannot be fathomed because they will be never-ending. Other costs to our country will include the loss of the nuclear energy industry and the clean, carbon-free electricity derived from nuclear power when we need it most to help mitigate global climate change. As we lose our base load nuclear energy, our country will be forced to increase the use of fossil fuels, thereby increasing carbon pollution and damage to the environment and human health that accompanies the use of dirty power sources. The costs of energy will rise and our country may again become dependent on other countries that have moved past the United States in securing their own energy supplies, including an increase in nuclear energy. Ultimately, if our country does not take the lead in a transition toward an all-electric economy, we will fall further behind the rest of the world and lose our influence abroad.

Direct Financial Costs

Let's start with the simple costs. First, the never-ending expense to the government (that is, the taxpayers) from losing lawsuits brought by utility companies for the government's failure to take their spent nuclear fuel as promised in the Nuclear Waste Policy Act (NWPA) has already begun to roll up to staggering amounts. As of 2011, 72 breach of contract claims had been filed by utilities against the U.S. Department of Energy (DOE), resulting in approximately $1.2 billion in damage awards and settlements. The DOE's own recommendations for additional settlements had already totaled nearly $250 million more at that time. Energy giants Exelon Corporation[345] and Next Era Energy,[346] owners of energy generating plants in almost every state in the union, have collected the largest amounts in breach of contract payments thus far—nearly $650 million. In addition, each of these companies has claims pending for even more payments. They have found a winning strategy, and are pursuing it vigorously. And why not? Compensation is due to these and other utilities. In 2012, two subsidiaries of the energy behemoth Entergy filed additional breach of contract claims against the DOE, as did Arizona Public Service Company[347] and Dairyland Power Cooperative.[348, 349]

The utilities are suing not just to recover the costs of storing their spent nuclear fuel, but also to garner the interest on these costs, "diminution of value" of their plants, fees for Nuclear Regulatory Commission (NRC) oversight of the spent nuclear fuel, and costs incurred to implement actions required by state legislatures as a condition of ongoing storage. Such costs can include mandatory emergency preparedness training and equipment for neighboring cities and counties. Additional costs exist, including at least $160 million that has been spent by the Department of Justice (DOJ) in litigating these utility cases. The DOJ conducted 39 spent nuclear fuel trials through the end of 2012, and employed staff to do so. In 2010, this agency requested $11.4 million in budget to hire 10 new lawyers to work on these lawsuits. Once again, the DOJ, as part of the federal government, is funded by taxpayers. Moreover, due to a technicality in contract law, utilities sue only for "partial" breach of contract, not total, because it is to their advantage. That way, the liability to the government is never fully closed. The DOE itself has estimated its ongoing liability to be at least $12.3 billion *if* it begins accepting spent nuclear fuel by 2020, a date no longer possible due to the termination of the Yucca Mountain Project. It also estimates ongoing costs of $500 million per year for each year beyond 2020, but added that "the government's obligation...[does] not encompass costs that may be unique to utilities with which the government has not settled...[and] may not fully account for the government's potential defenses." The utilities estimate the liability of the federal government to be closer to $50 billion for its failure to take possession of spent nuclear fuel.[350]

Who pays these damages to the utilities who successfully sue the government? Not the Nuclear Waste Fund, which was specified and collected as per the NWPA for the purpose of building a nuclear waste repository. As of 2013, it held approximately $30 billion in funds, unspent due to the political stalemate of the nuclear waste program. Payments to the utilities come out of the federal government's Judgment Fund, which is supplied by American taxpayers money. Likewise, the DOJ's expenses for hiring extra lawyers and defending against cases brought by the utilities are paid from regular DOJ appropriations, also supplied by taxpayers. In other words, these costs are paid by every American taxpayer, not just those who benefit from using the clean energy generated from nuclear power plants.[351] (There remain unanswered questions regarding the funds former Energy Secretary Chu and former NRC Chairman Jaczko used to terminate the Yucca Mountain Project and stop the license review, and how they might be held accountable for misuse of government funds.)

The delay in opening a repository provides nuclear utilities with another financial benefit that is not widely known. An obscure provision in the NWPA obligates each utility (or its holding company) to make a large payment to the government for taking the spent nuclear fuel that was generated before the NWPA was passed. Therefore, a delay in repository operation enriches the utilities in two ways: They can receive payments from the government for its failure to take their spent nuclear fuel, and they can delay paying the government the debt obligation they owe when it takes the fuel generated before 1983.[352]

Exelon is one of the utilities that benefits financially from the political nuclear waste stalemate. Exelon has reported to the Securities and Exchange Commission a liability of $1 billion if the DOE ever opens a repository to accept Exelon's spent nuclear fuel. Interestingly, Exelon has *not* used its considerable access to President Obama's administration to press for the resumption of the Yucca Mountain Project or the siting of another repository. White House records show that executives of Exelon have been able to secure an unusually large number of meetings with top administration officials at key moments in the consideration of environmental regulations. According to the *New York Times,* "with energy an increasingly pivotal issue for the Obama White House, a review of Exelon's relationship with the administration shows how familiarity has helped foster access at the upper reaches of government and how, in some cases, the outcome has been favorable for Exelon."[353] Note that the chairman of Exelon also is chairman of the Nuclear Energy Institute, and in this capacity has refused to object to the termination of the Yucca Mountain Project.

Costs We Cannot Measure: Building Up Greenhouse Gases that Will Change Our World

Next, the cost of the political stalemate in dealing with our nuclear high-level waste and spent nuclear fuel blocks us from moving ahead with development and deployment of newer, safer, and more reliable nuclear power plants. Nuclear power plants do not generate carbon dioxide (CO_2) and release it into the atmosphere like coal and gas plants. Natural gas generates less CO_2 than coal, but it still emits a significant amount of CO_2 into the atmosphere.

The climate changes produced by emissions of CO_2 can be explained by a concept called the "climate cycle." It operates something like a bank account—deposits and withdrawals are made, affecting the balance in the account. In the earth's carbon cycle, the deposits and withdrawals are in energy. In the pre-industrial, "balanced" state, energy was received by the earth from the sun, stored or moderated in the earth's atmosphere, land, and water, and partially released from the earth by escaping back into space (through reflections by clouds, the ground, and the atmosphere itself). Carbon dioxide was always a part of this cycle, as plants converted light to energy in photosynthesis. However, since the 1800s, humans in industrial societies have upset the climate cycle or the energy balance by adding larger and larger amounts of greenhouse gases to the atmosphere (primarily CO_2 but also methane and nitrous oxides). Greenhouse gases act to trap heat in the atmosphere, preventing its escape back to space in natural (balanced) levels. There is considerable scientific debate about the degree of man's influence on climate change, and I am not a scientific expert in this field. However, in my opinion, the disruptive effects of releasing billions of tons of CO_2 into the atmosphere each year cannot be ignored.

The Intergovernmental Panel on Climate Change (IPCC) is a scientific, multi-national organization established by member governments and operates through the United Nations. According to its charter, it provides "climate, socio-economic, and environmental data, both from the past and also in scenarios projected into the future...for climate change researchers, but...[also for] educators, governmental and non-governmental organizations, and the general public."[354] The IPCC was established in 1988, and since 1990 it has issued five Assessment Reports on the state of the global climate and probable causes for climate changes.

The IPCC's Fourth Assessment Report (AR4), issued in 2007, contains conclusions based on a broad array of the world's climate studies and literature. It reflected scientific consensus on the question of whether humans are causing climate change, stating that "most of the observed increase in global average temperatures since the mid-20th century is very likely due to the observed increase in anthropogenic [that is, man-made] greenhouse gas concentrations." In the report, the term "very likely" means that the scientific consensus is greater than 90 percent.[355] The report includes data showing that the earth's temperatures rose more during the 20th century than in any century going back 2,000 years. Since 1880, temperatures have risen about 0.9°C, and the pace of the rise is quickening. Since the early 1980s, temperatures have been rising about 0.18°C per decade. Based on an accelerating scale, albeit one filled with unknown factors, the report projected that the average global temperature will increase between 1.1°C and 6.4°C by the end of the 21st century.[356]

The main flaw in the 2007 report was not its uncertainty factors. According to the Fifth Assessment Report (AR5), issued in 2013, the 2007 report was much too conservative. More than a thousand scientists contributed to AR5, concluding that "warming of the climate system is unequivocal, and since the 1950s, many of the observed changes are unprecedented over decades to millennia. The atmosphere and ocean have warmed, the amounts of snow and ice have diminished, sea level has risen, and the concentrations of greenhouse gases have increased... It is *extremely likely* that human influence has been the dominant cause of the observed warming since the mid-20th century... The basic cause of the undisputed climate change was/is the emission of CO_2 from burning fossil fuels in modern industrial society. The atmospheric concentrations of CO_2, methane, and nitrous oxide have increased to levels unprecedented in at least the last 800,000 years. Carbon dioxide concentrations have increased by 40% since pre-industrial times, primarily from fossil fuel emissions."[357]

The effects of increased CO_2 emissions are being felt in two major ways. The first is higher earth temperatures. According to the AR5 report, "Continued emissions of greenhouse gases will cause further warming and changes in all components of the climate system." The report organized the data and made projections based on four representative concentration pathways depicting mildest to most severe conditions and predictions. The bottom line conclusions of AR5 are that global mean surface temperatures are very likely to rise 1.5°C to 4.5°C by the year 2100 (a high confidence assumption), are extremely unlikely to rise less than 1.0°C (less than a five percent chance) and very unlikely to rise more than 6.0°C (up to a 10 percent chance).[358]

The second major way that climate is and will be affected by continuing emissions of CO_2 is ocean warming and rising. The AR5 also concludes that "ocean warming dominates the increase in energy stored in the climate system, accounting for more than 90% of the energy accumulated between 1971 and 2010 (*high confidence*)... The rate of sea level rise since the mid-19th century has been larger than the mean rate during the previous two millennia (*high confidence*). Over the period 1901–2010, global mean sea level rose by 0.19 [0.17 to 0.21] meters... The ocean has absorbed about 30% of the emitted anthropogenic carbon dioxide, causing ocean acidification... ... Global mean sea level will continue to rise during the 21st century. Under all...scenarios the rate of sea level rise will *very likely* exceed that observed during 1971–2010 due to increased ocean warming and increased loss of mass from glaciers and ice sheets."[359] Consensus predictions now place expected rises in ocean levels between 0.8 and 2.0 meters by the year 2100.

In a balanced environment, trees and the oceans are the main vehicles that absorb CO_2. Deforestation through population and urban growth has vastly depleted the number of trees, at the same time that more CO_2 is released to the atmosphere, needing to be absorbed. The world's oceans, then, have become the main "sinks" for CO_2, which is converted to carbonic acid and causes increasing ocean acidification. Acidification is dissolving the calcium-based shells of clams, King Crab in Arctic waters, and coral reefs in tropical waters, and upsetting the eco-balance of the oceans in other damaging ways.[360]

The AR5 has been criticized by some for being too political, less scholarly, and not as scientifically sound as the previous IPCC reports. However, the report conveys well just how incredibly complicated and interconnected are earth's climate systems, and it shows how small changes in temperature profoundly affect the way we live on earth.

Examine, for example, how a rise in temperature of less than 1°C is already melting glaciers and, more important, the massive ice sheets of Greenland and Antarctica. These two ice sheets, the world's largest, are a lot larger and more integral to the planet than many people realize. The Antarctic ice sheet covers 5.4 million square miles—an area equivalent to almost 60 percent of the United States—and is about one-mile thick. The Greenland ice sheet is much smaller, but still covers an area 17 percent the size of the United States and one-half mile thick.[361] A complete melting of these ice sheets could raise world ocean levels by more than 80 meters, submerging so much habitable land mass that the some of the world's population would be insupportable. Even a rise of a few meters, caused by an increase of just a few degrees of earth's temperature, would melt enough ice to submerge many island nations and coastal areas that support literally billions of people. This result would occur because nearly all coastal regions are inhabited and often are the sites of large cities. For example, it is estimated that more than 17 percent of the country of Bangladesh would be inundated by a sea-level rise of one meter. Bangladesh has a rapidly growing population that stands at about 150 million, and about half of that number live in low-elevation areas.[362] In addition, more mega-storms, likely to be produced by climate change, could wash salt water into inhabited coastal areas, contaminating potable water supplies and damaging agricultural land. Climate refugees could be created by the thousands or millions, and other nations, already pressured by rising seas, would be unlikely to take them. Think of Bangladesh, if half of its people needed to leave the coastal areas they now inhabit. Refugee camps holding heretofore unimaginable numbers of people, would then breed disease (more prevalent *anyway* as world temperatures rise), extremism, terrorism, and poverty with all of its attendant outgrowths that threaten everyone else.

This cursory list doesn't begin to cover all of the major effects of even small rises in world temperatures. One effect can create or accelerate other effects, such as ice sheets that interact in complicated ways with their surroundings. They don't melt uniformly, but melt into existing crevices, making them wider, deeper, and more subject to "calving" or breaking off into ocean waters and thus melting more quickly. Land-based glaciers are also melting, depriving many areas of the world of their chief fresh-water supply, disrupting agriculture, and drying up rivers. Major fault lines of culture often lie along rivers, and wars over water are not just likely but inevitable as fresh water supplies shrink. The Middle East in particular with its arid climate creates great demand on a few large rivers—the Nile, Jordan, Tigris, and Euphrates—now shared by Iran, Iraq, Egypt, Israel, Syria, Lebanon, and other nations already infamous for not getting along. Think of the effects of just a small decrease in fresh water supplies in an area where every drop of water is already allocated by hard-fought treaties. Think of the Indus

River, which is the largest fresh water source for Pakistan's 183 million people. This river flows first through India, an even more populous nation with historical enmity to Pakistan. Anytime a critical river flows across a border, conflict is possible. If major rivers are disrupted by the effects of climate change (more flooding from mega-storms, but ultimately less fresh water supply), the possibility of conflict becomes almost a certainty.

Now mix in conflicts over rivers with disputes over oil production, and you have a toxic brew that could disrupt world-wide oil supplies and bring faraway rivalries into the heart of America's own economy. In the Niger Delta, where Nigeria produces 2.4 million barrels per day of oil, violence between Muslims and Christians is disrupting at least one-quarter of the production through theft and violence. Militias have formed, as the residents of Delta demand a share of the rich production that occurs in their midst, but whose profits go to rival Muslims who control most of the central government. Just a few years ago, the United States imported nearly one million barrels of oil per day from Nigeria, but today we import only about half that amount. Major United States and European oil companies are divesting their holdings in Nigeria, selling out to that country's state-owned oil companies, as conflicts over the river delta and its bounty (in oil and water), promise only to get worse.[363]

Other effects of climate change are important too, albeit not as obvious as rising global mean temperatures, rising oceans and melting glaciers. All of these conditions are interrelated. Ocean acidification destroys coral reefs, and coral reefs act as buffers for storm surges. Extreme storms and weather events are predicted to become more frequent as temperatures rise. Reefs also act as "nurseries" for the microscopic and small marine species that form the basis for the entire ocean food chain. A 2013 survey estimated that 80 percent of the coral reefs in the Caribbean have been lost already.[364] In late 2013, the environmental non-profit group called the Center for Biological Diversity filed a federal lawsuit in Seattle against the Environmental Protection Agency (EPA) over the threat to oysters and other sea life posed by ocean acidification. It is not the first or only such lawsuit.[365]

Extreme storm surges are destroying other natural buffers that have protected low-lying lands for millennia. The Sundarbans, the largest mangrove forests in the world, covering an area variously de-lineated between 3,800 and 8,000 square miles, sit along the coast strad-dling India and Bangladesh. Not only do these swamps support rich biodiversity and at least two million people, but they serve as buffers to reduce the effects of storm surges and flooding in one of the world's areas most prone to cyclones. It is estimated that a sea level rise of just 60 centimeters could destroy three-quarters of the Sundarbans, and a rise of one meter would essentially destroy them.[366]

Disease outbreaks and various other negative health effects also are predicted to accompany global climate change. Climate researcher Dr. Andrew Guzman of the University of California at Berkeley states, "...health is a complex thing, and it relies on just about everything around us...Each of the stresses that climate change imposes on in-dividuals and society threatens the systems we have built and upon which we rely to protect our health...This may not be immediately obvious, because for most of us, it is not changing climate itself that presents the greatest threat. It is, instead, the indirect effects of cli-mate change."[367]

Recognizing that refugee migration and makeshift living condi-tions breed disease, other indirect effects of climate change that could degrade health include food and fresh water shortages as fresh wa-ter glaciers melt and sea water encroaches on agricultural land. Heat waves take a disproportionate toll on the elderly and the already ill, especially in cities. The spread and prevalence of conditions ideally suited to produce pandemics and new, cross-species illnesses such as avian flu, severe acute respiratory syndrome (SARS), and other diseases could increase with climate change because alterations in ecosystems can produce quirky results favoring certain pathogens above others. Economic hardships that result from climate change could lower health care delivery systems.

The World Health Organization has estimated that if global temperatures increase by 2.0°C to 3.0°C, an additional three to five percent of the world's population will be at risk for malaria. If we just consider the low end of that range, it means that more than 216 million additional people will be at risk for malaria.[368]

The CO_2 in our atmosphere already measures just above 390 parts per million (ppm) with occasional spikes above 400 ppm at national observatories in the Arctic and at Mauna Loa, Hawaii. Leading climate scientists warn that a CO_2 level of 450 ppm would raise global temperatures another 1.0°C. The CO_2 level was about 310 ppm in 1960, and about 280 ppm in 1800.[369]

"Climate change will affect carbon cycle processes in a way that will exacerbate the increase of CO_2 in the atmosphere (*high confidence*)," according to the IPCC's AR5. "Most aspects of climate change will persist for many centuries even if emissions of CO_2 are stopped. This represents a substantial multi-century climate change commitment created by past, present, and future emissions of CO_2...Limiting climate change will require substantial and sustained reductions of greenhouse gas emissions."[370]

Decarbonization of electricity generation is one of the key climate change mitigation strategies discussed in the AR5 because differentials in carbon production occur more rapidly and visibly in electricity generation than in any other sector. In the majority of scenarios aimed at low-stabilization targets for CO_2, the list of low-carbon electricity suppliers comprising renewable energy, nuclear energy, and fossil fuels with carbon capture would need to increase from its current share of approximately 30 percent to more than 80 percent by 2050. Fossil fuel power generation without carbon capture and storage would need to be phased out almost entirely by 2100.[371]

Even if we had a large collection of nuclear power plants producing electricity right now, we wouldn't be able to stop burning fossil fuels because electricity can't yet power all of our energy needs. Most transportation vehicles still are powered by petroleum-based fuels. But if we had more nuclear plants, coal-fired plants that generate electricity could be phased out while new economic bases are built in regions economically dependent on coal production. Burning coal generates 37 percent of the electricity in the United States.[372] Today, nuclear energy generates 18–19 percent of the electricity in the United States in comparison, but it represents nearly 70 percent of U.S. carbon-free energy. More nuclear power plants producing electricity would lower the cost per unit, and spur the development of practical, all-purpose electric vehicles and the conversion of other portions of our activities to electric power. In other words, the implementation of climate change mitigation policies could increase the competiveness of nuclear energy technologies relative to other technology options that emit CO_2. The AR5 calls nuclear energy "a mature low-greenhouse gas emission source of base load power" and recommends that "nuclear energy could make an increasing contribution to the low-carbon energy supply, but a variety of barriers and risks exist."[373] The barriers and risks include operational risks, uranium mining risks, financial and regulatory risks, and *unresolved waste management issues*.

The Limitations of Natural Gas

Today, there is much talk about natural gas as a bountiful and cleaner substitute for oil and coal. The subject is popular because new technology has found ways to unlock large deposits of gas in rocks deep beneath at least three major areas of the United States and Canada. The Barnett Formation beneath north central Texas, the Eagle Ford shale deposits beneath the Permian Basin in west Texas, and other formations along the Texas-Louisiana Gulf Coast, had been thought to hold 23 percent of America's natural gas, until recently. These formations are huge, allowing Texas to produce up to seven trillion cubic feet per year.[374]

In just the last few years, vast additional deposits have been found. The Marcellus Formation is a huge unit of marine sedimentary rock extending underneath about 95,000 square miles of the eastern United States, including below parts of New York, Pennsylvania, Virginia, West Virginia, Ohio, Tennessee, and Maryland. From New York State, it also reaches under Lake Erie into southern Ontario. The shale contains largely untapped natural gas reserves, and its proximity to the high-demand markets along the East Coast of the United States makes it an attractive target for energy development. Estimates of the amount of natural gas in the Marcellus Formation differ so widely that it is difficult to have confidence in them at this time. It suffices to say the amount is many trillions of cubic feet. In 2013, 3.2 trillion cubic feet are expected to be extracted from the Marcellus Formation.[375] In addition, the Bakken Formation, lying beneath the Williston Basin in North Dakota and parts of Montana, Saskatchewan, and Manitoba in Canada, sprawls approximately 200,000 square miles. The U.S. Geological Service has estimated that the Bakken Formation in the United States alone could contain about two trillion cubic feet of gas and another 150 million barrels of natural gas liquids.[376]

Natural gas is a naturally occurring, carbon-based substance found in deep underground rock formations or in or near other hydrocarbon reservoirs such as coal beds and petroleum deposits. It can be used as a fuel (or energy source) for heating, cooking, electricity generation, vehicle propulsion, and as a chemical feedstock in the manufacture of plastics and other commercially important organic chemicals. It also can be used to make ethylene, an essential ingredient in plastics. Natural gas used to be considered so rare and precious that its use in new power generating facilities was curtailed in the Power Plant and Industrial Fuel Use Act of 1977. This Act also restricted the industrial use of natural gas in large boilers. However, sections of this law relating to natural gas were repealed a decade later.[377]

The recent discoveries of large gas deposits in underground shale and other rock formations, along with two key new technologies—fracking and horizontal drilling—to extract them, have caused gas prices to plummet and demand to soar."[378] Fracking and horizontal drilling (discussed later in this chapter) can release so-called "wet" gas from rock formations, adding to our supply of traditional "dry" gas. Dry gas is essentially methane. Wet gas also contains compounds such as butane and ethane. These "liquid natural gasses" can be separated and sold individually. The addition of significant amounts of wet gas production has driven down the price of natural gas to a 10-year low in spring 2012.[379]

As a result of these developments, some analysts say that natural gas will solve our energy dependence problem for the foreseeable future, or at least make the problem small enough to be easily managed. However, there isn't enough of it to last for generations. The U.S. Energy Information Administration (EIA) estimates that there are about 2,203 trillion cubic feet of natural gas that is technically recoverable in the United States. Proved reserves of wet gas rose to a new record high of 348.8 trillion cubic feet by the end of 2011.[380] Even combining these two numbers, and using the rate of U.S. natural gas consumption in 2011 of about 24 trillion cubic feet per year, our recoverable supply is enough to last about 106 years.[381] If demand rises due to attractive pricing, the supply will last even less time. If natural gas plants replace coal plants in substantial numbers, our projected supplies will last less than 70 years and gas prices will skyrocket. Either way, roughly a century or less isn't a time horizon on which to bet our nation's energy future. Even if we decided to burn all of our natural gas, we'd still be foolish not to be preparing now to secure a stable energy supply for the 22nd century.

Gas plants are relatively easy and quick to construct, so their capital costs are low. Pricing is controlled by the cost of the fuel, which can fluctuate. By contrast, nuclear plants are capital-intensive to construct, but once they are constructed fuel costs are relatively low, meaning that energy costs are stable. Stable pricing, which I'll discuss later in this chapter, is a key factor in whether an energy technology is sustainable.

Fracking and horizontal drilling are new technologies that are raising hopes about natural gas. Fracking is a contraction derived from the word fracturing. It refers to hydraulic fracturing of the shale and rocks below ground that contain natural gas. In this technique, sand or other grainy abrasives are mixed with water and chemicals and injected into a wellbore in the rock formations at high pressure, creating small fractures. When the pressure is withdrawn from the well, the sand grains remain behind, holding the fractures open once the rock achieves equilibrium. The gas can then escape and be captured.[302] In horizontal drilling, the massive boring tool essentially turns at a 90-degree angle once it has penetrated deep below ground. Since it is employed in conjunction with fracking, the two technologies are generally discussed together.

The main problem with fracking is the large amount of hazardous chemicals injected deep into the ground, along with the sand, to fracture the rock formations. These chemicals include some that are extremely dangerous to the environment, including hydrochloric, formic, citric, acetic, phosphoric, thioglycolic and boric acids, ethylene glycol (anti-freeze), benzene, lead, naphthalene, acetaldehyde, ammonium persulfate and other forms of ammonium, and 2-butoxyethanol.

In 2010, the Committee on Energy and Commerce of the U.S. House of Representatives asked 14 oil and gas service companies to disclose the chemicals they used in fracking between 2005–2009. The companies revealed that they used 2,500 hydraulic fracturing products containing 750 chemicals and other components, in a volume of 780 million gallons of liquids not including water added. Some of these components were common and generally harmless, such as salt and citric acid, but some were extremely toxic. The most widely used chemical in hydraulic fracturing was methanol, used in 342 products. Methanol is a hazardous air pollutant and is on the candidate list for potential regulation under the Safe Drinking Water Act. The other most widely used chemical was isopropyl alcohol, used in 274 products. In total, 29 of the chemicals are either known or possible human carcinogens, regulated under the Safe Drinking Water Act for their risks to human health, or listed as hazardous air pollutants under the Clean Air Act.

The BTEX compounds—benzene, toluene, xylene, and ethylbenzene—appeared in 60 of the hydraulic fracturing products, and each BTEX compound is a regulated contaminant under the Safe Drinking Water Act and a hazardous air pollutant under the Clean Air Act. Benzene also is a known human carcinogen. More than 11 million gallons of products containing at least one BTEX chemical were injected over the five-year period.

In some instances, the oil and gas service companies were unable to provide the Committee with a complete chemical makeup of the hydraulic fracturing fluids they used because the chemicals were proprietary to their chemical suppliers. In the period of interest, the companies used 94 million gallons of 279 products that were unknown to the user. "In these cases," the Committee report stated, "the companies are injecting fluids containing chemicals that they themselves cannot identify... questions about the safety of hydraulic fracturing persist, which are compounded by the secrecy surrounding the chemicals used."[383]

Because some of these chemicals can and have escaped into groundwater, and/or the air, many state legislatures, as well as the EPA, are putting regulations in place to curtail them. (The EPA already regulates the chemical components, but now may be readying plans to regulate the entire process of fracking.) Gas companies are drilling as fast as they can, and often simply capping the wells after drilling without harvesting them, to escape future regulations that are sure to come.

Pipelines are another issue that dulls the premise that natural gas is the answer to our energy woes. Even if gas is successfully retrieved from the deep underground environment, it must be transported to end users. Transport through pipelines is the cheaper alternative, or the gas can be liquefied and transported in trucks, trains, or ships to end users. The energy cost of capturing, liquefying, and transporting natural gas would be significant, and it would generate more CO_2 in the process of converting it. The problem is analogous to the use of ethanol as motor fuel. The amount of fossil fuel required to grow ethanol-producing crops (such as corn or switchgrass), and to harvest, ferment, process, and distribute the ethanol is significant, and the percent gain in fuel supply is consequently small due to the required energy input.

Pipelines have their own set of issues, including permit require-ments, environmental impact studies, pressurization, and accidents. Pipeline explosions and fires caused more than 80 incidents in 2012 alone, according to the Pipeline Hazardous Materials Safety Administration (PHMSA), a branch of the U.S. Department of Transportation that in-spects and regulates the nation's pipelines. Of the 80 incidents, 38 were classified as significant. They caused seven injuries, no fatalities, and more than $44 million in damages.

Natural gas distribution lines, the much smaller gas lines under lower pressure that bring gas directly to residential and commercial customers in and around major population centers, added another 71 incidents with nine fatalities and 21 injuries, according to PHMSA data. In the past 10 years, natural gas pipeline explosions and other accidents have killed 27 people and significantly injured more than 100 persons in the United States alone.[384] A December 2012 explosion and fireball from a pipeline rupture near in Sissonville, West Virginia (near Charleston), burned for hours, set several buildings on fire, and essentially melted portions of Interstate 77.[385]

Pipelines are controversial even when they don't leak or explode. Environmental concerns about construction and operation combine with concerns over pricing, capacity, flooding, escaping radon gas, and the effects on communities of "boom and bust cycles." They pro-duce a morass of issues that seem to grow exponentially as natural gas companies race to capture newly discovered gas in the Marcellus and Bakken formations.[386]

Mexico has huge natural gas reserves, but it isn't able to use them due to pipeline shortages. That nation has now become a net importer of expensive gas, mostly by ship from Yemen and Nigeria.[387]

However, the most significant issue for natural gas is that it is *not* a clean, carbon-free energy source. While its CO_2 emissions are less than those of coal and oil, it is still a carbon-based fossil fuel. Emissions from burning natural gas are about 30 percent less than those from oil, and according to the EPA, they are about half those from burning coal as fuel. Burning natural gas also emits nitrous oxides, and, according to the EPA, "methane, a primary component of natural gas and a greenhouse gas, can also be emitted into the air when natural gas is not burned completely. Similarly, methane can be emitted as the result of leaks and losses during transportation."[388]

Discovery Press warns that natural gas is not a "clean" fuel. "Though it doesn't have as much of an effect on global climate change per unit compared to other greenhouse gases, it is by far the most abundant greenhouse gas in our atmosphere…The destructive side effects of natural gas occur before it even makes it to the pipes that carry it to users; it's in the most commonly used and economical method of extracting natural gas, known as "fracking"…During the fracking process, small amounts of methane are released directly into the atmosphere. And methane is considered more dangerous to the environment than carbon dioxide because it captures the heat from the Earth."[389]

If we are truly concerned about global climate change and its long-term effects, then we can't afford to rely on, or have an energy policy that depends on, a fuel that is only half as bad as coal and 70 percent as bad as oil. We need to break the paradigm of dependence on fossil fuels and not look to another fossil fuel (natural gas) as if it were a viable answer. We should be developing the only fuels that are truly carbon-free—nuclear, solar, and wind—in phased time, doing first the things that we know will work, based on technical readiness and industrial capacity to produce them, to limit the damage to our environment and minimize disruption to capable, clean systems that already work.

Carbon Capture and Storage

Carbon capture and storage (CSS) is the practice of capturing the CO_2 released from fossil fuel-burning plants and sequestering (isolating or secluding) it in deep underground storage sites. Although a variety of carbon sequestration technologies exist, essentially all of them employ a three-step process: Capturing CO_2, compressing it into a liquid for transport (usually in pipelines) to the sequestration site, and injecting it into rock formations below ground. Some scenarios imagine that the liquid carbon stream could be used in other industrial processes, but the volume of CO_2 produced in U.S. coal plants alone is so vast (nearly two billion tons per year) that industry could absorb only a small part of it and most would have to be buried. As we have seen with natural gas, the promise is much greater than the reality.

For one thing, carbon capture is expensive. It would require retro-fitting the thousands of fossil fuel-burning installations in the United States with carbon capturing equipment. The CO_2 would have to be purified if it were going to be used in industry. According to an analysis by the Congressional Budget Office in 2013, the average capital cost of a coal plant equipped with CCS would be 76 percent higher than a conventional plant, and the levelized cost of energy from a CCS-equipped plant also would average 76 percent more than for a conventional plant. Studies by the Electric Power Research Institute, the Massachusetts Institute of Technology, Carnegie Mellon University, the National Energy Technology Laboratory, and the Global Carbon Capture and Storage Institute all reached similar conclusions.[390]

In a real-life example, a new clean-coal plant in Mississippi incorporates all the latest carbon capture technology and was supported with taxpayer dollars. However, the price of its output is $6,800 per kilowatt generated—nearly seven times the cost per kilowatt of the average gas-fired plant in the United States.[391]

In addition, the problems don't end with cost. A 2012 report by the National Research Council warns that the injection of millions of tons of supercritical liquid carbon dioxide from fossil-fuel plants into deep geological formations is likely to create earthquakes that will fracture the surrounding impermeable rock and allow the greenhouse gas to escape into the atmosphere.[392]

Pipelines constitute another problem because tens of thousands of miles of new pipelines and other infrastructure would be needed to transport the CO_2.[393] As discussed earlier in this chapter, pipelines come with their own set of environmental, permitting, construction, and leakage issues. Compressing CO_2 gas into a liquid is an energy-intensive process, meaning that the embodied energy quotient of the original coal is reduced. With all of these problems, even environmentalists like Greenpeace and the Sierra Club have doubts about the feasibility of CSS.[394]

The Limitations of Other Energy Sources

Acknowledging the limitations of natural gas, we can rule it out as a long-term solution to our energy woes, and we already know that coal and oil (though fairly abundant) emit large amounts of greenhouse gas. What energy sources should underpin our future? Clearly solar may be an important part of our energy mix in the long run, because the source of nuclear fusion energy from the sun is essentially limitless and free. Wind also is limitless, although intermittent. Biofuels may provide a source of fuel to replace gasoline. However, each of these sources does have serious limitations that preclude it from consideration as a long-term solution to providing abundant clean energy.

Solar Energy: Several major limitations plague the expansive or long-term use of solar energy as it stands today. One crucial issue is that of energy storage. Solar panels typically produce the most energy during the day, during the summer, and in open areas without dense clouds or tree cover. Some areas aren't suitable for producing solar energy at all because of location and climate, other places are suitable only for certain periods of the year, and all places experience a day/night cycle.

Technology may solve the energy storage issue and make solar power more viable in the future, but transmission to local users remains an economic and practical issue. A more plausible solution to the energy storage issue is to convert the solar energy into some form of chemical energy such as hydrogen. I hope and expect that solar technology will mature, but until that time, the use of solar energy isn't practical or deployable in many areas.

Another key issue concerns materials and manufacturing. Processes and techniques used in manufacturing solar panels share many characteristics with those used in making semi-conductor wafers. The array of toxic materials used in making the panels include silicon, a culprit in autoimmune illnesses; mercury, a carcinogen and mutagen (meaning it can cause cancer and birth defects); lead, a heavy metal that can cause mental retardation and nerve damage; cadmium, a poison implicated in lung, bone, and liver damage; copper, which attacks the kidneys; gallium, and other substances. Grinding, spraying, coating, and electroplating these materials as part of the solar manufacturing process, often in nano configurations that can easily enter the body, can expose workers and also consumers when the products fail or burn through in roof fires. The dangerous materials can also enter the environment and water sources when used panels are discarded in landfills. Since the average lifespan of a solar panel is now 20–25 years, many experts say we have yet to experience the spate of environmental impacts that will come as more panels age and are disposed. Solving disposal issues in an environmentally defensible manner will inevitably raise solar energy costs. Just as the cost to dispose of nuclear waste is being paid for by end users (ratepayers), so too should the cost of disposing of solar panels be included in the cost for solar end users/ratepayers.

For all these reasons, California's Silicon Valley Toxics Coalition and some other environmental groups now target the solar panel manufacturing industry for dangerous practices as it once did the semi-conductor industry.[395] Furthermore, poor quality in manufacturing is a problem world-wide, as coatings on panels disintegrate and other defects cause fires. The *New York Times* reported in 2013 that "worldwide, testing labs, developers, financiers and insurers are reporting similar problems and say the $77 billion solar industry is facing a quality crisis... The quality concerns have emerged just after a surge in solar construction...meaning any significant problems may not become apparent for years." Industry leaders, including the head of DuPont's billion-dollar photovoltaic division, admit and acknowledge that "corners are being cut."[396]

The manufacturing and disposal hazards of solar energy are in addition to a surge in industrial accidents, including falls from roofs and deadly contact with nearby power lines occurring as solar panels are installed on roofs.[397]

Energy density is also a significant limitation of solar energy. Energy density or power density refers to the energy flow that can be harnessed from a given unit of volume, area, or mass. For the generation of central power stations, arrays of solar panels must be spread over very large areas of land to collect enough of the sun's energy. In addition, the energy produced needs transportation and storage mechanisms. All credible calculations today place solar energy near the bottom of the list of energy sources in terms of ratio of energy derived to mass of land required for its production. In other words, solar energy's density ratio is extremely low—orders of magnitude below that of coal, oil, and gas—which in turn are orders of magnitude below that of nuclear energy.[398]

Another problem with solar energy concerns "embodied energy"— the amount of energy it takes to produce solar panels. Manufacturing solar panels is energy-intensive, with informed sources, including the DOE, estimating it takes at least 3.5 to 7 years' worth of energy production from the panel to "pay back" the energy used to produce it and come out with a positive energy gain. Some estimates place the payback time even further out.[399]

Finally, cost is an important issue with solar power. It continues to be much more expensive than most other energy sources, including coal, oil, natural gas, hydropower, and nuclear power. In Europe, where solar power has been promoted as an alternative to other power sources, costs have skyrocketed. Even hefty government subsidies, borne by taxpayers, have failed to make solar power economically competitive to consumers. In Germany, where solar and wind power are promoted by the government in perhaps the most enthusiastic, or flagrant, case in the world, consumers pay the highest electricity prices in Europe. *Der Spiegel*, the erstwhile German newspaper, stated in late 2013 that "electricity is becoming a luxury good in Germany."[400]

At nearly the same time, Ryan Carlisle, a hydraulics engineer with Subsea Ltd., an innovative energy company based in London, called Germany's "grand experiment in renewable energy...a catastrophe... useless, costly and counter-productive."[401] In addition, top executives at Europe's primary electricity producers called on politicians to end "distorting subsidies" for solar and wind power, saying the incentives have led to "whopping bills for households and businesses and could cause continent-wide blackouts."[402] In faraway New Zealand, where the Green Party is making a vigorous push for solar power in 2014 election campaigns, Prime Minister John Key has stated that "once you start looking at the market, it [solar power] doesn't work...it must involve a government subsidy."[403]

Wind Energy: Another non-carbon power source is wind, but it also has major limitations. Perhaps the most serious limitation is its unreliability because the wind doesn't blow at a steady rate all the time, sometimes it doesn't blow at all, and in some places it hardly ever blows. Because wind is intermittent, it must be supplemented with backup power, which in most cases and places in the world today is generated by fossil fuels. Because fossil fuel plants run most efficiently when they run steadily, stopping and starting them to accommodate the intermittence of wind actually increases their carbon "footprint."

A good example has followed from Washington State's Initiative 937, passed in 1996 as the second such state statute in the nation. It requires that utilities that serve more than 25,000 customers derive three percent of their power from renewable energy sources by 2012, nine percent by 2016, and 15 percent by 2020.[404] The result has been a proliferation of windmills that have to be used when available, to meet statutory requirements, but disrupt existing power sources, arrangements, and real-time contracts. Costs and inefficiencies have risen, along with the extra carbon output caused by stopping and starting other power sources.[405]

A 2013 study by the non-profit Civitas Institute reached the same conclusion, and Owen Patterson, Environment Secretary of the United Kingdom, says he agrees: "I am not convinced building wind farms…is the right way [forward] because you have more problems. You have to have back up from gas—that is operating inefficiently."[406] In addition, when windmills are operating at full power, utilities are forced to simply waste some of that power because it causes surges and imbalances that could cause grid instability and threaten to interrupt entire systems.

The non-profit Institute for Energy Research has developed a quirky illustration of wind power's intermittency in a piece titled "What If Your Life Were as Unreliable as Wind Power?" The scenario walks through a typical day in which electric power is available either not at all, not at the right times, or in insufficient quantities to perform necessary life tasks. In this script, the protagonist's alarm clock does not ring on time as wind power has slowed during the night, the coffee does not brew, there is not enough electricity to power a car for the full commute to work, the lights are dim and various other disruptions plague the actor's life. At the end of the day, however, the wind blows steadily, so the actor stays up reading all night because the lights are finally on at full power.[407]

In addition, wind power comes with its own environmental hazards. Although windmill blades appear to move slowly, they can reach up to 170 miles per hour at the tips, creating tornado-like vortexes. They are usually about 30 feet tall, with spinning rotor blades as wide as the wingspan of a passenger jet. A 2010 study by the Massachusetts Institute of Technology found that wind farms can raise temperatures in the areas around them. Health effects from noise and vibration of wind farms are being studied by the Oregon Public Health Department. In 2013, a citizen lawsuit was filed against the owners of the Willow Creek Wind Farm in northeast Oregon, claiming health and economic losses caused by the noise of the wind turbines. Attorneys for the plaintiffs presented evidence of "wind turbine syndrome," a series of symptoms including dizziness, nausea, body tingling and ringing in the ears allegedly caused by the low-frequency wind turbine noise. [408]

Wind turbines can also disrupt radar signals. In 2012, President Obama used the Defense Production Act to temporarily stop the sale of four wind farms in northern Oregon to Chinese investors, because the wind farms are located near the Naval Weapons Systems Training Facility in Boardman. The basis for his action was the radar-jamming potential of the wind farms. The Defense Production Act authorizes the president to suspend or prohibit certain acquisitions of U.S. businesses if there is credible evidence that the foreign purchaser might take action that threatens to impair national security.[409]

Bird damage and destruction of habitat are other concerns in areas near wind farms. The U.S. Fish and Wildlife Service estimated in 2010 that 400,000 birds per year are already being killed by wind turbines, even though the wind industry is in its infancy, and the American

Bird Conservancy has announced that three iconic American bird species—Golden Eagles, Whooping Cranes, and Great Sage-Grouse—face especially severe threats from wind farms.[410] A 2013 study published in the *Journal of Raptor Research* found that 85 golden and bald eagles have been killed in the last five years by wind turbines.[411]

In parts of Europe where wind's penetration into the energy market is much larger than it is in the United States, the problems with intermittency have become so large as to essentially "end the honeymoon," according to the *Wall Street Journal*. Grid operators normally rely on coal and nuclear plants to meet base load demand, while trying to interject small amounts of energy from renewable sources at the right times to ensure that power moves across the grid at the proper frequency. When renewables, which are intermittent, constitute small players in the grid, they can be accommodated, albeit sometimes not efficiently. However, when added to the grid in significant amounts, in nations such as Denmark and Germany, they are causing "frequency fluctuations, voltage support issues and inadvertent power flows" and even brownouts and blackouts. "It's one thing to ask consumers to pay more for cleaner energy; it's another to force them to endure blackouts," says the *Journal*. "High energy bills and threats of blackouts ended the honeymoon. America, take note."[412]

The reality is that wind power's energy density is even lower than that of solar. A recent credible estimate shows that to produce the same power as the twin nuclear reactors of the South Texas Project near Houston, a wind farm would need to occupy a land area nearly the size of Rhode Island.[413] Add the fact that most turbines used in U.S. wind farms are manufactured in China, and you have a technology that certainly isn't equipped, at least at this time, to carry our nation to the secure and independent energy future it needs. Perhaps technology can find ways to capture and store wind energy in a steady fashion in the future. I hope we can find some way to use this non-carbon technology, to eventually overcome the issues of noise, radar jamming, wildlife disturbance, and other impacts to the environment.

Biofuels: Another type of alternative fuel sometimes proposed as a substitute for coal, oil, and gas is fuel made from plant mass, or "biofuel." Ethanol, made from corn is one recent example, while sugarcane is used widely to make ethanol in Brazil. Ethanol can substitute for gasoline, or can be blended with gasoline. Grasses and saplings containing cellulose are also being examined as fuel sources. However, alternative fuels known as biofuels come with significant drawbacks since they are carbon-based. Carbon from the atmosphere is absorbed into plants as they grow and conduct their basic life function—photosynthesis. When plants are burned to make fuel, or as fuel, that carbon goes back into the atmosphere, adding to the carbon-based air pollution that makes fossil fuels so unattractive. In addition, planting millions of extra acres in corn in recent years to make ethanol doesn't allow these fields to lie fallow, revert to nature and regenerate, thereby depleting the environment. If these poor farming practices along with drought conditions continue, farmers could be setting the stage for another "dust bowl" era such as occurred in the 1930s.[414]

Additionally, many scientists, economists, and environmentalists point out that producing ethanol from corn—an early foray into energy production from biomass—consumes more energy than it yields. Among them is John Deutch, who was DOE's Undersecretary of Energy and Director of Energy Research. He has also served on numerous science advisory committees under both Democrat and Republican party presidents, and is now Institute Professor at the Massachusetts Institute of Technology. In a 2006 article for the *Wall Street Journal*, Deutch wrote:

> In the United States, cultivation of corn is highly energy-intensive and a significant amount of oil and natural gas is used in growing, fertilizing and harvesting it.

Moreover, there is a substantial energy requirement—much of it supplied by diesel or natural gas—for the fermentation and distillation process that converts corn to ethanol. These petroleum inputs must be subtracted when calculating the net amount of oil that is displaced by the use of ethanol in gasohol. …it is clear that it takes two-thirds of a gallon of oil to make a gallon equivalent of ethanol from corn. Thus one gallon of ethanol used in gasohol [10% ethanol and 90% gasoline] displaces perhaps one-third of a gallon of oil or less.

A federal tax credit of 10 cents per gallon on gasohol, therefore, costs the taxpayer a hefty $120 per barrel of oil displaced cost. Surely it is worthwhile to look for cheaper ways to eliminate oil.[415]

The energy density ratio of biomass is even less efficient than those of most other renewables, meaning that to match with corn ethanol, the power produced by the two reactors of the South Texas Project would require intensive farming of an area nearly the size of West Virginia (more than 15 million acres). A Rockefeller University researcher, Jesse Ausubel, also calculated that it would take a thousand square miles (640,000 acres) of prime Iowa farmland to produce as much electricity from biomass as from a single nuclear power plant.[416]

In addition to its inefficiency, using corn to make ethanol drove up the price of food nationwide in the mid-2000s, and could result in actual food shortages in drought years.[417]

Energy Pricing

When we ask the question of why our nation is harming and hamstringing itself by refusing to deal with its nuclear waste and spent nuclear fuel, and move ahead with clean, stable nuclear energy development, we have to consider not just political stubbornness, law-breaking, deal-making, and fear. One more factor is extremely important, and that is energy pricing. When the NWPA imposed the $0.001 per kilowatt hour (kWh) tax on ratepayers who receive energy from nuclear plants, it was the *first* time in our country's history that consumers had been taxed to manage the wastes and byproducts generated by a specific energy source. In other words, the coal, oil, and gas industries are not taxed to manage their waste streams, nor are the consumers who burn their products.

In the case of many renewable energy sources, including solar, wind, and biofuels, the industries not only are not taxed, they are heavily subsidized. The cost of these subsidies is shared broadly by taxpayers, and it artificially manipulates energy markets. In just one example, the Obama administration has tried to foster ethanol production from corn by granting subsidies in recent agricultural appropriations bills. In 2011, Senator John McCain (R-AZ) introduced an amendment to these appropriations forbidding such subsidies, because he believed the market should and would sort out which energy sources thrive and grow.[418]

In other cases, solar companies have received, and are receiving, huge U.S. government subsidies even when they don't make a profit and indeed go bankrupt, leaving taxpayers to pay the bill.[419]

In Europe in late 2013, executives of companies that provide half of Europe's electricity production capacity called on politicians to end "distorting" subsidies for wind and solar power. They cited sharply rising costs and the threat of continent-wide blackouts as these immature technologies are rushed to market before they are ready to perform in a steady manner just because their prices are kept low due to subsidies.[420]

Normally, in our country, pricing acts as a powerful incentive to change behaviors and shape markets. The problem today is that the market cannot see the true cost of any energy source, except nuclear energy. The full cost of fossil fuels is not reflected in their price, and so people see them as cheap and attractive. The prices at which fossil fuels are bought and sold is far below their true cost, because they do not reflect the costs of the damage that fossil fuels do to the planet. One way to correct this situation would be to impose a "carbon tax" on the units of CO_2 produced and emitted by various fossil fuels and biofuels. A waste-handling tax such as that imposed on the nuclear industry would not work in the same way, that is, to pay for a repository to dispose of or store nuclear waste and spent nuclear fuel, because there is no way to dispose of or store carbon waste once it enters the air or oceans. However, imposing a "polluter pays fee" on the consumers of fossil fuel-generated electricity, similar to the fee imposed on nuclear energy consumers (1 mil per kilowatt hour), would make fossil fuel less competitive and encourage the use of robust carbon-free sources of electricity such as nuclear.[421]

In 2007, an organization called Carbon Tax Center was formed in New York City to lobby and educate on behalf of a carbon tax. Many others, including legislators, have the same idea, but powerful industry influences have prevented carbon tax legislation thus far. Likewise, the major renewable energy sources are not priced fairly, but enjoy numerous government grants and tax breaks. Thus, perhaps the most powerful and effective weapon we have to influence buying and use behavior has been taken off the table, because no government regulation is as successful at controlling behavior as prices.

Toward an All-Electric Economy

The United States and the rest of the world needs to move toward an all-electric economy over the long term. Energy transitions are inevitable, and have been occurring since humans shifted from using their own energy to forage in the world to using the energy of domesticated animals. Harnessing fire, and then moving from burning simple biomass fuels like wood to extracting and burning fossil fuels enabled humans to accomplish the Industrial Revolution. According to many energy experts, including Vaclav Smil, Distinguished Professor of Environment at the University of Winnipeg in Manitoba, Canada, the relevant question is not whether we will transition to non-carbon based fuel but how well we will manage that transition. We simply have to make this transition over time, if for no other reason than fossil fuels will eventually run out. Nuclear, solar, and wind are the clean fuels of the future to which we inevitably must turn.[422] However, solar and wind aren't ready yet and have fundamental science-based limitations. The longer it takes to transition away from fossil fuels, the more serious the effects of CO_2 will be on global climate change. Nuclear energy, which is a mature and viable technology ready for expansion right now, can allow us to energize, accelerate, and afford the development of practical all-electric cars and start other major industrial transitions on the way to an all-electric economy.

Even President Obama agrees that we have to make this transition. He stated at Georgetown University in 2013 that "global carbon pollution rose to a record high [in 2012]. That's a problem… A low-carbon, clean energy economy can be an engine for growth for decades to come. And I want America to build that engine. I want America to build that future—right here in the United States of America. That's our task… My administration will…support the work already underway across America, not only to cut carbon pollution, but also to protect ourselves from climate change."[423] However, the goals he sets are not science-based and are not achievable without a commitment to nuclear energy.

The Role of Energy in America's Place in the World

A brief examination of our nation's history will confirm that energy has played a key role in establishing the United States as a world leader. Since World War II, when the United States came out of its isolationist stance and led the way to winning the war, it has been the dominant world economic power. Hopefully, for the most part we have used that power for good. While we don't want to be the world's policemen, we have presided over a fairly benevolent Pax Americana since World War II, keeping small wars small, brokering peace or at least co-existence in some of the world's most potentially explosive places, and not using our power to grab territory or rule other nations.

Consider that in 1947, the United States accounted for one-third of all world exports. Its exports more than doubled in value compared to its imports. It ranked first in the world among producers of oil, steel, airplanes, automobiles, and electronics. The United States was a net creditor among nations, had a foreign trade balance "in the black" (that is, on the positive [income] side of the ledger), possessed two-thirds of the world's gold reserves, and more than 50 percent of the entire manufacturing capacity of the world. It had unquestioned naval and air superiority and a nuclear weapons monopoly. The U.S. dollar had displaced the British pound sterling as the global reserve currency. In terms of personal wealth in 1948, the per capita (per individual) income in the United States exceeded *by a factor of four* the *combined* per capita income of Britain, France, West Germany, and Italy![424]

Still, personal income in terms of owning a car instead of a bicycle, or having meat every night, or hot water in a home or apartment is not a measure of the wealth of nations. The measures that count are manufacturing capacity, production of durable goods, exports, energy supplies, military power, and gold reserves. In all of these areas, America was in an enviable position. Britain, formerly the dominant world power, had spent itself in the "40-years war" that encompassed World Wars I and II. It was about to lose its colonies and was dependent on Americans to rebuild its peacetime economy. In the United States, by contrast, the Gross National Product (GNP) grew by nearly 70 percent between 1939 and 1945.[425] A nation's GNP is the estimated value of the total worth of production and services, by its citizens, on its land or on foreign land, calculated over the course of one year.

Through 1972, the United States continued to export more oil than it imported, and oil fueled our bursting prosperity. In 1973, that balance shifted, and the United States began importing more than six million barrels per day of oil from foreign sources.[426] The chief sources of our oil were Saudi Arabia and other Persian Gulf nations, who, along with Venezuela, had formed the Organization of Petroleum Exporting Countries (OPEC) in 1960. The other members of OPEC include Indonesia, Ecuador, and some African nations, notably Nigeria We imported some of the oil we consumed from those nations, as well as from Canada and Mexico. OPEC's "Declaratory Statement" was clearly nationalistic, even though it was an intergovernmental organization. It "emphasized the inalienable right of all countries to exercise permanent sovereignty over their natural resources in the interest of their national development." The OPEC manifesto stated that it was formed to wrest domination of the "international oil market...[from] the "Seven Sisters" multinational companies."[427] The Seven Sisters were large oil companies owned primarily in the United States and Britain. Prior to the formation of OPEC, these companies controlled about 85 percent of the world oil market.

Ironically, 1973 was also the year that the Arab members of OPEC, plus Egypt, Syria, and Tunisia decided to flex their muscles by imposing an "oil embargo" on the United States in retaliation for our support of Israel in its war against the invading nations of Egypt and Syria that October. The nations participating in the embargo immediately raised oil prices to the United States by 70 percent. In December, they raised prices another 130 percent, and some of the nations imposed a total embargo against the United States, The Netherlands, and Denmark. By early 1974, oil prices had quadrupled, triggering inflation and gasoline shortages in the United States, and worsening our economic recession. Intense diplomacy in 1974 by American Secretary of State Henry Kissinger negotiated agreements with Israel and some of its neighbors, moderating oil prices.

In 1979, a popular revolution in Iran replaced Shah Muhammad Reza Pahlavi with a fundamentalist Islamic Republic. The protests leading to the overthrow disrupted Iran so much that oil production dropped dramatically, again spiking prices and causing shortages in the United States The following year, Iraq invaded Iran, again disrupting the country and the oil supply. Thus, by 1980, the price of crude oil coming into the United States was still extremely high, and we were still importing more than six million barrels per day. Our oil imports peaked in 2005 at more than 12.5 million barrels per day, but have declined since that time to just over seven million barrels per day.[428]

In summary, the tide in oil imports turned against us in 1973, placing us at least partially at the mercy of other nations, some of whom don't like us very well and have shown their willingness to use oil as an economic weapon. In other words, we've known about our vulnerability since the year Skylab was launched (the first orbiting U.S. space station), since journalists Carl Bernstein and Bob Woodward won the Pulitzer Prize for exposing the Watergate scandal, and since Israel defeated Egypt and Syria in the Yom Kippur War. More than half of all Americans living today were born after 1973, meaning that they have known shortages and threats surrounding our oil supply all of their lives. Every president since Richard Nixon in 1973 has stated that we must free ourselves of dependence on foreign oil, and every presidential candidate has made it a part of his platform to set goals to do so.

Despite these statements, our nation has not mustered the political will to move ahead with realistic new energy sources. Today, the United States actually exports oil, and is not inordinately dependent on foreign sources. Yet, this situation is temporary. Oil reserves are finite, and our consumption is huge. We will need to move away from the use of oil eventually, so we need to think long term and take the steps that will lead us to an energy-independent future long before an oil-short future arrives. Nuclear plants take a long time to design, permit, construct, and license. By starting now, we can eventually replace electricity generated by coal with electricity generated by nuclear plants. In the meanwhile, we can transition those communities that are dependent on coal-production for their livelihoods toward different economies, and avoid the severe economic disruptions that occur in the absence of planning.

Chapter 2 revealed that nearly every developed nation and many developing nations are building nuclear plants to supply steady base load energy at a rapid pace. The United States is not doing so, and part of the reason is that we haven't implemented a system to deal with spent nuclear fuel and high-level nuclear waste. If the United States implemented a repository program, as it intended to do when the NWPA was passed in 1982 and amended in 1987, our nation might find more investors and more communities willing to site and build new nuclear power plants. At least we could have a fair debate on a level playing field about the merits and safety of nuclear power, without the debate being stopped in its tracks by "the waste issue." Not having a workable federal system for managing nuclear waste is a powerful argument not to build more nuclear plants. I recommend that we follow the law, forge ahead in solving the nuclear waste issue, and then have a discussion about the power sources of the future.

The Cost of Energy Dependence: Our National Debt

Dependence on foreign energy supplies has affected our standing as a creditor nation. The blunt fact is that we haven't been a net creditor nation since the 1978–1979 budget cycle. As a debtor nation, the United States has borrowed more money from other nations than they have borrowed from us, and every year we owe interest on our debts to other nations. Much of that debt between the late 1970s and the very recent past has been incurred buying oil from other countries. We have sold U.S. Treasury securities and other assets to investors, based on the belief and good faith that the U.S. government will pay them back, with interest. As of early 2014, the United States owed approximately $17.9 trillion in federal debt,[429] and more than 56 percent of that amount was owed to foreigners. Of the debt owed to foreigners, the vast majority (more than 72 percent) was owed to "official" investors (that is, countries), and only approximately one-quarter was owed to private foreign investors (businesses and individuals). The largest official holders of our foreign debt are China (21 percent) and Japan (19 percent).[430]

What do these mind-numbing statistics really mean? In 2012, oil magnate T. Boone Pickens stated that the amount of money we have paid to foreign nations for our oil (averaging about $700 billion per year for the last 40 years) amounts to the greatest transfer of wealth in human history.[431] He's either right or nearly right. Others express it differently. Economists often look at the ratio of public debt to Gross Domestic Product (GDP). A nation's GDP is the estimated value of the total worth of its production and services, within its boundary, by its nationals and foreigners, calculated over the course of one year. Thus, GDP is somewhat smaller than GNP. When the ratio of debt to GDP rises above 100 percent, a nation's economy will contract, or at least have trouble growing, because so much currency is being siphoned off to pay interest on the debt.

America came out of World War II with a huge public debt because the government, even though it raised taxes to historic highs during the war years, had borrowed so much money to pay for the conflict. The public debt exceeded GDP by 120 percent. However, two factors were much different than those of today. First, Americans owed much of that debt to themselves—in other words, to Americans who had bought war bonds. The transfer of wealth to pay that debt went from U.S. taxpayers to U.S. bondholders, who in turn paid taxes. The debt payments, for the most part, did not go offshore. Second, the booming postwar economy was growing expansively, providing more revenue for the government to pay down the debt. Indeed, sensible government policies did pay down a considerable portion of the debt from the war throughout the 1950s, 1960s, and into the early 1970s. However, public debt has climbed steadily since the late 1970s so that today it stands at about 120 percent of GDP. In Europe, economies have crashed at levels not too far above ours, with the worst example being Greece with a debt to GDP ratio of 182. Greece has had to impose severe austerity measures, including tax hikes and spending cuts, leading to mass protests, a shrunken middle class, and a sharp rise in homelessness and suicide rates. Other European countries with struggling economies include Italy with a ratio of 128, Portugal with 124, and Ireland with 119.[432]

According to the U.S. Congressional Research Service, "the burden of a foreign-financed deficit is borne by exporters and import-competing businesses... It is also borne by future generations, because future interest payments will require income transfers to foreigners. The federal debt is on an economically unsustainable path, meaning that it is projected to grow faster than GDP indefinitely. Were the debt to continue to grow faster than GDP, the government would eventually no longer be able to meet interest payments on the debt. At whatever point investors decided that this was the case, they would become unwilling to continue holding Treasury securities, driving down their price and likely prompting a financial crisis... This scenario has played out repeatedly in foreign countries, such as recently in Greece... The unsustainability of the federal debt is linked to the unsustainability of the whole of U.S. (private and public) borrowing from abroad...the United States...net foreign debt...grew to 27% of GDP in 2011...unsustainable federal borrowing and unsustainable foreign borrowing both pose separate...risks to financial stability."[433]

In other words, our debt is going to catch up with us and sentence future generations to pay more and more taxes just to pay interest on the federal debt to other nations. American dollars will be going to other nations, so they can build new roads, schools, hospitals, bridges, and other parts of their infrastructure, while our infrastructure ages and crumbles because we don't have the extra dollars to improve it. They will be able to fund better police and fire departments, and other services, while ours will shrink. Every sector of public spending will shrink. Eventually, if we persist in growing our debt and passing the costs on to our descendants, an actual financial crisis will occur for them, bringing austerity and contractions that shrink or eliminate pensions, investments, savings, and other assets. Other nations who hold our debt could trigger such a crisis to achieve their own national objectives, and the United States would have very few choices in terms of responses and outcomes. Thus, our independence and national security could be undermined.

Of course, buying oil from other countries isn't the only reason we have built up national debt, and I've pointed out that we actually export some oil today. Oil isn't the immediate culprit. However, if we secured a stable, independent, clean energy supply, we could grow our economy in astonishing ways. With abundant sources of nuclear-generated electricity, I'm convinced that American ingenuity would very quickly find ways to convert manufacturing industries and vehicles that now operate on oil to operate on electric power. We could revitalize those industries, provide much-needed jobs, and grow our economy to pay down and eventually eliminate the debt.

The Biggest Cost of All: The Rule of Law

In this chapter, I've pointed out the various costs resulting from our country's choice to allow the termination of the Yucca Mountain Repository Project. In summary, this action has left our nuclear waste and spent nuclear fuel in a vulnerable situation, caused our country to fall behind the rest of the world in nuclear energy technology development, and forced us to continue to rely on unsustainable energy sources that pollute the atmosphere. Some of the costs are obvious, such as the government's continuous payments to utilities for the DOE's failure to keep its promise to take their spent nuclear fuel. Some costs are more subtle but also more dangerous, such as the loss of America's clean nuclear energy leadership in the world. Other costs, including the costs of climate change and of chasing after dubious new energy technologies, could be even more dire because they threaten to drastically change how humankind must live on our planet. The science and long-term effects of global climate change are not yet well-understood, but the warning signs in nature and weather are disturbing.

A cost that may be even greater than all the others described here is the loss of protection for the rule of law in the United States—a result of allowing our Constitutional system to be ignored by the Executive branch of our government. Throughout our history, the separation of powers among the executive, legislative, and judicial branches of government has kept our democracy effective. Laws are made by a popularly elected Congress, and the elected president executes the government—a government of laws—albeit with some discretion because the American people choose the president based on political philosophy. Last, the federal judiciary, which is not elected because it must be impartial, hears disputes and settles them based on the rule of law. If we lose this system, we won't be able to count on the protection we have come to expect from the American constitutional system of laws.

John Adams, one of our founding fathers and the second president of the United States, recognized the righteousness of a "government of laws and not of men," and coined this phrase that we all remember. Supreme Court Justice John Marshall repeated it in a landmark court decision in 1803, saying "the government of the United States has been emphatically termed a government of laws, and not of men. It will certainly cease to deserve this high appellation if the laws furnish no remedy for the violation of a vested legal right." President Gerald Ford repeated the phrase again in announcing to the nation in 1974 that President Richard Nixon had left office because he was found to have violated the law. On the first day Ford became president, he said, "My fellow Americans, our long national nightmare is over. Our Constitution works. Our great Republic is a government of laws and not of men. Here the people rule."

Many Americans don't realize that we have a crisis on our hands today, and it's not just that we aren't dealing with our spent nuclear fuel and nuclear waste. We are not moving ahead with a clean and viable energy source for the future, and we're placing ourselves behind the rest of the developed world in nuclear technology. The real danger is that we are allowing our system of lawful government—the envy of the world—to be undermined by political cronyism, deal-making, and law-breaking. President Obama's termination of the Yucca Mountain Project clearly violated the law, and we used the court system to uphold the law and restore the government's separation of power. The NWPA now needs to be upheld or amended through Congress, because in the United States, no one—not even the president—is above the law.

## Chapter 5

Breaking the Stalemate—A Way Forward for Nuclear Waste Management

Simply put, we know what we have to do, we know we have to do it, and we even know how to do it.—Congressman Lee Hamilton and General Brent Scowcroft, Co-chairman of the Blue Ribbon Commission on America's Nuclear Future [434]

President Obama and Senator Reid's efforts to stop the Yucca Mountain Project have created a political stalemate for the U.S. nuclear waste program, but it also may have created an opportunity to break the stalemate by addressing issues that were debated at the time the Nuclear Waste Policy Act (NWPA) was enacted into law.

The issues debated in 1982 were about co-mingling defense waste with commercial nuclear waste and the permanent disposal of spent commercial fuel—issues that were controversial then and now. During the legislative debate leading to enactment of the NWPA, Senator

Henry "Scoop" Jackson (D-WA) expressed deep concern about requiring, by law, the co-mingling of defense waste with commercial nuclear waste. Both Senator Jackson and Admiral Hyman G. Rickover, known as the "Father of the Nuclear Navy," believed it was contrary to long-standing policy to require the Nuclear Regulatory Commission (NRC) to license defense activities. However, the argument prevailed that substantial cost savings could be obtained by co-mingling defense and commercial waste, and therefore NRC licensing was required in the ensuing legislation.

I recall that throughout most of the 1970s, when I was an official at the Energy Research and Development Administration (ERDA)—a predecessor agency to the U.S. Department of Energy (DOE)—the common assumption was that commercial spent nuclear fuel would someday be reprocessed. The waste resulting from that reprocessing would be stabilized and packaged for permanent disposal in the same process as that planned for defense waste. However, in April 1977, President Jimmy Carter indefinitely "deferred" spent nuclear fuel reprocessing out of concern that plutonium could be diverted into enemy hands to make nuclear weapons. He vetoed the ERDA Authorization Act of 1978, which would have appropriated funds to construct a federal reprocessing facility, and the NRC suspended license proceedings relating to spent nuclear fuel reprocessing.[435] These developments led to the policy drift that lawmakers tried to clarify and bound when they passed the NWPA in 1982, designating a deep geological repository as the destination for both high-level waste and spent nuclear fuel.

NWPA Decisions and Definitions Reverberate Today

Essentially then, the NWPA of 1982 was a compromise between those who adopted President Jimmy Carter's argument against reprocessing commercial spent nuclear fuel due to proliferation fears and those who argued that spent fuel should not be permanently discarded as waste because more than 90 percent of its energy value remains and is recoverable. The compromise between these two positions was to design a repository with two purposes: 1) permanent deep geologic disposal of high-level, defense nuclear waste; and 2) retrievable storage for commercial spent nuclear fuel to make it readily available for reprocessing at some future date; that is, if and when this process became economically feasible and politically acceptable. The much smaller amount of real waste left over from reprocessing the spent fuel rods would be sent back to the repository for permanent disposal.

An interesting but unfortunate result of Carter's policy decision is that it punished the United States by limiting our option in spent nuclear fuel processing, but it didn't stop nuclear weapons proliferation by other nations. Pakistan, North Korea, Iran, and possibly other nations have gained or are gaining nuclear weapons despite the U.S. ban on reprocessing.

In Chapter 1, the reprocessing cycle was briefly outlined. Reprocessing removes much or virtually all of the plutonium that has built up in irradiated fuel, thus rendering the resulting waste less hazardous. Spent nuclear fuel that has not been reprocessed still contains plutonium and other isotopes with long half-lives. Removing plutonium and these other isotopes would substantially reduce the risk profile that must be considered in disposing spent nuclear fuel to assure the health and safety of the public. Therefore, if the United States reprocessed spent nuclear fuel, it might be easier to site a repository to dispose of the waste once it had been reprocessed and used several times and was truly "spent." Also, mature technology now exists to vitrify the liquid wastes that result from reprocessing in forms that are just about impossible to undo, as long as the liquids are vitrified while they are fairly "fresh."[436] Maybe it's time the United States took another look at reprocessing, since an entire generation of leadership and population has emerged since President Carter stopped the practice 37 years ago.

Whether or not we reprocess spent nuclear fuel in the United States, we still must contend with the outdated legal definition of high-level waste established in the NWPA. This seminal law defines all waste that results from reprocessing spent nuclear fuel as "high-level waste."[437] The legal definition encompasses a wide spectrum of physical waste concentrations, lumping into the same category wastes that are vastly more or less radioactive. For example, reprocessing usually occurs in a series of cycles. The waste generated in the first cycle of reprocessing, essentially a "wash" cycle, is much less radioactive than waste generated in one of the final cycles where many chemicals have washed away fission byproducts and the waste sludge has been in contact with nearly purified plutonium.

Generally in science, physical properties of elements or chemicals govern classifications and safety considerations. To introduce some scientific and physical differentiation among the sludges resulting from reprocessing, this waste is now separated into categories called "high-activity waste" and "low-activity waste," but it is all legally defined as high-level waste. There is no single definition of low-activity waste because low-activity waste is divided into several sub-classes and the concentrations of radionuclides allowed in each sub-class vary by the specific radionuclide and are expressed in tables. In general, the U.S. Environmental Protection Agency (EPA) explains low-activity waste as "a category of radioactive wastes that contain very small concentrations of radionuclides. The concentrations are small enough that managing these wastes may not require all of the radiation protection measures necessary to manage higher-activity radioactive material to be fully protective of public health and the environment. Several classes of radioactive waste...that contain small enough concentrations of radionuclides may be considered low-activity waste."[438]

Redefining Waste: The WIR Issue

In 1999, the DOE tried to develop a process to manage some of the low-activity waste fractions of high-level waste in different ways.

Treating all high-level waste according to the rigorous regulations, equipment specifications and inspections, and other requirements of nuclear-grade work is slow and expensive. Most difficult of all, as we have seen, is siting a repository to permanently dispose of it. For these reasons, DOE promulgated Order 435.1, *Radioactive Waste Management,* and DOE *Radioactive Waste Management Manual* 435.1-1, identifying the Waste Incidental to Reprocessing (WIR) process.[439]

The WIR principle stated that "waste resulting from reprocessing spent nuclear fuel that is determined to be *incidental to reprocessing is not high-level waste,* and would be managed under DOE's regulatory authority in accordance with the requirements for transuranic (TRU) waste or low-level waste (LLW), as appropriate."[440] Determinations of which high-level waste fractions could be managed as TRU or LLW would be made based on levels or radioactivity or contamination, and not on the legal definition embedded in the NWPA. Therefore, radioactive wastes resulting from reprocessing plant operations, such as contaminated job wastes, laboratory clothing, tools, equipment, and other relatively "mild" or indirect activities, could be managed differently than hot streams of liquids directly contacting or containing dissolved spent fuel.

Some less radioactive wastes could be processed to remove key radionuclides to the maximum extent that is technically and economically practical, and incorporated in a solid physical form such that their concentration did not exceed statutory limits for Class C LLW as set out in 10 CFR 61.55, *Waste Classification.*[441] Other radioactive wastes could be processed to remove key radionuclides to the maximum extent technically and economically practical, and incorporated in a solid physical form and meet alternative requirements such that they could be managed as TRU waste.[442, 443]

Disagreeing with the WIR concept, the Natural Resources Defense Council (NRDC) and others filed a lawsuit in 2002 against Energy Secretary Spencer Abraham, charging that he was violating the NWPA and challenging DOE's authority to manage any of its high-level waste through an "incidental"–WIR–process. The lawsuit alleged that DOE was using or would use the WIR process to improperly or inadequately treat high-level waste as LLW or TRU waste, and not dispose it in a repository. The suit asserted that all wastes resulting from reprocessing spent nuclear fuel should be managed as high-level waste and disposed in a repository. The lawsuit had been filed originally in 2000 in the Ninth Circuit Court of Appeals (covering nine western states including Washington, Oregon, and Idaho), but was subsequently transferred to the Federal District Court in Idaho. Other parties to the lawsuit were the Snake River Alliance, the Confederated Tribes and Bands of the Yakama Nation, and the Shoshone-Bannock Tribes. The states of Washington, Oregon, Idaho, and South Carolina participated as *amicus curiae* ("friends of the court").

Senator Maria Cantwell (D-WA) objected strongly, saying: "They [DOE and the administration] are trying to create a loophole in the definition of nuclear waste big enough to drive a truck through and leave Washington State to deal with a mess that we don't want."[444] A primary concern of the plaintiffs and the Senator was that DOE would use the WIR process to permanently leave behind high-level waste in aging waste tanks at the Hanford and Savannah River sites, and the Idaho National Laboratory.[445]

The Federal District Court in Idaho found for the plaintiffs in July 2003, and declared DOE's WIR process to be invalid.[446] The DOE appealed the decision, and in November 2004, the U.S. Court of Appeals for the Ninth Circuit vacated the lower court's decision on "ripeness" grounds (meaning that adjudication could not occur until actual actions by DOE had produced results—presumably results harmful to the plaintiffs).[447]

Meanwhile, in October 2004, while the NRDC lawsuit was under review, the Congress passed the National Defense Authorization Act (NDAA) of 2005. Section 3116 of the NDAA, which had been developed in consultation with Idaho and South Carolina officials, allowed DOE to "reclassify" certain high-level waste at federal sites in those states, and thus manage some of them as LLW or TRU wastes. Reclassification meant that certain high-level waste could be managed as LLW or TRU waste if it met specified criteria. These criteria included a determination by the Secretary of Energy, in consultation with the NRC, that the high-level waste in question did not require disposition in a repository, had high-level radionuclides removed to the maximum extent practical and did not exceed criteria for Class C LLW. In addition, certain high-level waste that did exceed criteria for Class C LLW, could be managed as LLW or TRU waste if it was disposed according to a plan and permit approved by the state, pursuant to plans developed by the Secretary of Energy and the NRC.[448]

Section 3116 of the NDAA of 2005 has allowed state agencies in Idaho and South Carolina, in conjunction with DOE and the NRC, to handle some of their tank wastes in ways different than originally planned. The Savannah River Site operates a process called "saltstoning" that solidifies certain liquid salt wastes that have resulted from cleaning and pumping out high-level waste from underground storage tanks. Tank cleaning and pumping inevitably increase waste volumes, as water must be added to mobilize the high-level waste that has settled into sludges and crusts. In the absence of NDAA Section 3116, this site would need to vitrify all wastes produced by contacting the high-level waste in tanks, and prepare it for disposal in a national repository. Similarly in Idaho, joint state and federal determinations have allowed cementitious grouting, calcining, steam reforming, and other solidification treatments for some high-level waste deemed incidental to reprocessing.

Section 3116 does not apply to the Hanford Site, nor to the West Valley Demonstration Project Site in New York State. However, the Hanford Site is wrestling with the same issues that prompted DOE Order 435.1 in the first place. One good example is Waste Management Area C (WMAC), a World War II tank "farm" (collection of tanks) and the associated infrastructure, piping, contaminated soils, and other media at Hanford. As state and federal regulators try to "close" WMAC, they are discussing the most appropriate ways to treat and dispose of certain wastes that are not highly radioactive but may have contacted high-level waste from the tanks. Common sense says that these wastes do not merit that same level of expense and effort to permanently isolate them from the environment as is expended on highly radioactive waste. These discussions are being played out against a backdrop of animosity, shrinking budgets, revelations of additional tank leaks into the ground, and immense technical difficulties and delays with Hanford's Waste Treatment Plant (WTP). Naturally, these discussions are contentious, and often veer far from the actual merits of the WIR principle. Nevertheless, compromise that allows varying waste determinations (and therefore treatment and disposal options) within the broad high-level waste definition, may be reached if Congress amends the NWPA.

Moving Forward: Amending the NWPA

The opportunity now presents itself for Congress to amend the existing NWPA to address the issues, definitions, and strictures that have proved expensive and unnecessary to assure the health and safety of the public, and provide a way for both the defense waste and commercial nuclear waste programs to move forward. The amendments to the NWPA that I propose are as follows:

1. Remove the requirement to co-mingle the disposal of defense and commercial nuclear waste (but retain the option) and assign responsibility for the disposal of defense waste to the National Nuclear Security Administration (NNSA), the organization responsible for managing the nuclear weapons program. I also propose that the NNSA, an agency within the DOE, become a completely separate agency.

2. Remove the requirement to treat all waste resulting from reprocessing spent nuclear fuel as high-level waste, and allow differentiation of categories based on physical properties within the broad definition of high-level waste.

3. License the Yucca Mountain site as planned, but delay the requirement to construct the repository until the state of Nevada is offered incentives as recommended by the Blue Ribbon Commission on America's Nuclear Future (BRC). Even though incentives should be offered, provisions of the NWPA that give the Congress the authority to make the final decision on repository location should be maintained.

4. Adopt the recommendations of the BRC and the DOE to construct large-scale, interim storage facilities.

The Blue Ribbon Commission on America's Nuclear Future

The recommendations I propose to amend the NWPA to break the stalemate and get the nuclear waste program moving again fit very well with some of the recommendations made by the BRC. The BRC delivered its final report to President Obama in January 2012, offering precisely what the president and former Energy Secretary Chu had asked for—a long- and short-term strategy for nuclear waste management.[449]

Secretary Chu's stated assumption in choosing the high-level BRC panel was that "we know a lot more today than we did 25 or 30 years ago..."[450] when the NWPA was amended to designate Yucca Mountain as the repository site to be studied. However, Chu's assumption was incorrect. The BRC's report did not provide any new discoveries, advanced knowledge, or new technologies that had not already been considered and recommended by the DOE and others, including Secretary Chu and his former colleagues at the nation's national laboratories when he was director of Lawrence Berkeley National Laboratory.[451] The Executive Summary of the BRC's report acknowledged that "The elements of this strategy will not be new to those who have followed the U.S. nuclear waste program over the years."[452] However, the report did provide some of the best ideas that had been recommended previously but not implemented.

The eight key recommendations in the BRC's final report stated that the United States should implement or develop:

1. A new, consent-based approach to siting future nuclear waste management facilities.[453]
2. A new organization dedicated solely to implementing the waste management program and empowered with the authority and resources to succeed.
3. Access to the funds nuclear utility ratepayers are providing for the purpose of nuclear waste management.
4. Prompt efforts to develop one or more geologic disposal facilities.
5. Prompt efforts to develop one or more consolidated storage facilities.
6. Prompt efforts to prepare for the eventual large-scale transport of spent nuclear fuel and high-level waste to consolidated storage and disposal facilities when such facilities become available.
7. Support for continued U.S. innovation in nuclear energy technology and for workforce development.
8. Active U.S. leadership in international efforts to address safety, waste management, non-proliferation, and security concerns.

In a special letter to the president, the commissioners strongly urged him to act on the recommendations "without further delay,"[454] acknowledging that presidents and Congress have a poor track record in implementing the recommendations they commission:

> "All of them [the eight recommendations] are necessary
> to establish a truly integrated national nuclear waste

management system, to create the institutional leadership and wherewithal to get the job done, and to ensure that the United States remains at the forefront of technology developments and international responses to evolving nuclear safety, non-proliferation, and security concerns."[455]

The BRC specifically named two of its recommendations as the most urgent for immediate implementation: "Creating a new federal corporation dedicated solely to implementing the waste management program and empowered with the authority and resources to succeed," and giving the new federal corporation "access to the funds nuclear utility ratepayers are providing for the purpose of nuclear waste management," that is, the Nuclear Waste Fund (NWF). At this writing, more than two years later, neither of these recommendations has been proposed by the Obama administration, let alone implemented.

The DOE's Implementation Strategy

In 2011, in authorizing DOE's budget for fiscal year (FY) 2012, Congress directed the DOE to "develop a strategy for the management of spent nuclear fuel and other nuclear waste within six months" of the publication of the BRC's final report.[456] In April 2012, Secretary Chu announced that he had established a DOE working group to conduct an in-depth review of the BRC's strategy recommendations. Chu stated that the internal DOE process review would include "the full range of public comments, commissioned papers, and policy perspectives received by the BRC during their investigation."[457] He said that the working group was expected to take until the end of July 2012 to complete a "new national strategy that accounts for the Commission's recommendations," which would then be addressed in partnership with Congress. Secretary Chu did not promise that the new national strategy would "implement" the BRC's recommendations, but that it would "account" for the Commission's recommendations. Many of us saw this full review of work that had already been performed by the BRC as unnecessary and another delaying tactic.

When DOE finally issued its "nuclear waste strategy" in January 2013, it was six months late and merely consisted of a 14-page outline of a strategy. The *Strategy for the Management and Disposal of Used Nuclear Fuel and High-Level Radioactive Waste*[458] described itself as "a framework for moving toward a sustainable program to deploy an integrated system capable of transporting, storing, and disposing of spent nuclear fuel and high-level radioactive waste from civilian nuclear power generation, defense, national security, and other activities."

The sketchy strategy set out broad steps to be taken in the future rather than near-term action. It called for selecting and constructing a pilot-scale (small) consolidated storage facility for spent nuclear fuel and nuclear high-level waste, to begin accepting waste by 2021, with a high priority given to spent nuclear fuel "stranded" at shut down nuclear plants. A larger consolidated storage facility, prepared to hold 20,000 metric tons (MT) of spent nuclear fuel would begin accepting waste by 2025—enough waste, according to the plan, "to reduce expected government liabilities."[459] Under this gradual plan, a permanent repository would not be available to begin accepting waste until 2048[460]—50 years after the NWPA's original deadline of 1998 for a national repository to begin accepting high-level waste, and more than 100 years after the United States led the world in opening the nuclear age. The fatal flaw of the new DOE waste *Strategy* is that, by law, it can't be implemented until and unless the NWPA is revised or repealed by the Congress. To date, neither the president nor the DOE has proposed legislation to implement either the *Strategy*, or the BRC recommendations.

The nuclear waste situation is growing urgent for many states. Even if a 20,000-MT consolidated storage facility were to begin accepting waste by 2025, the United States already has three and a half times that much spent nuclear fuel stored at reactors. By 2025, industry and government projections estimate we'll have about 25,000 more MT, which increases the backlog to nearly five times the capacity of DOE's proposed facility.[461]

The Nuclear Waste Administration Bill

In 2013, a bipartisan group of four powerful Senators introduced a new bill aimed at finding solutions to the nuclear waste storage and disposal impasse. Senators Ron Wyden (D-OR) and Dianne Feinstein (D-CA) teamed with Lamar Alexander (R-TN) and Lisa Murkowski (R-AK) to propose legislation to implement the BRC recommendations for a new nuclear waste administration (separate from the politicized DOE) and a consent-based process for siting nuclear waste facilities.

"Our country can't wait any longer to find a long-term solution for disposing nuclear waste," said Wyden.

"The government's failure to address our nuclear waste issues is damaging to the development of future nuclear power and simultaneously worsening [sic] our nation's financial situation," said Murkowski.

The bill "establishes a desperately needed nuclear waste policy… The time is now to find a solution that safely stores this material [used nuclear fuel and high-level nuclear waste]," said Feinstein.

"We need to solve the problem of where to put the used nuclear fuel…putting an end to what's become a decades-long stalemate," said Alexander.[462]

The bipartisan *Nuclear Waste Administration* bill proposed an entirely new law—the Nuclear Waste Administration Act of 2013[463]—implementing several of the BRC's recommendations, including forming an independent agency known as the Nuclear Waste Administration (NWA) to manage nuclear waste storage and disposal. Consent-based siting of waste facilities was paramount in the bill, as it advocated working assiduously with state, local, and tribal governments. The new agency would begin immediately to site facilities to temporarily store "priority waste," such as that left behind at closed nuclear plants. Temporary storage facilities could continue to be sited for 10 years, provided parallel funds were being allocated to site a permanent repository. After 10 years, temporary facilities could continue to be sited only after a permanent repository site had been selected for study. Interestingly, the bill would authorize the Secretary of Energy to conduct studies to revisit the earlier decision that co-mingles the storage of commercial spent nuclear fuel with waste created in national defense programs. (I have recommended an even simpler approach in amending the NWPA to separate these materials.)

Funding, always an important consideration, would come from both the NWF, already established in the NWPA, and from a new Working Capital Fund to be established in the Treasury. This latter fund would be fed by the $0.001 per kilowatt hour (kWh) tax assessed on electric ratepayers, and would be available to the new NWA without further appropriation. The NWF, totaling about $30 billion, would be available, but only through Congressional appropriation as it is now.[464]

Although the bipartisan *Nuclear Waste Administration* bill was a good first step on the part of the Senate, it had little chance of passing in Congress because it did not address the current NWPA and the Yucca Mountain Project. Furthermore, at the beginning of 2014, the *Nuclear Waste Administration* bill was still in the Senate Energy Committee, with no plans to bring it to the floor of the Senate. Even with perseverance, it could take years before this proposal became a law and any of the BRC recommendations could be implemented. In addition, Energy and Natural Resources Chairman Ron Wyden left this committee to take over the tax-writing committee, further delaying action on the bill.

In the meantime, the continued delay in the ability of the government to take possession of the high-level waste and spent nuclear fuel stored at multiple sites across the United States is costing money on an ongoing basis. Successful lawsuits from utilities, as already pointed out, have so far cost taxpayers more than $2 billion, and the clock is running.

Even the DOE conservatively estimates that the taxpayers' liability from successful utility lawsuits will likely approach $21 billion, even if the government starts accepting high-level waste and spent nuclear fuel in 2020. With the Yucca Mountain Project terminated or in limbo and no alternative in place, meeting the 2020 deadline is not possible. The government's liability is expected to grow by at least $500 million per year.[465]

Ratepayers have been taxed approximately $750 million per year to pay for a nuclear waste repository. In November 2013, in another lawsuit brought by the Nuclear Energy Institute and the National Association of Regulatory Utility Commissioners, the D.C. Court of Appeals ruled that the U.S. government can no longer require nuclear power plant operators to pay fees into the NWF. The court said the fees could not currently be justified because of the government's long-stalled plan to build a national waste facility at Yucca Mountain in Nevada had not come to fruition. In January 2014, the DOE agreed to reduce the fees to zero but asked the court to consider a new hearing on the matter at a later date.[466]

Moving Forward: Restarting the Yucca Mountain Project Licensing Process

While new bills to implement the recommendations of the BRC are negotiated and debated in the Congress, I believe that the simple amendments I recommended to the existing NWPA, would provide a compromise, a logical path forward, and invite a speedier implementation of a pilot consolidated nuclear waste storage facility. These steps can be taken right now to move forward in solving our nuclear waste dilemma. Licensing the Yucca Mountain repository still is important because doing so would demonstrate that it's possible to license a repository without risk to the health and safety of the public, and that the bulk of objections have been political. Furthermore, licensing the Yucca Mountain site would satisfy the requirement of the NWPA to license a repository before other storage facilities can be built.

The BRC as well as most of the nuclear community believe as I do, that the next step in managing spent nuclear fuel is to establish one or more secure storage locations for dry cask storage until a responsible decision can be made regarding reprocessing the fuel—whether to remove the long-lived isotopes or to recover the energy content. Additionally, after spending $15 billion to study and prepare a license application for the Yucca Mountain site, it would be irresponsible to abort the project and waste so much time, effort, and money based purely on political interests.

On August 13, 2013, the NRC was court-ordered to resume the Yucca Mountain license review. Senator Harry Reid of Nevada, long the Yucca Mountain Project's nemesis, stated that "the place [Yucca Mountain] is locked up...Yucca Mountain is an afterthought."[467] He also made sure listeners understood that, as Senate Majority Leader, he would block appropriations for any further money. Even if the Obama administration moves forward on the application, "there's no money" for Yucca Mountain, Reid said. "We've cut out funding for many years now and there's none in our budget to start it."[468]

Indeed, Reid has successfully blocked Senate budgets regarding Yucca for the past five years. Even Senator Wyden, through his spokesman, said that the $11.1 million left in the NRC's study fund won't go very far, "which means the ball is still in Congress's court when it comes to deciding the direction of U.S. nuclear waste policy."[469]

Yet *Wall Street Journal* columnist Kimberly Strassel stated in her August 15, 2013, column that staff members inside the NRC and Congress have told her the license review could be completed in six to eight months at a cost of less than $7 million. True, this amount isn't enough to finish the licensing project, but, as Strassel says, "there is more than enough money to get that crucial document into the public debate."[470] She was referring to the NRC's Safety Evaluation Report that was nearly complete before the review was stopped.

Other knowledgeable industry and Washington insiders have said the same thing. Carryover funding of approximately $11.1 million in the NRC and $15 million from DOE could certainly restart the license review, while NRC and DOE assess the full funding needs and request them from Congress, as agencies should do. Congress then can appropriate the remainder of the licensing review costs from the NWF whether or not the NRC or DOE budgets request them. By law, these funds can only be used to support licensing, construction, and operation of a repository at Yucca Mountain. The funds exist and are available—Congress just needs to appropriate them for the purpose for which they were intended.

Another objection sometimes raised to restarting the licensing review—that the process is too complicated—is also easy to debunk. Both DOE and the NRC have stipulated to the courts and Congress that they could restart the review if so ordered. It is exponentially cheaper to restart this process than to start the entire repository siting and characterization process from the beginning. Pertinent documents have been preserved by DOE's Office of Legacy Management and can be retrieved as needed. Any issues involving data and documentation can be expediently addressed and mitigated within the bounds of NRC requirements.

Strassel agrees, stating: "Congressional staff who have seen a redacted report tell me the staff's answer is yes [the Yucca Mountain Project is a safe location for a nuclear waste repository]. Mr. Reid is determined to keep this report from going public, since he knows it could dramatically increase the pressure—in particular from Congress—to move forward with Yucca...Congress has the tools...[and] a willing ally in the NRC staff, which remains furious that the [Gregory] Jaczko-Reid duo tanked years of its work. The NRC staffers have publicly called on Congress to help get their product to the public, and they can surely be enlisted now in a campaign to finish the safety review."[471]

The experts and the expertise needed to conclude licensing is limited to a small number of individuals who are well known to the process and not too scattered to retrieve. The DOE still has active contracts for outside counsel for licensing support, and for a management and operations contractor. Any additional expertise needed can be procured through these contracts. Current licensing experts, engineers, and managers intimately involved with the project over many years estimate that waste could be accepted at Yucca Mountain by 2023. Moreover, if Congress and the administration fully support the project and provide funding on the order of $930 million per year (from the existing NWF) over the next six years, waste could be accepted at Yucca Mountain perhaps as early as 2019. In comparison to starting the entire national repository site selection process all over, which both the DOE *Implementation Strategy* and the bipartisan *Nuclear Waste Administration* bill would require, restarting the licensing process leading to approval of the Yucca Mountain site would be a fiscal (and operational) bargain for the United States. Nuclear waste shipping out of the multiple, scattered locations across the nation could start some 28 years earlier than the DOE projection of 2048.

A last pertinent reason to re-start the Yucca Mountain Project licensing process is that the existing U.S. law—the NWPA—requires that at least one permanent repository be licensed before any interim consolidated storage facilities can be built. This requirement was included in the Act to ensure that interim storage did not become permanent storage by default if no repository was ever licensed.[472] (Such conditions already exist at the nation's major nuclear defense sites—the Hanford Site in the state of Washington and the Savannah River Site in South Carolina.)

Legally, even if Congress were to adopt the DOE *Implementation Strategy* or the bipartisan *Nuclear Waste Administration* bill, the stipulation to license a permanent repository would still have to be met. Further, demonstrating that a deep geological facility can be licensed would be of great value to those communities considering hosting consolidated storage facilities, because it would show that the stringent public health and safety standards required for safe storage of high-level waste and spent nuclear fuel can be met. Licensing Yucca Mountain also would provide a benefit to the rate payers using nuclear power for the $15 billion already spent, rather than allowing this enormous investment to be wasted. Additionally, achieving a repository license would help the United States regain some of its lost scientific prestige and technological leadership in the worldwide nuclear energy community.

Moving Forward: Interim Storage

Given my strong belief that this country should immediately restart the Yucca Mountain Project licensing process, there is a crucial activity that I think should happen at nearly the same time. Key organizations and individuals who have looked closely at America's nuclear waste dilemma since the Yucca Mountain Project was terminated have advocated centralized interim storage, especially for some high-priority waste. The BRC recommended taking immediate steps to create consolidated storage facilities, as did the DOE *Strategy* and the bipartisan *Nuclear Waste Administration* bill. Given that the NWPA requires licensing a permanent repository, my recommendation is to license the Yucca Mountain site but delay constructing it until an incentive package has been presented to Nevada. Licensing the repository would clear the path for centralized interim storage.

The BRC report made it clear that storage means temporary and disposal means permanent:

> "Disposal, intended as the final stage of waste management, is isolation that relies in the long term only on the passive operation of natural environmental and man-made barriers, does not permit easy human access to the waste after final emplacement, and does not

require continued human control and maintenance. Storage, intended as an intermediate step in waste management, is isolation that permits managed access to the waste after its emplacement, with active human control and maintenance to assure isolation. After a period in storage, waste is subject to disposal....the term "disposal" is understood to mean permanent disposal; the term "storage" is understood to mean storage for an interim period prior to disposal or other disposition.[473]

The BRC recommended that consolidated storage facilities were essential to solving the nuclear waste storage dilemma. Implementing regional consolidated storage facilities for commercial spent nuclear fuel is the best way for the government to take possession of spent fuel from utilities pending the construction of one or more deep-geologic permanent repositories. Moreover, siting at least one consolidated interim storage facility would provide the opportunity for further research and evaluation of the pros and cons of reprocessing commercial spent nuclear fuel as part of a waste management disposal strategy. As described in Chapter 2, many nations are either reprocessing or moving toward reprocessing as a way to extract more value from their nuclear fuel and reduce the volumes of spent nuclear fuel that require long-term storage.

Moving Forward: Defense Waste

As explained in Chapter 1, most of the high-level waste at government defense production sites—where materials for U.S. nuclear weapons were produced—exists in forms quite different from commercial spent nuclear fuel. First, the government sites contain about 2,465 MT of spent nuclear fuel, but most of it consists of solid metallic fuel elements or rods in aluminum or zirconium cladding or "jackets." Most commercial spent fuel consists of tiny pellets or sintered powders inside tubes or jackets incorporating many different metals alloyed in blends. Still, spent nuclear fuel is spent nuclear fuel, and the defense and commercial forms aren't that different. The real divergence between commercial spent fuel and defense nuclear waste is that the vast majority of defense waste at government sites exists as soupy liquids or sludges stored in large underground tanks. They are the initial products or byproducts of "reprocessing" of irradiated fuel from reactors to extract plutonium for use in nuclear weapons. Some of these sludges have been vitrified, or solidified at high temperatures with other materials to become an extremely hard and impervious "glass-like" material. Thus, vitrification has created a third waste form—glass logs. Spent nuclear fuel elements from the nuclear ships in the U.S. Navy, and the calcined products of reprocessed Navy fuel, all stored at the Idaho National Laboratory, constitute yet another defense waste form.

It is unfortunate that the NWPA co-mingled the management and disposal of commercial and defense waste. Not enough consideration was given to the physical properties of the waste and the fact that defense waste was ready to be solidified into its final form and disposed, while commercial "waste" (spent nuclear fuel) needed to be preserved to keep open the option of reprocessing. In addition, the size of the first repository, which was to be at Yucca Mountain, was limited on purpose—administratively although not technically—to force the opening of a second repository, in the interests of environmental justice. The reality, even if we now had the Yucca Mountain Project, is that a single repository is not large enough to hold all the defense and commercial materials.

The point is that governing all of the wastes in the same way ties our hands in unfortunate ways. Waste left over from reprocessing is "real" waste, sometimes called "legacy waste," since it is from the past and has no more energy value. This waste should be disposed of permanently. Commercial spent nuclear fuel, on the other hand, is now sometimes called "used nuclear fuel," because it is really not spent and is really not waste. The spent nuclear fuel rods or elements retain 90 percent of their original energy, and can be reprocessed to produce more energy for nuclear plants by extracting the fissile and fertile material from the spent fuel. In addition, the co-mingling of defense and civilian waste causes a great deal of confusion to the public. The bureaucratic, technical, and administrative bungling that has resulted in years of delay and cost overruns in waste management at the Hanford and Savannah River Sites leads people to believe that all nuclear plants make, or could make, the same types and amounts of "messes" that are found at these old defense sites. This confusion seriously impacts the public's belief that there is a credible solution to the commercial waste and spent nuclear fuel dilemma, and holds back acceptance of nuclear power.

I am sure that nuclear waste storage and eventual disposal could be furthered if the NWPA were amended to separate commercial from defense waste, assign responsibility for the disposal of defense waste to DOE's NNSA, and re-define high-level waste to account for the physical, isotopic, and radiological differences between low-activity waste and very high-activity waste. If the NWPA were thus amended, we could treat low-activity waste sludges differently than high-activity sludges, all of which currently must be treated by the complicated and expensive vitrification process. Low-activity waste sludges could be treated with other, cheaper immobilization technologies, including steam reforming, grouting, or calcining in facilities much more readily available than vitrification facilities. We could develop a fast-track approach to disposing of vitrified, high-activity defense waste, which is ripe for disposal because it has no residual value.

Congress would have to amend the NWPA to define the low-activity waste fraction of high-level waste as a different waste than the "rest" of high-level waste, and allowing different regulation, treatment, and disposal of it. At the same time, Congress could direct the establishment of an expert team of scientists and engineers to determine which defense waste requires vitrification and which could be safely treated more quickly and cost effectively with other solidification technologies.

Currently, Hanford Site waste treatment plans are governed by a decision made in a DOE Environmental Impact Statement (EIS) issued in 1997, stating that all 57 million gallons of tank wastes at the Site would be vitrified.[474] This EIS reversed the decision in an EIS one decade earlier, which had stated that the low-activity waste fraction of tank waste would be placed in grout (a type of cement), and only the high-activity fraction would be vitrified.[475] However, early tests with grout showed technical problems. Instead of keeping the waste fractions separate and looking for a treatment alternative to grouting, the 1997 EIS simply combined all the wastes and said they must be vitrified. A subsequent EIS dealing with the tanks at Hanford did not change the 1997 decision.[476]

The problem, however, is that the "simple" 1997 decision is not simple at all, and it is unnecessarily expensive. It resulted in an implementation strategy that is constructing the world's largest vitrification facility, the Hanford WTP. The design requirements for the WTP were a mistake from the beginning, driven by bureaucrats and not scientists and engineers. Ground was broken for the plant in 2000, with a projected operational date of 2007. Yet, new projections show that no parts of it will be operating until at least 2020, and major portions will not begin operating until after that time because intrinsic technical and safety issues have not been solved. The plant's cost was supposed to be $4.4 billion but is now projected to be nearly three times that amount, with no assurance that recent cost estimates of approximately $13 billion are realistic either.[477]

The Hanford WTP project has been one of the most heavily criticized in modern U.S. history. Its first process step, according to plans, will be to separate the low-activity waste and high-activity fractions of the tank waste, and *treat them separately!* Both fractions will be vitrified, but in separate processes and separate buildings, because the low-activity waste fraction is chemically more complex and will require vast additional additives ("glass-formers") to achieve an impermeable product. The low-activity waste and high-activity fractions will also be disposed of separately, with the low-activity waste fraction permitted in a special field of earthen trenches at Hanford,[478] and the high-activity portion is now orphaned because the Yucca Mountain Project was terminated. Given that the NWPA combines the low-activity waste and high-activity fractions administratively, while they cannot be combined and treated physically, doesn't it make sense to amend the law and separate them legally? The NWPA is a superior document to an EIS because the former is a law and the latter is an agency product. All kinds of flexibility could be gained by thus amending the NWPA.

One adaptation that could be considered, if the definition of high-level waste was changed in the NWPA, would be the possibility of disposing some of the waste, in solidified form, as mixed TRU waste. The Waste Isolation Pilot Plant (WIPP) in New Mexico is the disposal facility for the nation's defense TRU waste. The WIPP facility began receiving shipments in 1999, and has since received nearly 10,000 shipments of TRU waste from 29 nuclear weapons production sites across the United States, in a deep salt repository 2,150 feet underground.[479] More than 82,000 cubic meters of TRU waste have been safely disposed of thus far. If the NWPA were amended to separate defense and commercial wastes, then certain solidified tank wastes from Hanford (and other defense sites) could be disposed in WIPP-like facilities. This concept already has some support in the most recent Hanford Waste Management EIS, which states that "DOE prefers to consider the option to retrieve, treat and package waste that may be properly and legally designated as mixed TRU waste from specific tanks for disposal at WIPP."[480]

Another adaptation that could come from redefining high-level waste in the NWPA would be that "secondary waste" generated during vitrification and other solidification processes could be treated and disposed by various, scientifically appropriate means. Secondary waste volumes at Hanford's WTP will not be trivial, and could surpass even the waste volumes now stored in Hanford's tanks. At this time, there is no mitigation plan for this secondary waste. Surely creative and sound treatment and disposal methods can be found if the strict definition that everything that touches high-level waste becomes high-level waste could be revised.[481]

The largest benefit in amending the NWPA's definition of high-level waste would come from loosening the regulatory bottleneck now existing for low-activity waste, created at Hanford by the Washington State regulators' distrust of DOE. Nearly 90 percent of the waste in Hanford's tanks is low-activity waste, and should not, in terms of common sense, be subject to the same treatment and disposal requirements as high-activity waste.

Moving Forward: Consent with Benefits

First among the BRC's recommendations was that the United States implement "a new, consent-based approach to siting future nuclear waste management facilities." The original NWPA provided that a state in which a repository site had been chosen could veto the selection, but that veto could be overridden by a majority vote of both houses of Congress. The 1987 amendments to the NWPA gave Nevada the right to disagree, but took away its power to veto the Yucca Mountain site, provided the site proved to be scientifically sound. The science would be judged by the NRC via the license application review.[482]

In addition, the BRC recommended that "the United States establish a program that leads to the timely development of one or more consolidated storage facilities."[483] Multiple benefits would occur, including starting to meet federal obligations, stopping the flow of money to utilities who sue successfully for the government's failure to take the waste, fostering a technical learning curve and technology development, gaining flexibility to respond to lessons learned from nuclear events around the world, and other plusses. The BRC urged that we move quickly to begin a safe, sound program to store spent nuclear fuel and solidified high-level waste in states/communities that volunteer to house these materials (with economic and social rewards) until a national repository is available.

As stated earlier, the issue of consent is viewed with at least irony if not outright sarcasm by residents of Washington State, because the Hanford Site was located there in complete secrecy during World War II. The same is true of the Oak Ridge Site in Tennessee and the Los Alamos Site in New Mexico. However, these latter two sites are tiny compared to behemoth Hanford, which is 14 to 50 times larger than the other two World War II, U.S. nuclear defense sites. More important, Hanford contains approximately two-thirds of the waste in the entire DOE complex, and Hanford's waste is uniquely complicated and unruly because it is so old and has been fed by more chemical and physical processes than any other site in the nation. No one in the state of Washington consented to host any of it.

After World War II, "atomic" activities had cachet, and they came with federal dollars, so communities fought to have new nuclear defense facilities located near them. In the cases of the Idaho National Laboratory (formerly the Reactor Testing Station), the Savannah River Site, and the Rocky Flats Site near Denver, communities lobbied to be chosen, and some communities even protested when they were not chosen as homes to nuclear defense sites. Even if these communities didn't know about all of the waste they would be getting in the bargain, they at least had some choice in the siting processes of the 1950s.

Across the world today, as presented in the first chapter, many nations are deciding to site nuclear waste storage and disposal sites with at least some participation by potentially affected communities. Consent may not mean much in China, but it is a major factor in communities in Canada, the United Kingdom, Finland, Spain, Sweden, and other European countries that have asked for—and received—voluntary self-selection and active engagement of potential host communities. Incentives, mainly economic, motivate communities to volunteer.

First of all, siting studies alone will bring in geologists, hydrologists, engineers, drillers, excavators, and other skilled workers and their families, and these people will feed businesses in the communities as they meet their everyday needs. Becoming a host community can bring all sorts of financial benefits such as local college endowments and scholarships, new roads and railroads, buildings and emergency equipment for local police and fire, many jobs, local hiring preferences, taxes or payments in lieu of taxes to local governments, funding for state and local oversight boards, and other rewards. The BRC recognized these benefits as powerful stimulants for communities to volunteer when it stated that "siting processes for waste management facilities should include a flexible and substantial incentive program."[484]

The BRC report also stated that the responsibilities of the new waste management administration it recommended should "include promoting the social and economic well-being of communities affected by waste management facilities."[485]

There are many communities in the United States that might be interested in hosting an interim, consolidated storage facility for spent nuclear fuel—particularly stranded spent nuclear fuel—along with some high-level waste, provided the benefits were right and safety was assured. Such communities might include those communities now storing nuclear byproducts without the benefit of incentives, such as the communities near the Hanford and Savannah River Sites. Benefits to these communities could include those mentioned above as well as direct payments, preferential consideration for siting new energy projects in wind, solar, energy storage, and other nuclear technologies, to support a clean energy park. This park would present a unique opportunity to demonstrate the commercial viability of integrating and distributing solar and wind energy with base load nuclear power.

One of the difficulties in implementing a consent-based approach that the BRC neglected to address is the possibility of a future situation that parallels Nevada's experience. Initially, Nevada supported a repository, but then politics of support changed to objection, except in Nye County where Yucca is located. Nye County has consistently supported a repository in Nevada because the region has benefitted from the economic and social incentives such as those recommended by the BRC. The success of licensing, construction, and operation of any repository will ultimately need to rely on the preemption of federal law over state political or legal objections.

Summary and Conclusion

In summary, I propose that Congress amend the NWPA to maintain the licensing requirement for the Yucca Mountain site, but delay the decision to construct it until Nevada has received and responded to an incentive package for hosting it. Most important, the process of amending the NWPA in the four ways I have recommended, instead of violating it, would re-assert the rule of law in this matter and the principle of separation of powers that are crucial to maintaining our democracy.

Afterword

On November 3, 2013, four top environmental scientists—three Americans and an Australian—released an Open Letter to world leaders advocating that nuclear power is the best hope for reversing the looming threats from global climate change. James Hansen, formerly of the National Aeronautics and Space Administration; Ken Caldeira, the Carnegie Institution; Kerry Emanual, the Massachusetts Institute of Technology; and Tom Wigley, the University of Adelaide, stated that "in the real world there is no credible path to climate stabilization that does not include a substantial role for nuclear power... Renewables like wind and solar and biomass...cannot scale up fast enough to deliver cheap and reliable power at the scale the global economy requires."[486]

Their open letter captures the theme of this book. The world needs nuclear energy urgently, right now, and the United States should be a leader in promoting nuclear energy. Our nation led the world in developing nuclear technology, but it has lost its edge in this field to developed and developing countries throughout the world that are clearly setting courses toward generating clean energy and achieving energy independence fueled by nuclear power. It's not that scientists and engineers in these nations are smarter than those in America. We've fallen behind because we're leaving the stage—or the laboratory—and simply not competing. We're closing nuclear plants, building precious few new ones, leaving our spent nuclear fuel spread around the country next to population centers, taxing the nuclear industry in ways no other energy industries are taxed, and then not delivering back to the nuclear rate-payers any of the benefits for which they were taxed. This situation is one of the most short-sighted and self-destructive that I've seen during my 50-year career in nuclear energy. I've written this book as a call to action for our nation to protect its own self-interests by promoting nuclear energy as well as to lead the rest of the world in carbon-free energy production.

Japan, the third largest economy in the world, announced that it will not meet its target for reduction of CO_2 emissions because most of its nuclear power plants have remained closed since the March 2011 accident at the Fukushima Power Station. In fact, Japan's emissions are expected to rise by three to four percent by 2020, against a 1990 baseline, instead of meeting its reduction goal of 25 percent.[487] The deficit of nuclear power in Japan has directly and immediately affected the world community's efforts to reduce greenhouse gas emissions. The United States contribution to reduction efforts will be similarly affected if we continue to prematurely shut down nuclear power plants without building new nuclear power plants to replace them. And as President Obama noted at the beginning of his first term in office, *"there is no future for expanded nuclear without first addressing … security of nuclear fuel and … waste storage…"*

On a more positive note, on November 18, 2013, the U.S. Nuclear Regulatory Commission (NRC) directed staff to complete the Safety Evaluation Report associated with the construction authorization application for the Yucca Mountain repository and requested that the U.S. Department of Energy (DOE) complete the supplemental Environmental Impact Statement (EIS) needed to address the potential impacts of the construction authorization on groundwater and from surface discharges of groundwater.[488] This action was in direct response to the writ of mandamus issued by the U.S. Court of Appeals for the District of Columbia Circuit on August 13, 2013, resulting from the lawsuit I filed as a private citizen, which was combined with the suits of other affected parties. The next day, the D.C. Circuit Court directed that the Secretary of Energy submit to Congress a plan to reduce the payments from utilities into the NWF "to zero until such a time as either the Secretary chooses to comply with the [Nuclear Waste Policy] Act as it is written, or until Congress enacts an alternative waste management plan."[489]

A more fair, reasonable, and resounding victory for the rule of law can hardly be imagined. Our country seems to have lost interest in the civil art of discussion and debate, though we have broader access to the means of communicating our thoughts and opinions far and wide than ever before. As citizens of a democracy, it is essential that we think, discuss, and act.

Our country's apathy toward falling behind the rest of the world in a transition from fossil fuels to clean nuclear energy is somewhat analogous to the situation Winston Churchill faced when he was Prime Minister of Britain during World War II. He wrote a book in 1938 entitled *While England Slept* warning his nation that its lack of attention to military preparedness was perilous and foolhardy while German Chancellor Adolf Hitler built a huge military force and bullied neighboring countries. Indeed, when war came, England was nearly destroyed.

Using the Churchill analogy, the United States is sleeping as mounting evidence supports the conclusion that we have an energy policy in disarray and that our goals to reduce CO_2 emissions will not be met, causing irreversible impact to our environment. As the late James Schlesinger, the first Secretary of Energy, wrote in 1992, "Every nation will have an energy policy—if it is not explicit and (presumably) coherent, it will simply be haphazard… Will a nation embrace a de facto policy of drift, especially under rapidly changing conditions?"[490]

We need a serious debate about our national energy policy, not only because of the nuclear issues I've raised in this book, but because we must heed history's stark lessons about the role of energy supply in maintaining international security and economic stability. We are currently observing in our country the situation Schlesinger feared: "a de facto policy of drift" regarding energy.

At the beginning of this book, I introduced four themes: the importance of upholding the separation of powers among the three branches of our government—the cornerstone of our democracy; the value of nuclear energy to U.S. national security and its potential to mitigate global climate change; the dangers of letting the rest of the world bypass the United States in essentially every area of nuclear technology; and President Obama's disturbing record of ignoring laws and bypassing legislative procedures that the founding fathers of our country set out in the U.S. Constitution. I contend that these themes represent a good place to start in an essential national debate about a new energy policy that will enable the United States to maintain its energy independence and regain its leadership in nuclear energy.

References

Introduction

1. Two of my most trusted friends and longtime business colleagues, Bill Lampson, president and CEO of Lampson, International, with headquarters in Kennewick, WA, and operations worldwide; and Gary Petersen, vice-president of Hanford Programs at the Tri-Cities Development Council in Kennewick, WA.

2. Court Order, Aiken County et al. vs. Nuclear Regulatory Commission, No. 11-1271, U.S. District Court of Appeals for the District of Columbia Circuit, September term 2012, Filed August 13, 2013.

3. Joint Congressional Committee on Inaugural Ceremonies, *President's Swearing-In Ceremony*, U.S. Senate, Washington, D.C., January 21, 2013, at www.inaugural.senate.gov/days-events/days-event/presidents-swearing-in-ceremony

4. Obama, Barack, *State of the Union Address*, White House (Washington, D.C.), January 28, 2014, at www.washingtonpost.com/wp-apps/say-what/2014-state-of-the-union/

5. Judge Brett Kavanaugh, *On Petition for Writ of Mandamus*, Document 1451347, Aiken County, et al. vs. Nuclear Regulatory Commission, No. 11-1271, U.S. District Court of Appeals for the District of Columbia Circuit, August 13, 2013, at www.cadc.uscourts.gov/internet/opinions.nsf/BAE0CF34F762EBD985257BC6004DEB18/$file/11-1271-1451347.pdf.

6. Meeting in the Roosevelt Room at the White House-February 2, 1982. Attendees: T. Louis Austin, Jr., Chairman of the Texas Utilities Co.; William R. Gould, Chairman of the Southern California Edison Co.; Robert Baldwin, President of Morgan Stanley & Co.; Robert E. Kirby, Chairman of Westinghouse Electric Corporation; Stephen O. Bechtel, Jr., Chairman of Bechtel Corporation; William S. Lee, President of Duke Power Co.; Edward F. Burke, Chairman of the Rhode Island Public Utilities Commission; Lelan F. Sillin, Jr., Chairman of Northwest Utilities; Charles H. Dean, Jr., Chairman of the Tennessee Valley Authority; Sherwood H. Smith, Jr., Chairman of Carolina Power & Light Co.; **Robert L. Ferguson**, Managing Director of the Washington Public Power Supply System; Larry J. Wallace, Indiana Public Service Commission; Robert M. Gardiner, President of Dean Witter Reynolds Organization; John F. Welch, Chairman of General Electric Co.; and W.S. White, Jr., Chairman of the American Electric Power Co.

7. Ronald Reagan: "Letter to the Speaker of the House and the President of the Senate on Nuclear Waste Legislation," April 28, 1982. *The American Presidency Project, at* www.presidency.ucsb.edu/ ws/?pid=42459

8. Nuclear Waste Policy Act (NWPA), Public Law 97-425, 97th Cong., 2nd Session, January 7, 1983.

9. Shippingport Atomic Power Station was an exception because it was completely decommissioned in the 1980s, and its waste was removed. The station was a joint project between private industry and the federal government, so the government shipped the waste to federal nuclear sites in other states for storage. This fuel is still in storage, and has never been permanently disposed. This situation is not typical, as in most cases nuclear power plants are purely private ventures and the waste still resides at the plant sites where it was generated.

10. Reagan, Ronald, "Remarks on Signing the Nuclear Waste Policy Act of 1982," January 7, 1983, *The American Presidency Project*, University

of California at Santa Barbara, at www.presidency.ucsb.edu/ws/?pid=40954

11. Majority Staff, U.S. Senate Committee on Environment and Public Works, *Yucca Mountain, the Most Studied Real Estate on the Planet*, Report to the Chairman James Inhofe, March 2006, at www.epw.senate.gov/repwhitepapers/YuccaMountainEPWReport.pdf

12. U.S. Department of Energy (DOE), May 1986, *Multi-attribute Utility Analysis of Sites Nominated for Characterization for the First Radioactive Waste Repository—A Decision-Aiding Methodology* (DOE/RW-0074), Washington, D.C., at energy.gov/downloads/multiattribute-utility-analysis-sites-nominated-characterization-first-radioactive-waste-0

13   Nuclear Waste Policy Act, Public Law 100-203, 100th Cong., 1st Session, December 22, 1987.

14. U.S. Atomic Energy Commission (AEC), *Draft Environmental Impact Statement, Management of Commercial High-level and Transuranic Contaminated Radioactive Waste*, WASH-1539, 1974; Nevada Legislature, *Assembly Joint Resolution No.15*, 58th Session, 1975.

15. U.S. DOE, Office of Civilian Radioactive Waste Management, *Spending to Date*, February 10, 2001, Washington, D.C.

16. Clinton vs. Jones, 520 U.S. 681, 1997; Baker, Peter, "Clinton Settles Paula Jones Lawsuit for $850,000," *Washington Post*, November 14, 1998, at www.washingtonpost.com/wp-srv/politics/special/clinton/stories/jones111498.htm

17. Froomkin, Dan, "Case Closed," *Washington Post*, December 8, 1998, at www.washingtonpost.com/wp-srv/politics/special/pjones/pjones.htm

Chapter 1

18. Obama '08: *Barack Obama's Plan to Make America a Global Energy Leader*, at obama.3cdn.net/4465b108758abf7a42_a3jmvyfa5.pdf

19. Blue Ribbon Commission on America's Nuclear Future (BRC), "Letter of Transmittal," to Steven Chu, January 2012, at cybercemetery.unt.

edu/archive/brc/20120620220235/http://brc.gov/sites/default/files/documents/brc_finalreport_jan2012.pdf

20. World Nuclear Association (WNA), "World Nuclear Power Reactors and Uranium Requirements," October 2012, at www.world-nuclear.org/info/reactors.html; Nuclear Energy Institute (NEI), "U.S. Nuclear Plant Operators, Owners, and Holding Companies," March 2012, at www.nei.org/resourcesandstats/documentslibrary.

21. For technical simplicity, we describe spent fuel inventories in terms of metric tons (MT) instead of the more accurate metric tons heavy metal (MTHM). Heavy metal refers to the mass of actinide elements with atomic numbers greater than 89 in spent fuel. See the U.S. Environmental Protection Agency's (EPA's) *Yucca Mountain Background Information Document*, p. 5-1, at www.epa.gov/radiation/docs/yucca/bid/yucca_bid_060501_ch5.pdf

22. NEI, *Nuclear Waste: Amounts and On-Site Storage*, at nei.org/resourcesandstats/nuclear_statistics/nuclearwasteamountsandonsitestorage; U.S. Nuclear Regulatory Commission (NRC), *Spent Fuel Storage in Pools and Dry Casks: Key Points and Questions and Answers*, March 29, 2012, at www.nrc.gov/waste/spent-fuel-storage/faqs.html

23. *Blue Ribbon Commission on America's Nuclear Future (BRC), Report to the Secretary of Energy*, p. 35, at cybercemetery.unt.edu/archive/brc/20120620220235/http://brc.gov/sites/default/files/documents/brc_finalreport_jan2012.pdf

24. *Blue Ribbon Commission on America's Nuclear Future (BRC), Report to the Secretary of Energy*, p. 35, at cybercemetery.unt.edu/archive/brc/20120620220235/http://brc.gov/sites/default/files/documents/brc_finalreport_jan2012.pdf

25. NEI, *Map: Used Nuclear Fuel in Storage*, at www.nei.org/getmedia/0e936169-02de-492f-a600-42f89d95a86a/Used-Fuel-Map-2012?width=1100&height=850&ext=.png

26. NEI, *U.S. State by State Used Fuel and Payments to the Nuclear Waste Fund*, at www.nei.org/Knowledge-Center/Nuclear-Statistics/On-Site-Storage-of-Nuclear-Waste/US-State-by-State-Used-Fuel-and-Payments-to-the-Nu

27. U.S. Energy Information Administration (EIA), *Frequently Asked Questions*, May 16, 2012, at www.eia.gov/tools/faqs/faq.cfm?id=228&t=21; Johnson, Jeff, "Nuclear Retirement Anxiety," *Chemical & Engineering News*, Vol.91, Issue 13, pp. 14-17, American Chemical Society (ACS), Washington, D.C.

28. NEI, *License Renewal*, 2013, at www.nei.org/resourcesandstats/nuclear statistics/License-Renewal; NEI, *New Nuclear Plant Status*, May 2013, at www.nei.org/resourcesandstats/Documentlibrary/New-Plants/graphicsandcharts/New-Nuclear-Plant-Status; Tennessee Valley Authority (TVA), *Watts Bar Nuclear Unit 2: The Way Forward to Complete TVA's Seventh Reactor*, April 2012, at www.tva.com/power/nuclear/pdf/Watts_Bar_2_White_Paper.pdf; Burris, Roddy, "Slowdown at V.C. Summer Nuclear Plant Brings Layoffs," *The State*, Columbia, SC, January 25, 2013, at www.thestate.com/2013/01/25/2603871/slowdown-at-vc-summer-nuclear.html

29. NEI, *Nuclear Units Under Construction Worldwide*, January 2014, at www.nei.org/Knowledge-Center/Nuclear-Statistics/World-Statistics/Nuclear-Units-Under-Construction-Worldwide

30. NEI, *Watts Bar 2 Reactivation*, March 29, 2012, at www.nrc.gov/info-finder/reactor/wb/watts-bar.html

31. 10 CFR 51.23, U.S. NRC: Temporary storage of spent fuel after cessation of reactor operation—generic determination of no significant environmental impact, at www.nrc.gov/reading-rm/doc-collections/cfr/part051/part051-0023.html

32. Wald, Matt, "Court Forces a Rethinking of Nuclear Fuel Storage," *New York Times*, June 8, 2012, at www.nytimes.com/2012/06/09/science/earth/court-says-nuclear-agency-must-rethink-fuel-storage.html?_r=1; New York vs. NRC, 681 F.3d 471 (D.C. Cir. 2012). Final Rule, Consideration of Environmental Impacts of Temporary Storage of Spent Fuel After Cessation of Reactor Operation, 75 Fed. Reg. 81,032 (Dec. 23, 2010); Waste Confidence Decision Update, 75 Fed. Reg. 81,037 (Dec. 23, 2010).

33. Tetreault, Steve, "Ruling Reopens Debate on Yucca Mountain," *Las Vegas Review-Journal*, June 8, 2012, at www.lvrj.com/news/court-throws-out-nuke-waste-storage-rule-158236255.html

34. U.S. NRC, 42 FR 34391, July 5, 1977.

35. U.S. NRC, Memorandum and Order - CLI-12-16, at www.nrc.gov/reading-rm/doc-collections/commission/orders/2012/2012-16cli.pdf

36. Wald, Matt, "An Uncertain Phase for Nuclear Power Licenses," *New York Times,* August 9, 2012, at green.blogs.nytimes.com/2012/08/09/an-uncertain-phase-for-nuclear-power-licenses/?_php=true&_type=blogs&_r=0

37. Stars Alliance, *APS: Palo Verde Nuclear Generating Station,* 2012, at www.starsalliance.com/members/paloverde.asp

38. National Academy of Sciences (NAS), *Safety and Security of Commercial Spent Nuclear Fuel Storage: Public Report,* 2006, NAS Press, Washington, D.C. (ISBN-10: 0-309-09647-2).

39. U.S. Government Accountability Office (GAO), *Highlights: Spent Nuclear Fuel—Accumulating Quantities at Commercial Reactors Present Storage and Other Challenges,* GAO-12-797, August 2012, at www.gao.gov/assets/600/593745.pdf.

40. NEI, "Uncertainty Over Accelerating Dry Storage of Used Nuclear Fuel," *NEI Magazine,* September 17, 2012 (citing Electric Power Research Institute [EPRI]).

41. U.S. GAO, *Spent Nuclear Fuel: Accumulating Quantities at Commercial Reactors Present Storage and Other Challenges,* GAO-12-797, August 2012, at www.gao.gov/assets/600/593745.pdf

42. U.S. NRC, *Map of U.S. Independent Spent Fuel Storage Installations,* July 2013, at www.nrc.gov/waste/spent-fuel-storage/locations.pdf

43. U.S. NRC, *Spent Fuel Storage in Pools and Dry Casks,* at www.nrc.gov/waste/spent-fuel-storage/faqs.html

44. NEI, *Costs, Fuel, Operation and Waste Disposal,* 2013, at www.nei.org/resourcesandstats/nuclear_statistics/Costs-Fuel,-Operation-and-Waste-Disposal

45. U.S. GAO, *Key Attributes, Challenges, and Costs for the Yucca Mountain Repository and Two Potential Alternatives,* GAO-10-48, November

4, 2009, at www.gao.gov/products/GAO-10-48; U.S. GAO, *Spent Nuclear Fuel: Accumulating Quantities at Nuclear Reactors Present Storage and Other Challenges*, GAO-12-797, August 2012, at www.gao.gov/assets/600/593745.pdf; U.S. GAO, *Observations on the Key Attributes and Challenges of Storage and Disposal Options*, GAO-13-532T, April 11, 2013, p. 10, at www.gao.gov/products/GAO-13-532T

46.   NEI, *Nuclear Plant Security*, 2013, at www.nei.org/resourcesandstats/Documentlibrary/Safety-and-Security/factsheet/powerplant-security; U.S. NRC, *Fact Sheet on Safety and Security Improvements at Nuclear Plants*," March 29, 2012, at www.nrc.gov/reading-rm/doc-collections/fact-sheets/safety-scurity.html; U.S. NRC, *Security Orders*, U.S. NRC, *Order Modifying Licenses*, EA-02, 104 (March 16, 2002), and *Interim Safeguards and Compensatory Measures*, EA-02-77 (May 23, 2002), and *Decommissioning Nuclear Power Plants with Spent Fuel in the Spent Fuel Pool*, EA-03-99 (August 18, 2004), at www.nrc.gov/reading-rm/doc-collections/enforcement/security-orders

47.   A gigawatt is equivalent to one billion watts.

48.   NEI, *U.S. Nuclear Operating Plant Basic Information*, 2013, at www.nei.org/resourcesandstats/graphicsandcharts/plantinformation; U.S. EIA, *Nuclear and Uranium State Nuclear Profiles*, April 26, 2012, at www.eia.gov/nuclear/state/; NEI, *U.S. State by State Commercial Nuclear Used Fuel and Payments to the Nuclear Waste Fund*," March 2012, at www.nei.org/resourcesandstats/Documentlibrary/Nuclear-Waste-Disposal/graphicsandcharts/Nuclear-Waste-Fund-Payment-Information-by-State

49.   Exelon Corp., *Dresden Generating Station*, 2013, at www.exeloncorp.com/powerplants/dresden/Pages/profile.aspx

50.   Exelon Corp., 2013, *LaSalle County Generating Station*, at www.exeloncorp.com/powerplants/lasalle/Pages/profile.aspx | *Braidwood Generating Station*, at www.exeloncorp.com/powerplants/braidwood/Pages/profile.aspx; NEI, *U.S. Nuclear Power Plants*, 2013, at www.nei.org/resourcesandstats/nuclear_statistics/U-S-Nuclear-Power-Plants; American Electric Power (AEP), *Cook Nuclear Plant Opens Dry Cask Storage Facility for Used Fuel*, August 1, 2012,

at www.indianamichiganpower.com/info/news/viewRelease. aspx?releaseID=1292

51.   U.S. EIA, *Nuclear and Uranium State Nuclear Profiles*, April 26, 2012, at www.eia.gov/nuclear/state/

52.   U.S. GAO, *Spent Nuclear Fuel: Accumulating Quantities at Nuclear Reactors Present Storage and Other Challenges*, GAO-12-797, August 2012, at www.gao.gov/assets/600/593745.pdf

53.   A curie is a measure of the amount of radioactivity.

54.   U.S. DOE, *Final Environmental Impact Statement for a Geologic Repository for the Disposal of Spent Nuclear Fuel and High-Level Radioactive Waste at Yucca Mountain, Nye County, Nevada*, DOE/EIS-0250F, February 2002, Volume II, Appendix A.

55.   NEI, *Fact Sheet: Status of Used Nuclear Fuel Storage at U.S. Commercial Nuclear Plants*, November 2011, at www.nei.org/resourcesandstats/ Documentlibrary/Nuclear-Waste-Disposal/factsheet/statuso-fusednuclearfuelstorage; Exelon Corp., *Braidwood Station to Host Community Information Night March 5*, March 2, 2009, at www.exe-loncorp.com/Newsroom/Pages/pr_20090302_GenerationA; Wald, Matthew, "A Safer Nuclear Crypt," *New York Times*, July 5, 2011, at www.nytimes.com/2011/07/06/business/energy-environment/ 06cask.html?pagewanted=all; AEP, *Cook Nuclear Plant Opens Dry Cask Storage Facility for Used Fuel*, August 1, 2012, at www.indiana-michiganpower.com/info/news/viewRelease.aspx?releaseID=1292; Exelon Corp., *Zion Station*, 2013, at www.exeloncorp.com/power-plants/zion/Pages/profile.aspx

56.   Union of Concerned Scientists (UCS), *Nuclear Power Safety in Illinois*, Cambridge, MA, March 2012, at www.ucsusa.org/assets/ documents/nuclear_power/nuclear-power-safety-in-illinois

57.   Exelon Corp., 2013, *Byron Generating Station*, at www.exeloncorp. com/powerplants/byron/Pages/profile.aspx |*Quad Cities Generating Station*, at www.exeloncorp.com/powerplants/quadcities/Pages/ profile.aspx | Clinton Power Station, at www.exeloncorp.com/ powerplants/clinton/Pages/profile.aspx

58. Ford, Sarah, "Cordova Exelon Taking Steps to Store Spent Fuel On-Site," *Quad-Cities Online Mobile (Dispatch and Rock Island Argus* (Moline, IL), October 17, 2009, at qconline.com/archives/qco/dosplay_mobile.php?id=462739; Simmons, Jennifer, "Nuclear Plant Officials Share Details on Spent Fuel Storage Plan," *Rochelle News-Leader* (Rochelle, IL), July 17, 2008, at www.rochellenews-leader/com/V2_news_articles_php?heading=0&story_id=18788(page= ; Landis, Tim, "Nuclear Plant in Clinton Running Out of Space for Spent Fuel," *The State Journal-Register* (Springfield, IL), April 23, 2011, at www.sj-r.com/top-stories/x1274368437/Nuclear-plant-in-Clinton-running-out-of-space-for-spent-fuel

59. NEI, *U.S. State by State Commercial Nuclear Used Fuel and Payments to the Nuclear Waste Fund*, March 2012, at www.nci.org/rcsource-sandstats/Documentlibrary/Nuclear-Waste-Disposal/graphicsand-charts/Nuclear-Waste-Fund-Payment-Information-by-State; U.S. EIA, *Nuclear and Uranium State Nuclear Profiles*, April 26, 2012, at www.eia.gov/nuclear/state/; U.S. GAO, *Spent Nuclear Fuel: Accumulating Quantities at Nuclear Reactors Present Storage and Other Challenges*, GAO-12-797, August 2012, at www.gao.gov/assets/600/593745.pdf; Schmitt, R.C., G.J. Quinn, and M.J. Tyacke, *Historical Summary of the Three Mile Island Unit 2 Core Debris Transportation Campaign*, DOE/ID-10400, March 1993, U.S. DOE, Idaho Field Office, Idaho Falls, ID; Kingrey, K.I., *Fuel Summary for Peach Bottom Unit I High Temperature Gas-Cooled Reactors Cores 1 and 2*, INEEL-EXT-03-00103, April 2003, Idaho National Laboratory (INL), Idaho Falls, ID, at www.inl.gov/technicalpublications/Documents/2699826.pdf

60. Noria Corp. "PPL's Susquehanna Unit 1 is Now the Nation's Largest Boiling Water Reactor," *Reliable Plant Newsletter 2010,* (Tulsa, OK), at www.reliableplant.com/Articles/Print/24969; Exelon Corp., 2013, *Three Mile Island*, at www.exeloncorp.com/powerplants/threemileisland/Pages/profile.aspx | *Peach Bottom Atomic Power Station*, at www.exeloncorp.com/powerplants/peachbottom/Pages/profile.aspx

61.   First Energy, *Beaver Valley: Continuing a Legacy of Nuclear Power*, February 2012 (Akron, OH), at www.firstenergycorp.com/content/ fecorp/about/generation_system/FENOC/beaver_valley.html; Exelon Corp., 2013, *Limerick Generating Station*, at www.exeloncorp. com/powerplants/limerick/Pages/profile.aspx

62.   U.S. GAO, *Spent Nuclear Fuel: Accumulating Quantities at Nuclear Reactors Present Storage and Other Challenges*, GAO-12-797, August 2012, at www.gao.gov/assets/600/593745.pdf; NEI, *Fact Sheet: Status of Used Nuclear Fuel Storage at U.S. Commercial Nuclear Plants*, November 2011, at www.nei.org/resourcesandstats/Documentlibrary/ Nuclear-Waste-Disposal/factsheet/statusofusednuclearfuelstorage

63.   NEI, *U.S. State by State Commercial Nuclear Used Fuel and Payments to the Nuclear Waste Fund,"* March 2012, at www.nei.org/resource-sandstats/Documentlibrary/Nuclear-Waste-Disposal/graphicsand-charts/Nuclear-Waste-Fund-Payment-Information-by-State; NEI, *U.S. Nuclear Power Plants*, at www.nei.org/Knowledge-Center/ Nuclear-Statistics/US-Nuclear-Power-Plants

64.   NEI, *U.S. Nuclear Plant Information*, May 2013, at www.nei.org/ resourcesandstats/Documentlibrary/Reliable-and-Affordable-Energy/graphicsandcharts/U-S-Nuclear-Plant-License-Information; Duke Energy, *Robinson Nuclear Plant*, (Charlotte, NC), August 2012, at www.duke-energy.com/power-plants/nuclear/robinson.asp; South Carolina Electric & Gas (SCG&E), *Nuclear Plants*, SCANA (Cayce, SC), 2013, at www.sceg.com/en/about-sceg/power-plants-nuclear/; U.S. GAO, *Spent Nuclear Fuel: Accumulating Quantities at Nuclear Reactors Present Storage and Other Challenges*, GAO-12-797, August 2012, at www.gao.gov/assets/600/593745.pdf; NEI, *Fact Sheet: Status of Used Nuclear Fuel Storage at U.S. Commercial Nuclear Plants*, November 2011, at www.nei.org/resourcesandstats/Documentlibrary/ Nuclear-Waste-Disposal/factsheet/statusofusednuclearfuelstorage

65.   NEI, *U.S. State by State Commercial Nuclear Used Fuel and Payments to the Nuclear Waste Fund*, March 2012, at www.nei.org/resource-sandstats/Documentlibrary/Nuclear-Waste-Disposal/graphicsand-charts/Nuclear-Waste-Fund-Payment-Information-by-State; NEI,

U.S. Nuclear Plant Information, May 2013, at www.nei.org/resource-sandstats/Documentlibrary/Reliable-and-Affordable-Energy/graph-icsandcharts/U-S-Nuclear-Plant-License-Information; U.S. GAO, *Spent Nuclear Fuel: Accumulating Quantities at Nuclear Reactors Present Storage and Other Challenges*, GAO-12-797, August 2012, at www. gao.gov/assets/600/593745.pdf; Entergy, *Indian Point Energy Center*, (New Orleans, LA), 2013, at www.safesecurevital.com/respources/fags/dry-cask-storage-faqs; Public Service Enterprise Group (PSEG), *Salem Nuclear Generating Station Facts*, (Newark, NJ), 2012, at www. pseg.com/family/power/nuclear/pdf/salem_factsheet.pdf; Johnson, Tom, "Public Hearing on Oyster Creek Nuclear Plant Slated to Convene Today," January 7, 2013, *NJSpotlight* (Montclair, NJ), at www.njspotlight.com.stories/13/01/06/public-hearing-on-oys-ter-creek-nuclear-plant-slated-to-convene-today; Entergy, *James A. Fitzpatrick Nuclear Power Plant*, 2012, at www.entergy-nuclear.com/plant_information/fitzPatrick.aspx; U.S. NRC, *R.E. Ginna Nuclear Power Plant*, 2012, at www.nrc.gov/info-finder/reactor/ginn.html; U.S. NRC, *Nine Mile Point Nuclear Station*, December 2012, at www. nrc.gove/infor-finder/reactor/nmp2.html

66. NEI, *U.S. State by State Commercial Nuclear Used Fuel and Payments to the Nuclear Waste Fund*," March 2012, at www.nei.org/re-sourcesandstats/Documentlibrary/Nuclear-Waste-Disposal/graphicsandcharts/Nuclear-Waste-Fund-Payment-Information-by-State; NEI, *Fact Sheet: Status of Used Nuclear Fuel Storage at U.S. Commercial Nuclear Plants*, November 2011, at www.nei.org/resourcesandstats/Documentlibrary/Nuclear-Waste-Disposal/factsheet/statusofusednuclearfuelstorage; NEI, *U.S. Nuclear Plant Information*, May 2013, at www.nei.org/resource-sandstats/Documentlibrary/Reliable-and-Affordable-Energy/graphicsandcharts/U-S-Nuclear-Plant-License-Information."

67. NEI, *U.S. Nuclear Plant License Information*, at www.nei.org/Knowledge-Center/Nuclear-Statistics/US-Nuclear-Power-Plants/US-Nuclear-Plant-License-Information; U.S. EIA, *Nuclear and Uranium State Nuclear Profiles*, April 26, 2012, at www.eia.gov/

nuclear/state/; CBS Radio, *Indian Point to become First Nuclear Plant to Operate with Expired License*, May 13, 2013, at www.newyork.cbslocal.com/2013/05/13/indian-point-to-become-first-nuclear-plant-to-operate-with-expired-license

68.   U.S. GAO, *Spent Nuclear Fuel: Accumulating Quantities at Nuclear Reactors Present Storage and Other Challenges*, GAO-12-797, August 2012, at www.gao.gov/assets/600/593745.pdf; NEI, *Fact Sheet: Status of Used Nuclear Fuel Storage at U.S. Commercial Nuclear Plants*, November 2011, at www.nei.org/resourcesandstats/Documentlibrary/Nuclear-Waste-Disposal/factsheet/statusofusednuclearfuelstorage

69.   NEI, *U.S. State by State Commercial Nuclear Used Fuel and Payments to the Nuclear Waste Fund*," March 2012, at www.nei.org/resourcesandstats/Documentlibrary/Nuclear-Waste-Disposal/graphicsandcharts/Nuclear-Waste-Fund-Payment-Information-by-State; U.S. GAO, *Spent Nuclear Fuel: Accumulating Quantities at Nuclear Reactors Present Storage and Other Challenges*, GAO-12-797, August 2012, at www.gao.gov/assets/600/593745.pdf; Browder, Cullen, "Spent Nuclear Fuel Stored at Wake County Plant," *WRAL.com* (Raleigh, NC), March 31, 2011, at www.wral.com/news/local/wral_investigates/story/9366238

70.   NEI, *U.S. State by State Commercial Nuclear Used Fuel and Payments to the Nuclear Waste Fund*," March 2012, at www.nei.org/resourcesandstats/Documentlibrary/Nuclear-Waste-Disposal/graphicsandcharts/Nuclear-Waste-Fund-Payment-Information-by-State; NEI, *U.S. Nuclear Plant License Information*, at www.nei.org/Knowledge-Center/Nuclear-Statistics/US-Nuclear-Power-Plants/US-Nuclear-Plant-License-Information

71.   TVA, *Browns Ferry Nuclear Plant*, 2012, at www.tva.gov/sites/brownsferyy.htm; Southern Company, *Plant Farley*, 2013, at www.southerncompany.com/about-us/our-business/southern-nuclear/farley.cshtml

72.   Florida Power and Light (FPL), *About Turkey Point*, (Miami, FL), 2012, at www.fpl.com/environment/nuclear/about_turkey_point.shtml; FPL, *St. Lucie*, 2012, at www.fpl.com/environment/nuclear/

about_st_lucie.shtml; Penn, Ivan, "Duke Energy Announces Closing of Crystal River Nuclear Power Plant," *Tampa Bay Times* (Tampa, FL), February 5, 2013, at www.tampabay.com/news/business/energy/duke-energy-announces-closing-of-crystal-river-nuclear-power-plant/1273794

73. Southern Company, 2012, *Plant Hatch*, at www.southerncompany.com/about-us/our-business/southern nuclear/hatch.cshtml | *Plant Vogtle*, at www.southerncompany.com/about-us/our-business/southern-nuclear/vogtle.cshtml; NEI, *Fact Sheet: Status of Used Nuclear Fuel Storage at U.S. Commercial Nuclear Plants*, November 2011, at www.nei.org/resourcesandstats/Documentlibrary/Nuclear-Waste-Disposal/factsheet/statusofusednuclearfuelstorage

74. NEI, *U.S. State by State Commercial Nuclear Used Fuel and Payments to the Nuclear Waste Fund*, March 2012, at www.nei.org/resourcesandstats/Documentlibrary/Nuclear-Waste-Disposal/graphicsandcharts/Nuclear-Waste-Fund-Payment-Information-by-State; NEI, *U.S. Nuclear Plant License Information*, at www.nei.org/Knowledge-Center/Nuclear-Statistics/US-Nuclear-Power-Plants/US-Nuclear-Plant-License-Information

75. Mufson, Steven, "San Onofre Nuclear Power Plant to Shut Down," *Washington Post*, June 7, 2013, at articles.washingtonpost.com/2013-06-07/business/39807950_1_atlas-cops-n-kids-louis-cruz-news-golden-gloves-finals; California Energy Commission, *Nuclear Energy in California*, 2012 (Sacramento), at www.energy.ca.gov/nuclear/california.html; WNA, "Cleanup Complete at Rancho Seco," October 2009, *World Nuclear News* (London, UK), at www.world-nuclear-news.or/WR-Cleanup_complete_at_rancho_seco; NEI, *Fact Sheet: Status of Used Nuclear Fuel Storage at U.S. Commercial Nuclear Plants*, November 2011, at www.nei.org/resourcesandstats/Documentlibrary/Nuclear-Waste-Disposal/factsheet/statusofusednuclearfuelstorage

76. NEI, *U.S. State by State Commercial Nuclear Used Fuel and Payments to the Nuclear Waste Fund*," March 2012, at www.nei.org/resourcesandstats/Documentlibrary/Nuclear-Waste-Disposal/graphicsandcharts/Nuclear-Waste-Fund-Payment-Information-by-State;

NEI, *U.S. Nuclear Plant License Information*, at www.nei.org/ Knowledge-Center/Nuclear-Statistics/US-Nuclear-Power-Plants/ US-Nuclear-Plant-License-Information; Zipp, Yvonne, "Small Crack Found in Tank at Palisades Nuclear Plant: Inspection Still Ongoing, Executives Say," May 13, 2013, *MLive Media Group* (Flint, MI), at www.mlive.com/news/kalamazoo/index.ssf/2013/05/ small_crack_found_in_tank_at_p.html; DTE Energy, *Fermi 2 Power Plant*, Utilities Service Alliance (Overland Park, KS), 2012, at www.usainc.org/members/index.html?organization_id=47197; U.S. NRC, *Fermi, Unit 3 Application*," April 15, 2013, at www.nrc.gov/ reactors/new-reactors/col/fermi.html

77. U.S. NRC, *Big Rock Point*, March 29, 2012, at www.nrc.gov/in-fo-finder/decommissioning/power-reactor/big-rock-point.html; AEP, *Cook Nuclear Plant Opens Dry Cask Storage Facility for Used Fuel*, August 1, 2012, at www.indianamichiganpower.com/info/ news/viewRelease.aspx?releaseID=1292; U.S. GAO, *Spent Nuclear Fuel: Accumulating Quantities at Nuclear Reactors Present Storage and Other Challenges*, GAO-12-797, August 2012, at www.gao.gov/as-sets/600/593745.pdf; NEI, *Fact Sheet: Status of Used Nuclear Fuel Storage at U.S. Commercial Nuclear Plants*, November 2011, at www.nei.org/ resourcesandstats/Documentlibrary/Nuclear-Waste-Disposal/ factsheet/statusofusednuclearfuelstorage

78. NEI, *U.S. State by State Commercial Nuclear Used Fuel and Payments to the Nuclear Waste Fund*," March 2012, at www.nei.org/resource-sandstats/Documentlibrary/Nuclear-Waste-Disposal/graph-icsandcharts/Nuclear-Waste-Fund-Payment-Information-by-State; NEI, *U.S. Nuclear Operating Plant Basic Information*, 2013, at www. nei.org/resourcesandstats/graphicsandcharts/plantinformation; Dominion Power, 2012, *Surry Power Station*, (Richmond, VA) at www.dom.com/about/stations/nuclear/surry/ | *North Anna Power Station*, (Richmond, VA) at www.dom.com/about/stations/nuclear/ north-anna/; NEI, *Fact Sheet: Status of Used Nuclear Fuel Storage at U.S. Commercial Nuclear Plants*, November 2011, at www.nei.org/

resourcesandstats/Documentlibrary/Nuclear-Waste-Disposal/
factsheet/statusofusednuclearfuelstorage

79. NEI, *U.S. State by State Commercial Nuclear Used Fuel and Payments to the Nuclear Waste Fund,"* March 2012, at www.nei.org/resourcesandstats/ Documentlibrary/Nuclear-Waste-Disposal/graphicsandcharts/ Nuclear-Waste-Fund-Payment-Information-by-State

80. NEI, *U.S. Nuclear Power Plants,* at www.nei.org/Knowledge Center/Nuclear-Statistics/US-Nuclear-Power-Plants; Luminant Co., *Comanche Peak Nuclear Power Plant,* 2008, (Dallas, TX) at www. luminant.com/news/cpe/cpexpansionfactsheet.pdf; STP Nuclear Operating Company, *STP Unit 2 Returns to Service,* April 23, 2013, (Wadsworth, TX) at www.stpnoc.com/

81. U.S. NRC, *Combined License Application Documents for Comanche Peak Nuclear Power Plant, Units 3 and 4 Application,* April 16, 2013, at www. nrc.gov/rectors/new-reactors/col/comanche-peak/documents; U.S. NRC, *2013 Applicant Documents for Comanche Peak Nuclear Power Plant, Units 3 and 4 Application,* April 17, 2013, at www.nrc.gov/rectors/ new-reactors/col/comanche-peak/documents; Osborne, James. "NRC Shoots Down Texas Nuclear Plant Expansion," *DallasNews* (*Dallas Morning News*) April 30, 2013, at www.bizbeatblog.dal- lasnews.com/2013/04/nec-shoots-down-texas-nuclear-plant-ex- pansion; Luminant, Letter to U.S. NRC: *Comanche Peak Nuclear Power Plant (CPNPP) and Independent Spent Fuel Storage Installation (ISFSI) Docket Nos. 50-445, 50-446, 72-74,* October 11, 2012; Weiss, Jeffrey, "Spent Nuclear Fuel at Comanche Peak is Safer than the Design at the Wrecked Japanese Reactors, Plant Officials Say," *DallasNews,* March 25, 2011, at www.dallasnews.com/news/local- news/20110325-spent-nuclear-fuel-at-comanche-peak; U.S. GAO, *Spent Nuclear Fuel: Accumulating Quantities at Nuclear Reactors Present Storage and Other Challenges,* GAO-12-797, August 2012, at www.gao. gov/assets/600/593745.pdf; NEI, *Fact Sheet: Status of Used Nuclear Fuel Storage at U.S. Commercial Nuclear Plants,* November 2011, at www.nei. org/resourcesandstats/Documentlibrary/Nuclear-Waste-Disposal/ factsheet/statusofusednuclearfuelstorage

82. PNM Resources Inc., "Palo Verde Nuclear Generating Station," (Albuquerque, NM), 2012, at www.pnm.com/systems.pv.htm; Stars Alliance, *APS: Palo Verde Nuclear Generating Station*, 2012, at www.starsalliance.com/members/paloverde.asp; NEI, *Fact Sheet: Status of Used Nuclear Fuel Storage at U.S. Commercial Nuclear Plants*, November 2011, at www.nei.org/resourcesandstats/Documentlibrary/Nuclear-Waste-Disposal/factsheet/statusofusednuclearfuelstorage

83. U.S. EPA, "Vermont Yankee Nuclear Plant Closure in 2014 Will Challenge New England Energy Markets," *Today in Energy*, September 6, 2013, (Washington, D.C.) at www.eia.gov/todayinenergy/detail.cfm?id=12851; Wald, Matt, "Vermont Yankee Plant to Close Next Year as the Nuclear Industry Retrenches," *New York Times*, August 27, 2013, at www.nytimes.com/2013/08/28/science/entergy-announces-closing-of-vermont-nuclear-plant.html?_r=0

84. NEI, *U.S. Nuclear Power Plants*, at www.nei.org/Knowledge-Center/Nuclear-Statistics/US-Nuclear-Power-Plants

85. NEI, *U.S. State by State Commercial Nuclear Used Fuel and Payments to the Nuclear Waste Fund*," March 2012, at www.nei.org/resourcesandstats/Documentlibrary/Nuclear-Waste-Disposal/graphicsandcharts/Nuclear-Waste-Fund-Payment-Information-by-State; U.S. Census Bureau, "U.S. and World Population Clock," U.S. Department of Commerce (Washington, D.C.), 2013, at www.census.gov/popclock/; *U.S. States (plus Washington D.C) Area and Ranking*, Enchanted Learning LLC (Mercer Island, WA), 2013, at www.enchantedlearning.com/usa/states/area.shtml

86. NEI, *U.S. State by State Commercial Nuclear Used Fuel and Payments to the Nuclear Waste Fund*," March 2012, at www.nei.org/resourcesandstats/Documentlibrary/Nuclear-Waste-Disposal/graphicsandcharts/Nuclear-Waste-Fund-Payment-Information-by-State

87. NEI, *Fact Sheet: Status of Used Nuclear Fuel Storage at U.S. Commercial Nuclear Plants*, November 2011, at www.nei.org/resourcesandstats/Documentlibrary/Nuclear-Waste-Disposal/factsheet/statusofusednuclearfuelstorage; U.S. GAO, *Spent Nuclear Fuel: Accumulating*

Quantities at Nuclear Reactors Present Storage and Other Challenges, GAO-12-797, August 2012, at www.gao.gov/assets/600/593745.pdf.

88. NEI, *U.S. Nuclear Plant License Information*, at www.nei.org/ Knowledge-Center/Nuclear-Statistics/US-Nuclear-Power-Plants/US-Nuclear-Plant-License-Information; Haber, Gary, "Feds Deny Appeal for Third Calvert Cliffs Nuclear Reactor," *Baltimore Sun*, March 11, 2013, at www.bizjournals.com/baltimore/news/2013/03/11/feds-deny-appeal-for-third-calvert. html; Wheeler, Timothy, "Used Nuclear Fuel to be Put in Bunkers; Calvert Cliffs Faced with Storage Crisis," *Baltimore Sun*, December 8, 1992, at articles.baltimoresun.com/1992-12-08/ news/1992343015_1_calvert-cliffs-temporary-storage-nuclear-fuel

89. Mufson, Steven, "San Onofre Nuclear Power Plant to Shut Down," *Washington Post*, June 7, 2013, at articles.washingtonpost.com/2013-06-07/business/39807950_1_atlas-cops-n-kids-louis-cruz-news-golden-gloves-finals; NEI, *U.S. Nuclear Plant License Information*, at www. nei.org/Knowledge-Center/Nuclear-Statistics/US-Nuclear-Power-Plants/US-Nuclear-Plant-License-Information; Penn, Ivan, "Duke Energy Announces Closing of Crystal River Nuclear Power Plant," *Tampa Bay Times* (Tampa, FL), February 5, 2013, at www.tampabay.com/news/business/energy/duke-energy-announces-closing-of-crystal-river-nuclear-power-plant/1273794; Wald, Matthew, "As Price of Nuclear Energy Drops, a Wisconsin Plant is Shut," *New York Times*, May 7, 2013, at www.nytimes.com/2013/05/08/business/ energy-environment/kewaunee-nuclear-power-plant-shuts-down. html?_r=0; Content, Thomas, "A Month After Kewaunee, Another Nuclear Plant Shutters," *Journal-Sentinel* (Milwaukee, WI), June 8, 2013, at www.jsonline.com/blogs/business/210706981.html; Exelon Corp., *Zion Station*, 2013, at www.exeloncorp.com/powerplants/ zion/Pages/profile.aspx; U.S. NRC, *Millstone Unit 1*, March 29, 2012, at www.nrc.gov/info-finder/decommissioning/power-reactor/millstone-unit-1.html

90. U.S. NRC, *Locations of Power Reactor Sites Undergoing Decommissioning*, August 1, 2012, at www.nrc.gov/info-finder-decommissioning/

power-reactor; NEI, *Reactors Shut Down or Decommissioned*, 2013, at nei.org/resoucesandstats/nculear_statistics/reactorsshut-downdecommissioned; U.S. NRC, *Peach Bottom Unit 1*, March 29, 2012, at www.nrc.gov/info-finder/decommissioning/power-re-actor/peach-bottom-atomic-power-station-unit.html; Schmitt, R.C., G.J. Quinn, and M.J. Tyacke, *Historical Summary of the Three Mile Island Unit 2 Core Debris Transportation Campaign*, DOE/ID-10400, March 1993, U.S. DOE, Idaho Field Office, Idaho Falls, ID; Abrahamson, Dean, "Minnesota and Nuclear Power," *MinnPost* (Minneapolis, MN), January 20, 2011, at www.minnpost.com/community-voices/2011/01/minnesota-and-nuclear-power

91. U.S. NRC, *Haddam Neck—Connecticut Yankee*, March 29, 2012, at www.nrc.gov/info-finder/decommissioning/power-reactor/hadd-am-neck-connecticut-yankee.html; Yankee Company, *Welcome to Yankee Rowe*, 2012, at www.yankeerowe.com; U.S. NRC, *Dresden-Unit 1*, March 29, 2012, at www.nrc.gov/info-finder/decommis-sioning/power-reactor/dresden-nuclear-power-station-unit-1.html; Portland State University, "Trojan Nuclear Power Plant," *Oregon Encyclopedia* (Portland, OR), 2005, at www.oregonencyclopedia.org/entry/view/trojan_nuclear_power_plant; Kindelspire, Tony, "Colorado Nuke Plant at Ft. St. Vrain has Short, Troubled Ride," *Longmont Weekly*, March 28, 2011, (Longmont, CO) at www.long-mostweekly.com/ci_17701792

92. Hubbuch, Chris, "A Nuclear Option: After 25 Years, Genoa Reactor's Waste gets New Home," *LaCrosse Tribune*, July 15, 2012, (LaCrosse, WI) at lacrossetribune.com/news/local/a-nuclear-option-after-years-genoa-reactor-s-waste-gets/article_38fce0e2-ce37-11e1-8c0c-0019bb2963f4.html

93. U.S. Department of Justice (DOJ), *Response to Request for Information from the Blue Ribbon Commission on America's Nuclear Future*, December 20, 2011, at www.brc.gov/sites/default/files/comments/attachments/doj_response.12.20.11_0.pdf; Barwell, Owen, *Liability Estimate*, U.S. DOE, Washington, D.C., October 11, 2011.

94. Maine Yankee, *Federal Government Urged to Remove Spent Nuclear Fuel*, (Wiscasset), 2012, at www.maineyankee.com/public

95. King, Jessie, "Murphy Calls for National Storage Facility for Spent Nuclear Fuel," *Waterford Patch*, May 21, 2013, (Waterford, CT) at waterford.patch.com/groups/business-news/p/murphy-calls-for-national-storage-facility-for-spent-nuclear-fuel

96   Government Printing Office (GPO), *Hearing Before the Subcommittee on Energy and Air Quality of the Committee on Energy and Commerce, House of Representatives, 100th Congress, 2nd Session, July 15, 2008*, Serial 110-135 (citing Fred Upton), pp 2, 4.

97. *Ibid* (citing Anne George), p. 62.

98. Wernau, Julie, and Lisa Black, "Spent Nuclear Fuel Storage Comes Under Scrutiny," *Chicago Tribune*, March 19, 2011, at articles.chicagotribune.com/2011-03-19/news/ct-met-0320-spent-fuel-20110319_1_nuclear-fuel-dry-casks-nuclear-reactors; Exelon Corp., *Zion Station*, 2013, at www.exeloncorp.com/powerplants/zion/Pages/profile.aspx

99. Shimkus, John, "Nuclear Waster: Thy Name is Yucca Mountain," *Chicago Tribune*, June 5, 2013, at www.chicagotribune.com/news/opinion/commentary/ct-perspec-0605-nuclear

100. Restuccia, Andrew, "Official: Lack of Nuclear Waste Dump is a 'Serious Failure of the American Government'," *The Hill*, February 1, 2012, (Washington, D.C.), (citing Lee Hamilton) at thehill.com/blogs/e2-wire/e2-wire/207963-official-delay-in-establishing-nuke-waste-dump-serious-failure-of-the-american-government

101. Hamilton, Lee, and Brent Scowcroft, "Build Disposal Facilities to Deal with Nuclear Waste: Guest Opinion," *The Oregonian* (Portland), June 15, 2013, www.oregonlive.com/opinion/index.ssf/2013/06/build_disposal_facilities_to_d.html

102. Gram, Dave, "Federal Nuclear Waste Rules Need to be Improved, Attorneys General Petition NRC," *Huffington Post*, May 23, 2013 (citing William Sorrell and Eric Schneiderman), at www.huffingtonpost.com/2013/05/23/federal-nuclear-waste-rules_n_3328495.html

103. Cummings, Bill, "Storage of Spent Fuel Rods at New England Nuclear Power Plants Generates Fear," *Mass Live.com* (*The Republican*: Springfield, MA) May 3, 2011, at www.masslive.com/news/index. ssf/2011/04/storage_of_spent_fuel_rods_at_new_england_nuclear_power_plants_generates_fear.html

104. Whitfield, Ed, *Yucca Mountain: Error of Judgment by the Obama Administration*, Congressman Ed Whitfield Media Center, February 16, 2012, at whitfield.house.gov/yucca-mountain-error-judgment-obama-administration

105. Gerber, Michele, *Plutonium Production at the Hanford Site: A Processes and Facilities History*, WHC-MR-0521, June 1996, Westinghouse Hanford Co., Richland, WA, at www.osti.gov/energycitations/servlets/purl/664389-jAx4J1/webviewable/664389.pdf

106. U.S. DOE, *Long-Term Management of High-Level Radioactive Waste (HLW) and Spent Nuclear Fuel (SNF)*, 2010, at energy.gov/gc/long-term-management-high-level-radioactive-waste-hlw-and-spent-nuclear-fuel-snf

107. U.S. DOE, U.S. EPA, and Washington Department of Ecology, *Hanford Federal Facility Agreement and Consent Order*, Ecology (Olympia, WA), 1989, and as amended; U.S. DOE, U.S. EPA, and South Carolina Department of Health and Environmental Control (DHEC), *Federal Facility Agreement for the Savannah River Site*, 89-05-FF, DHEC (Columbia, SC), August 16, 1993; U.S. DOE, U.S. Navy, Idaho Department of Environmental Quality (IDEQ), *Idaho Settlement Agreement and Consent Order*, IDEQ (Boise), 1995.

108. U.S. DOE, U.S. Navy, IDEQ, *Idaho Settlement Agreement and Consent Order*, IDEQ (Boise), 1995; U.S. GAO, *Better Information Needed on Waste Storage at DOE Sites as a Result of Yucca Mountain Shutdown*, GAO-11-230, March 23, 2011, at www.gao.gov/products/GAO-11-230; Hain, Kathleen, *Idaho Site Spent Nuclear Fuel Management*, June 2010, U.S. DOE, at www.nwtrb.gov/meetings/2010/june/hain.pdf

109. U.S. GAO, *Better Information Needed on Waste Storage at DOE Sites as a Result of Yucca Mountain Shutdown*, GAO-11-230, March 23, 2011, at www.gao.gov/products/GAO-11-230; U.S. DOE, *Agreement Between*

the *Department of Energy and the State of Colorado Regarding Shipping Spent Fuel out of Colorado*, February 13, 1996.

110. U.S. GAO, *Better Information Needed on Waste Storage at DOE Sites as a Result of Yucca Mountain Shutdown*, GAO-11-230, March 23, 2011, at www.gao.gov/products/GAO-11-230; U.S. DOE, *West Valley Demonstration Project Nuclear Timeline*, 2007, at www.wv.doe.gov/Site_History.html; U.S. Congress, *West Valley Demonstration Project Act*, Public Law 96-368, 96th Congress, 2nd Session, Washington, D.C., October 1, 1980.

111. U.S. GAO, *Better Information Needed on Waste Storage at DOE Sites as a Result of Yucca Mountain Shutdown*, GAO-11-230, p. 26, March 23, 2011, at www.gao.gov/products/GAO-11-230.

112. Associated Press, "Energy Department Says Worst Hanford Tank May Be leaking Nuclear Waste into the Soil," *Washington Post*, June 22, 2013, at www.washingtonpost.com/business/energy-dept-says-worst-hanford-tank-may-be-leaking-nuclear-waste-into-the-soil/2013/06/21/192cb068-dad8-11e2-b418-9dfa095e125d_story.html

113. U.S. GAO, *Better Information Needed on Waste Storage at DOE Sites as a Result of Yucca Mountain Shutdown*, GAO-11-230, March 23, 2011, at www.gao.gov/products/GAO-11-230; U.S. NRC, *Hanford Site Disposal Facility for Waste Incidental to Reprocessing*, March 29, 2012, at www.nrc.gov/waste/incidental-waste/wir-process/wir-locations/wir-hanford.html; U.S. NRC, *Savannah River Site Disposal Facility for Waste Incidental to Reprocessing*, March 29, 2012, at www.nrc.gov/waste/incidental-waste/wir-process/wir-locations/wir-srs.html

114. Cary, Annette, "Tank Leak Found," *Tri-City Herald*, February 16, 2013, (Kennewick, WA); Cary, Annette, "Inslee Says Tank Leak Worrisome," *Tri-City Herald*, February 28, 2013, (Kennewick, WA); Cary, Annette, "Murray Calls for Tank Farm Plan," *Tri-City Herald*, May 31, 2013, (Kennewick, WA).

115. Washington Department of Ecology (WDOC), *Integrated Disposal Facility Operating Unit Group 11*, Access Washington (Washington Ecology: Olympia, WA), 2011, at www.ecy.wa.gov/Programs/NWP/Permitting/HDWP/OU/IDF.html; Dahl, Suzanne, Rabindra

Biyani, and Erika Holmes, "Full Focus Needed on Finishing Hanford's Waste Treatment Plant," Washington Department of Ecology, Paper #12196, in *Proceedings of the Waste Management Conference 2012*, Phoenix, AZ, February 2012, at https://www.wm-sym.org/archives/2012/papers/12196.pdf

116. Gerber, Michele, *On the Home Front: The Cold War Legacy of the Hanford Nuclear Site*, Lincoln: University of Nebraska Press, 1992, 1997, 2002, 2007.

117. Associated Press, "Energy Department Says Worst Hanford Tank May Be leaking Nuclear Waste into the Soil," *Washington Post*, June 22, 2013, (citing Washington Governor Jay Inslee) at www.washingtonpost.com/business/energy-dept-says-worst-hanford-tank-may-be-leaking-nuclear-waste-into-the-soil/2013/06/21/192cb068-dad8-11e2-b418-9dfa095e125d_story.html.

118. Energy Communities Alliance (ECA), *Energy Communities Alliance Position Paper: Yucca Mountain and the Future of Geologic Disposal of High Level Waste in the U.S.*, December 2011, (Washington, D.C.) at www.energyca.org/policies_hiwaste.htm

119. Citizens Advisory Board (CAB), *Yucca Mountain as Interim Storage Site*, Recommendation #286, May 22, 2012, (Aiken, SC) at cab.srs.gov/library/recommendations/recommendation_286.pdf

120. Firestone, David, "Governor Threatens to Bar U.S. Plutonium Shipments," *New York Times*, August 11, 2011; "South Carolina Governor Sues to Stop Plutonium," *New York Times*, May 2, 2002, at www.nytimes.com/2002/05/02/us/national-briefing-south-south-carolina-governor-sues-to-stop-plutonium.html

121. Jordan, Jacob, "Judge Thwarts S.C. Governor's Attempts to Block Plutonium Shipments," *OnlineAthens*, June 19, 2002, (Athens, Georgia); Defense Nuclear Facilities Safety Board (DNFSB), *Plutonium Storage at the Department of Energy's Savannah River Site: First Annual Report to Congress*, June 2004, (Washington, D.C.) at www.hss.energy.gov/deprep/2004/fb04y28b.pdf; "More Plutonium Shipped to S.C., *South Carolina Radio Network*, July 9, 2009, (Columbia) at www.southcarolinaradionetwork.com/2009/07/09/more-plutonium-shipped-to-sc

122. Harder, Amy, "Energy Nominee Blocked Over Cuts at S.C. Nuclear Waste Plant," *National Journal*, April 24, 2013, (Washington, D.C.) at www.govexec.com/technology/2013/04/obamas-pick-energy-secretary-blocked-over-cuts-sc-nuclear-waste-plant/62745/

123. U.S. Senate, "Graham Introduces Legislation Providing a 'Rebate' to Consumers, Utilities, and Communities for the Administration's Refusal to Open Yucca Mountain," *Senate Press Room*, April 23, 2009, at www.lgraham.senate.gov/public/index.cfm?FuseAction=PressRoom.PressReleases&ContentRecord_id=d4508482-802a-23ad-438a-bd6ff3ddfe1e; Rosen, James, "Sen. Graham Wants Yucca Fees Rebated to SC Electricity Customers," *The State*, March 12, 2013, at www.thestate.com/2012/03/14/2190848/sen-graham-wants-yucca-fees-rebated.html

124. "Idaho Doesn't Want More Nuclear Waste," *Seattle Times*, May 11, 1991, at community.seattletimes.nwsource.com/archive/?-date=19910511&slug=1282582; "Nuclear Shipments Halted," *Seattle Times*, June 29, 1993, at community.seattletimes.nwsource.com/archive/?date=19930629&slug=1708815

125. Hain, Kathleen, *Idaho Site Spent Nuclear Fuel Management*, U.S. DOE, June 2010, at www.nwtrb.gov/meetings/2010/june/hain.pdf; "Nuclear Waste Arrives in Idaho," *Seattle Times*, October 25, 1995, at community.seattletimes.nwsource.com/archive/?date=19951025&slug=2148782

126. Messick, Molly, "Former Idaho Govs Andrus, Batt Oppose Changes to 1995 Nuclear Agreement," *State Impact* (Boise State Public Radio), December 10, 2012, at stateimpact.npr.org/idaho/2012/12/10/former-idaho-govs-andrus-batt-oppose-changes-to-1995-nuclear-agreement/; Barker, Rocky, "Door Closed on Revising Batt's 1995 Nuclear Waste Agreement," *Idaho Statesman* (Boise), May 24, 2012, at voices.idahostatesman.com/2012/05/24/rockybarker/door_closed_revising_batts_1995_nuclear_waste_agreement; Carlson, Chris, "Standing Tall for Idaho," *Idaho State Journal*, December 21, 2012, (Pocatello) at http://www.pocatelloshops.com/new_blogs/politics/?p=9977; Leadership in Nuclear Energy

(LINE) Commission, *Full Report*, Idaho State Government (Boise), January 2013, at www.line.idaho.gov/pdf/LINE%20Full%20Report. pdf; Richert, Kevin, "Otter Praises Idaho Nuclear Commission for Answering 'Some Tough Questions'," *Idaho Statesman*, December 3, 2012, at voices.idahostatesman.com/2012/12/03/krichert/otter_praises_idaho_nuclear_commission_answering_some_tough_ques

127. U.S. Senate, "Schumer Announces $74 Million in Economic Recovery Act Funding Coming to West Valley Demonstration Project," *Senate Press Room*, March 31, 2009, at www.schumer.senate.gov/Newsroom/record.cfm?id=310832; Gram, Dave, "Federal Nuclear Waste Rules Need to be Improved, Attorneys General Petition NRC," *Huffington Post*, May 23, 2013, at www.huffingtonpost.com/2013/05/23/federal-nuclear-waste-rules_n_3328495.html

Chapter 2

128. Moniz, Ernest, "Why We Still Need Nuclear Power," *Foreign Affairs*, Council on Foreign Affairs (Washington, D.C.), November-December 2011, at www.foreignaffairs.com/articles/136544/ernest-moniz/why-we-still-need-nuclear-power

129. World Nuclear Association (WNA), *World Nuclear Power Reactors and Uranium Requirements*, October 2012, at www.world-nuclear.org/info/reactors.html; Nuclear Energy Institute (NEI), *World Nuclear Power Plants in Operation*, August 2012, at www.nei.org/resourcesandstas/documentslibrary; Stanway, David, "Special Report: In China the Big Nuclear Question is 'How Soon'?" *Reuters*, May 3, 2011, at www.reuters.com/article/2011/or/o3/us-china-nuclear-idUSTRE7240V420110503; Kidd, Steve, "Nuclear in East Asia—the Hotbed?" *NEI Magazine*, December 2011, at www.neimagazine.com/story.asp?stpryCode=2061333

130. WNA, *World Nuclear Power Reactors and Uranium Requirements*, October 2012, (London) at www.world-nuclear.org/info/reactors.html; "India Foresees Sharp Rise in Nuclear Power," *American Free*

Press (AFP), August 20, 2009, at www.google.com/hostednews/afp/article/ALeqM5jDcQmyGqCr4CbK0zHDYJillfg

131. WNA, *World Nuclear Power Reactors and Uranium Requirements*, October 2012, at www.world-nuclear.org/info/reactors.html; Weir, Fred, "Russia Plans Big Nuclear Expansion," *Christian Science Monitor*, July 7, 2007, at www.csmonitor.com/2007/0717/p01s04-woeu.htm; WNA, *Nuclear Power in Russia*, September 2012, at world-nuclear-org/info/inf45.html

132. Bodeen, Christopher, "China Says It Has Mastered Nuclear Fuel Reprocessing," *Associated Press (AP)*, January 3, 2011, at news.yahoo.com/s/ap/20110103/ap_on_re_as/as_china_nuclear_fuel_1/print; Ying, Yuan, and Wang Haotong, "China's Nuclear Waste Rush," *Chinadialogue*, March 21, 2011, (London and Beijing); WNA, *Nuclear Power in India*, September 2012, at www.world-nuclear.org/info/inf53.html; International Atomic Energy Agency (IAEA), *The National Report of the Russian Federation on Compliance with the Obligations of the Joint Convention on the Safety of Spent Fuel Management and the Safety of Radioactive Waste Management*, Moscow, 2006, p. 12, at www-ns.iaea.org/downloads/rw/conventions/Russian-federation-national-report; Baryshnikov, M., A. Suvorova, A. Khaperskaya, A. Shorokhov, *Intermediate Results and Prospects for Handling Bilibino NPP Spent Fuel*, September 2012, Sosny R&D Co. (Dimitrovgrad Office) at www.sosnycompany.com/at_bilibino_en.html; WNA, *Nuclear Waste in France*, May 2013; Fairley, Peter, "Nuclear Wasteland: The French Are Recycling Nuclear Waste," *Spectrum*, February 2007 (IEEE: New Jersey).

133. NEI, *Nuclear Waste: Amounts and On-Site Storage*, at nei.org/resource-sandstats/nuclear_statistics/nuclearwasteamountsandonsitestorage; U.S. NRC, *Spent Fuel Storage in Pools and Dry Casks: Key Points and Questions and Answers*, March 29, 2012, at www.nrc.gov/waste/spent-fuel-storage/faqs.html

134. WNA, *World Nuclear Power Reactors and Uranium Requirements*, October 2012, at www.world-nuclear.org/info/reactors.html; NEI,

U.S. Nuclear Plant Operators, Owners and Holding Companies, March 2012, at www.nei.org/resourcesandstats/documentslibrary.

135. Wang, Ju, "High-Level Waste Disposal in China: Update 2010," *Journal of Rock Mechanics and Geotechnical Engineering*, Vol. 2:1, March 2010, pp. 1-11; Ying, Yuan, and Wang Haotong, "China's Nuclear Waste Rush," *Chinadialogue*, March 21, 2011, (London and Beijing); Ray, Kalyan, "India Keen on Having Nuclear Waste Repository," *Deccan Herald*, February 14, 2012, (Bangalore, India) at www.deccan-herald.com/content/227293/india-keen-having-nuclear-waste.html; Bhabha Atomic Research Centre (BARC), "Nuclear Fuel Cycle," *BARC Highlights* (Mumbai, India), 2006-2007, at wwwbarc.ernet.in/publications/eb/golden/nfc/toc/...6.pdf; WNA, *Russia's Nuclear Fuel Cycle*, August 30, 2012, at www.world-nuclear.org/info/inf45a_Russia_nuclear_fuel_cycle.html; National Agency for Management of Nuclear Waste (ANDRA—France), *Mastering Radioactive Waste*, ANDRA International, July 12, 2012, at www.andra.fr/international/pages/en/menu21/international-consultancy/operational; Capitol Press, "France," *Nuclear Waste News*, February 9, 2006, (Washington, D.C.), p. 23; WNA, "Next Phase for French Geological Disposal," *World Nuclear News*, January 5, 2012, at www.world-nuclear-news.org/WR-Next_phase_for_French_geological_disposal-0501

136. WNA, *World Nuclear Power Reactors and Uranium Requirements*, October 2012, (London) at www.world-nuclear.org/info/reactors.html

137. *Ibid*; NEI, *Nuclear Units Under Construction Worldwide*, May 2013, at www.nei.org/resourcesandstats/graphics and charts; NEI, *World Nuclear Power Plants in Operation*, August 2012, (Washington, D.C.) at www.nei.org/resourcesandstas/documentslibrary; Stanway, David, "Special Report: In China the Big Nuclear Question is 'How Soon'?" *Reuters*, May 3, 2011, at www.reuters.com/article/2011/or/o3/us-china-nuclear-idUSTRE7240V420110503; Kidd, Steve, "Nuclear in East Asia—the Hotbed?" *NEI Magazine*, December 2011, at www.neimagazine.com/story.asp?stpryCode=2061333

138. Grossman, Elaine, "Taiwan Ready to Forgo [sic] Nuclear Fuel-Making in U.S. Trade Pact Renewal," *Global Security Newswire*, July 19, 2012, (Nuclear Threat Initiative [NTI]: Washington, D.C.) at www.nti.org/gsn/article/taiwan-ready-forgo-nuclear-fuel-making-us-pact-renewal

139. WNA, *World Nuclear Power Reactors and Uranium Requirements*, October 2012, (London) at www.world-nuclear.org/info/reactors. html; "Kudankulam Nuclear Plant: Commissioning Delayed by a Month," *Business Standard*, May 16, 2013, at www.business-standard. com/article/economy-policy/kudankulam-nuclear-plant

140. Weir, Fred, "Russia Plans Big Nuclear Expansion," *Christian Science Monitor*, July 7, 2007, at www.csmonitor.com/2007/0717/p01s04-wocu.htm; WNA, *Nuclear Power in Russia*, September 2012, at world-nuclear-org/info/inf45.html

141. WNA, *World Nuclear Power Reactors and Uranium Requirements*, October 2012, (London) at www.world-nuclear.org/info/reactors. html; Chazan, Guy, "Nuclear Programme Sparks More Uncertainty," *Financial Times*, October 2, 2012, (London) at www.ft.com/intl/cms/s/0/e976cb98-0ca5-11e2-b175-00144feabdc0.html; "Industry Profile," Cogent-SSC, 2012, at www.cogent-ssc.com/industry/nuclear/industry-profile.php

142. WNA, *World Nuclear Power Reactors and Uranium Requirements*, October 2012, at www.world-nuclear.org/info/reactors.html; EDF Group, *EDF-Taking a Closer Look*, at about-us.edf.com/about-us-43666. html

143. WNA, *World Nuclear Power Reactors and Uranium Requirements*, October 2012, at www.world-nuclear.org/info/reactors.html; Swiss Federal Office of Energy, *Energy Strategy 2050*, September 28, 2012, at www.bfe.admin.ch/themen/00526/00527/index.html?lang=en; Baetz, Juergen, "Germany Set to Abandon Nuclear Power for Good," *Associated Press (AP)*, March 23, 2011, at www. hanfordnews.com/2011/03/23/v-print/16386/germany-set-to-abandon-nuclear; WNA, *Nuclear Power in Belgium*, July 27, 2012, pp. 1-2, at www.world-nuclear.org/info/inf94.html; WNA, *Nuclear*

Power in Switzerland, June 2012, at www.world-nuclear.org/info/ inf86.html; Areva, *Used Fuel Shipment from Australia to France*, September 2012, at www.AREVA.com/EN/operations-1379/nu-clear-used-fuel-shipment-from-australai-to-e; "Convoy Taking Italian Spent Nuclear Fuel to France: Reports," *Expatica.com* (France), July 24, 2012, at www.expatica.com/fr/news/french-news/ convoy-taking-italian-spent-nculear-fuel-to-France

144. WNA, *World Nuclear Power Reactors and Uranium Requirements*, October 2012, at www.world-nuclear.org/info/reactors.html; Maeda, Risa, "Japan Government Appears to Waver on Commitment to Quit Nuclear," *Reuters*, September 19, 2012, at www.reuters.com/ assets/print?aid=USL4E8KJ0BI20010919

145. WNA, *World Nuclear Power Reactors and Uranium Requirements*, October 2012, at www.world-nuclear.org/info/reactors.html; Kidd, Steve, "Nuclear in East Asia—the Hotbed?" *NEI Magazine*, December 2011, at www.neimagazine.com/story.asp?stpryCode=2061333; WNA, *Nuclear Power in South Korea*, September 2012, at www. world-nuclear.org/info/inf81.html

146. WNA, *World Nuclear Power Reactors and Uranium Requirements*, October 2012, at www.world-nuclear.org/info/reactors.html; NEI, "Indonesian Government Approves Nuclear Construction Plan," *NEI Magazine*, December 5, 2011, at neimagazine.com/story.as-p?storyCode=2061327; "Vietnam, Russia Sign Deal on First Nuclear Plant," *ChannelNewsAsia*, November 1, 2010, (Singapore) at www. channelnewsasia.com/stories/afp_asiapacific/print/1090517/1/. html

147. WNA, *World Nuclear Power Reactors and Uranium Requirements*, October 2012, at www.world-nuclear.org/info/reactors.html; Campbell, Robert, "Mexico Eyes Up to 10 New Nuclear Plants by 2028," *Reuters*, May 12, 2010, at www.reuters.com/assets/ print?aid=USTRE64B6CF20100512

148. Davis, Will, "Argentina Carries Torch for SMR Construction," *ANS Nuclear Café*, February 13, 2014, at ansnuclearcafe.org/2014/02/13/ carem-25-carries-torch-for-smr-construction/

149. Hinshaw, Drew, "Africa Looks to Nuclear Power," *Christian Science Monitor*, April 2010, at www.csmonitor.com/layout/set/print/content/view/print/291721

150. Al-Khalidi, Sulieman, and Keiron Henderson, "Jordan Shortlists Three Nuclear Plant Designs," *Reuters*, May 12, 2010, at www.reuters.com/assets/print?aid=USLDE64B0NC20100512; Associated Press, "UEA Pushes on With Plan for First Nuclear Reactors, Bases Design on Korean Plants," *Chicago Tribune*, December 27, 2010, at www.chicagotribune.com/business/sns-ap-ml-emirates-nuclear,0,2131043,print.story; NEI, "Saudi Arabia Plans Nuclear Tender for 2012," *NEI Magazine*, December 2011, at www.neimagazine.com/story.asp?storyCode=2061326; Associated Press, "Iran's Nuclear Reactor Reaches Full Capacity," *New York Daily News*, Sept 1, 2012, at articles/nydailynews.com/2012-09-01/news/33539245_1_nuclear-reactor-mohammad; WNA, *Nuclear Power in Pakistan*, April 16, 2013, at www.world-nuclear.org/info/Country-Profiles/Countries-O-S/Pakistan/

151. WNA, *World Nuclear Power Reactors and Uranium Requirements*, October 2012, at www.world-nuclear.org/info/reactors.html

152. *Ibid*; WNA, *Nuclear Power in Canada*, October 2012, at www.world-nuclear.org/info/inf49a_Nuclear_Power_in_Canada.html

153. WNA, *World Nuclear Power Reactors and Uranium Requirements*, October 2012, at www.world-nuclear.org/info/reactors.html; NEI, *U.S. Nuclear Plant Operators, Owners and Holding Companies*, March 2012, at www.nei.org/resourcesandstats/documentslibrary

154. Lovell, Jeremy, "Nuclear Waste: Bury It and Forget?" *Reuters*, March 8, 2006, at today.reuters.com/misc/PrinterFriendlyPopup.aspx?type=scienceNews&storyID=uri:2; WNA, *Nuclear Waste in France*, May 2013; Fairley, Peter, "Nuclear Wasteland: The French Are Recycling Nuclear Waste," *Spectrum*, February 2007 (IEEE: New Jersey); International Atomic Energy Agency (IAEA), *The National Report of the Russian Federation on Compliance with the Obligations of the Joint Convention on the Safety of Spent Fuel Management and the Safety of Radioactive Waste Management*, Moscow, 2006, p. 12, at www-ns.

iaea.org/downloads/rw/conventions/Russian-federation-national-report; Baryshnikov, M., A. Suvorova, A. Khaperskaya, A. Shorokhov, *Intermediate Results and Prospects for Handling Bilibino NPP Spent Fuel*, September 2012, Sosny R&D Co. (Dimitrovgrad Office) at www.sosnycompany.com/at_bilibino_en.html; WNA, *Nuclear Power in India*, September 2012, at www.world-nuclear.org/info/inf53.html; "The Sellafield Plan," Nuclear Decommissioning Authority (NDA), Sellafield Sites, and NMP (UK), August 1, 2011, at www.sellafieldsites.com/publications/sellafieldplan/Sellafield_Plan.pdf

155. WNA, *Nuclear Power in Japan*, p. 17, September 2012, at www.world-nuclear.org/info/inf79.html; Idei, Yas, "Japan's Other Nuclear Disaster," *Forbes*, April 6, 2011, at forbes.com/forbes/2011/0425/technology-rokkasho-japan-electric-nuclear-disaster; Bodeen, Christopher, "China Says It Has Mastered Nuclear Fuel Reprocessing," *Associated Press (AP)*, January 3, 2011, at news.yahoo.com/s/ap/20110103/ap_on_re_as/as_china_nuclear_fuel_1/print

156. WNA, *Processing of Used Nuclear Fuel*, May 2012, at www.world-nuclear.org/info/inf69.html

157. *Ibid*; "Canada to Reprocess Other Nations' Waste," *The Globe and Mail*, September 5, 2007, at www.theglobeandmail.com/servlet/story/RTGAM.20070905.wuranium05/BNstory/National/home; Nuclear Waste Management Organization (NWMO), "Used Nuclear Fuel Reprocessing," 2012, at www.nwmo.ca/uploads_managed/MediaFiles/1965_backgrounder_usednuclearfuelreprocessing2012.pdf; Fieveson, Harold, Zia Mian, M.V. Ramana, and Frank von Hippel, *Managing Spent Fuel From Nuclear Power Reactors: Experience and Lessons from Around the World*, ISBN 978-0-9819275-9-6, IPFM, September 2011, pp. 117-120, at www.fissilematerials.org; GNS (Gesellschaft fur Nuklear-Service), "A Major Project Is About to Be Completed: Last Shipment of High Active Waste from France to Germany," *GNS Media Release* (Essen, German), November 17, 2011, at www.gns.de/language=en/taps=4986/9135; Pomper, Miles, Ferenc Dainoki-Veress, Stephanie Lieggi, and Lawrence Scheinman, "Nuclear Power and Spent Fuel in East Asia:

Balancing Energy, Politics and Nonproliferation," *The Asia-Pacific Journal: Japan Focus* (Tokyo), June 21, 2010, at www.japanfocus. org/-Stephanie-Lieggi/3376

158. IAEA, *Storage and Disposal of Spent Fuel and High Level Waste*, 2006, at www.iaea.org/About/Policy/GC/GC50InfDocuments/English/ gc50inf-3-att5>en.pdf

159. Ying, Yuan, and Wang Haotong, "China's Nuclear Waste Rush," *Chinadialogue*, March 21, 2011.

160. Lakshmi, Rama, and Steven Mufson, "U.S., India Reach Agreement on Nuclear Fuel Reprocessing," *Washington Post*, March 30, 2010, at www.washingtonpost.co/wp-dyn/content/article/2010/03/29/ AR2010032901744.html; WNA, "India Opens New Reprocessing Plant," *World Nuclear News*, January 7, 2011, at www.world nucle- ar-news.or/WR_India_opens_new_reprocessing_plant_1601111

161. IAEA), *The National Report of the Russian Federation on Compliance with the Obligations of the Joint Convention on the Safety of Spent Fuel Management and the Safety of Radioactive Waste Management*, Moscow, 2006, p. 12, at www-ns.iaea.org/downloads/rw/con- ventions/Russian-federation-national-report; Baryshnikov, M., A. Suvorova, A. Khaperskaya, A. Shorokhov, *Intermediate Results and Prospects for Handling Bilibino NPP Spent Fuel*, September 2012, Sosny R&D Co. (Dimitrovgrad Office) at www.sosnycompany.com/ at_bilibino_en.html

162. "The Sellafield Plan," Nuclear Decommissioning Authority (NDA), Sellafield Sites, and NMP (UK), August 1, 2011, at www.sella- fieldsites.com/publications/sellafieldplan/Sellafield_Plan.pdf; Jones, Alan, and Emily Beament, "Sellafield's THORP Plant to Close," *The Independent*, June 7, 2012, at www.independent.co.uk/news/uk/ home-news/sellafields-thorp-plant-to-close-7827505.html; WNA, *National Policies: Radioactive Waste Management*, 2008, p. 6, at www. world-nuclear.org/info/inf04ap3.html

163. Lovell, Jeremy, "Nuclear Waste: Bury It and Forget?" *Reuters*, March 8, 2006, at today.reuters.com/misc/PrinterFriendlyPopup.aspx?type=- scienceNews&storyID=uri:2; WNA, "Nuclear Waste in France,"

World Nuclear News, May 16, 2013, at www.world-nuclear-news. org/WR_Public_comment_on_French_waste_disposal_16051311. html; Fairley, Peter, "Nuclear Wasteland: The French Are Recycling Nuclear Waste," *Spectrum*, February 2007 (IEEE: New Jersey).

164. GNS, "A Major Project Is About to Be Completed: Last Shipment of High Active Waste from France to Germany," *GNS Media Release* (Essen, German), November 17, 2011, at www.gns.de/language=en/ taps=4986/9135

165. WNA, *Nuclear Power in Belgium*, July 27, 2012, pp. 1-2, at www. world-nuclear.org/info/inf94.html; WNA, *National Policies: Radioactive Waste Management*, 2008, pp. 6-7, at www.world-nu-clear.org/info/inf04ap3.html; Fieveson, Harold, Zia Mian, M.V. Ramana, and Frank von Hippel, *Managing Spent Fuel From Nuclear Power Reactors: Experience and Lessons from Around the World*, ISBN 978-0-9819275-9-6, IPFM, September 2011, pp. 117-120, at www.fis-silematerials.org; WNA, "Swiss Radwaste Consultation Opens," *World Nuclear News*, June 19, 2012, at www.world-nuclear-news.org/ WR-Swiss_radwaste_consultation_opens-1906127.html

166. Fieveson, Harold, Zia Mian, M.V. Ramana, and Frank von Hippel, *Managing Spent Fuel From Nuclear Power Reactors: Experience and Lessons from Around the World*, ISBN 978-0-9819275-9-6, IPFM, September 2011, pp. 117-120, at www.fissilematerials.org

167. WNA, *Nuclear Power in Ukraine*, July 2012 at www.world-nuclear. org/info/inf46.html; Fieveson, Harold, Zia Mian, M.V. Ramana, and Frank von Hippel, *Managing Spent Fuel From Nuclear Power Reactors: Experience and Lessons from Around the World*, ISBN 978-0-9819275-9-6, IPFM, September 2011, pp. 117-120, at www.fissilematerials.org

168. WNA, *Japanese Waste and MOX Shipments From Europe*, August 2011, at www.world-nuclear.org/info/inf39.html; Pomper, Miles, Ferenc Dainoki-Veress, Stephanie Lieggi, and Lawrence Scheinman, "Nuclear Power and Spent Fuel in East Asia: Balancing Energy, Politics and Nonproliferation," *The Asia-Pacific Journal: Japan Focus* (Tokyo), June 21, 2010, p. 4, at www.japanfocus.org/-Stephanie-Lieggi/3376

169. WNA, *Nuclear Power in Japan*, p. 17, September 2012, at www.world-nuclear.org/info/inf79.html; Idei, Yas, "Japan's Other Nuclear Disaster," *Forbes*, April 6, 2011, at forbes.com/forbes/2011/0425/technology-rokkasho-japan-electric-nuclear-disaster

170. Pomper, Miles, Ferenc Dainoki-Veress, Stephanie Lieggi, and Lawrence Scheinman, "Nuclear Power and Spent Fuel in East Asia: Balancing Energy, Politics and Nonproliferation," *The Asia-Pacific Journal: Japan Focus*, June 21, 2010, p. 4, at www.japanfocus.org/-Stephanie-Lieggi/3376

171. "Canada to Reprocess Other Nations' Waste," *The Globe and Mail*, September 5, 2007, at www.theglobeandmail.com/servlet/story/RTGAM.20070905.wuranium05/BNstory/National/home; Nuclear Waste Management Organization (NWMO), "Used Nuclear Fuel Reprocessing," 2012, at www.nwmo.ca/uploads_managed/MediaFiles/1965_backgrounder_usednuclearfuelreprocessing2012.pdf.

172. WNA, *Processing of Used Nuclear Fuel*, May 2012, at www.world-nuclear.org/info/inf69.html; "Factbox—Timeline of U.S. Nuclear Reprocessing," *Reuters*, August 17, 2010, at www.reuters.com/assets/print?aid=USN0499528

173. Munger, Frank, "Nuke Fuel Recycling Project a 'Spectacular Success' So Far," *Knoxville News Sentinel*, January 28, 2008; Fahey, Jonathan, "GE's Nuclear Waste Plan," *Forbes.com* (New York), February 16, 2010, at www.forbes.com/2010/02/14/general-electric-reactors-technology-ecotech

174. Grossman, Elaine, "Taiwan Ready to Forgo [sic] Nuclear Fuel-Making in U.S. Trade Pact Renewal," *Global Security Newswire*, July 19, 2012, (Nuclear Threat Initiative [NTI]: Washington, D.C.) at www.nti.org/gsn/article/taiwan-ready-forgo-nuclear-fuel-making-us-pact-renewal; Pomper, Miles, Ferenc Dainoki-Veress, Stephanie Lieggi, and Lawrence Scheinman, "Nuclear Power and Spent Fuel in East Asia: Balancing Energy, Politics and Nonproliferation," *The Asia-Pacific Journal: Japan Focus*, June 21, 2010, p. 4, at www.japanfocus.org/-Stephanie-Lieggi/3376.

175. WNA, *Nuclear Power in France*, September 2012, pp. 12-13, at www.world-nuclear.org/info/inf40.html

176. Department of Energy and Climate Change (DECC), *Managing Radioactive Waste Safely: UK Radioactive Waste Inventory*, (UK government: London), November 24, 2011 at http://mrws.decc.gov.uk/en/mrws/cms/Waste/UK_radioactive/UK_radioactive.aspx; Plesch, Dan, "Britain's Nuclear Waste Dangerous, Vulnerable," Global Beat Syndicate, *Tri-City Herald*, July 29, 2002.

177. WNA, *Mixed Oxide (MOX) Fuel*, May 2012, at www.world-nuclear.org.info/inf29.html; WNA, *China's Nuclear Fuel Cycle*, August 2012, at www.world-nuclear.org/info/inf63b_china_nuclearfuelcycle.html

178. Nuclear Threat Initiative (NTI), *Advanced Fuel Fabrication Facility (AFFF)*, 2011, at www.nti.org/facilities/81/

179. U.S. NRC, *Frequently Asked Questions About Mixed Oxide Fuels*, October 3, 2012, at www.nrc.gov/materials/fuel-cycle-fac/mox/faq.html; WNA, *Mixed Oxide (MOX) Fuel*, May 2012, at www.world-nuclear.org.info/inf29.html.

180. International Nuclear Network (INN), "Rosatom Head Backs Mayak Reprocessing Plant," *Nuclear Waste Review*, Vol. 1:4, May 2005, p.5 (Note: International Nuclear Network is now Nucnet.org); U.S. DOE, "U.S., Russia to Eliminate Surplus Plutonium," *DOE This Month*, Vol. 23:8, October 2000, p. 3; Horner, Daniel, "DOE Set to Award Contract to Cogema for Data to Design MOX Plant in Russia," *Inside Energy*, January 30, 2006, p. 11; U.S. DOE, "U.S. and Russia Sign Plan for Plutonium Disposition," *DOE Media Release*, November 19, 2007.

181. WNA, *Nuclear Power in Japan*, p. 17, September 2012, at www.world-nuclear.org/info/inf79.html.

182. *Ibid*, p. 19.

183. WNA, *Nuclear Power in Canada*, October 2012, at www.world-nuclear.org/info/inf49a_Nuclear_Power_in_Canada.html; Bailey, April, "Construction Begins on MOX," *Aiken Standard*, August 22, 2007; "Ground Broken on Key Portion of MOX Facility," *Aiken Standard*, January 19, 2009; Stewart, Joshua, "MOX Plant 60% Done," *Georgia*

Public Broadcasting, July 24, 2012, at www.gpb.org/news/2012/07/24/mox-plant-60-done; Pavey, Rob, "H Canyon Gets Temporary Mission That Will Retain 90 SRS Jobs," *Augusta Chronicle*, October 31, 2011.

184. "Westinghouse Sold to Toshiba for $5.4-B," *Pittsburgh Business Times*, February 6, 2006, at www.bizjournals.com/pittsburgh/stories/2006/02/06/daily3.html

185. Associated Press (AP), "Exxon Corp Selling Exxon Nuclear to West German Firm," *AP News Archive*, December 23, 1986, at www.apnewsarchive.com/1986/Exxon-Corp-Selling-Exxon-Nuclear-Co-to-West-German-Firm/id-6b4edcd7930d464d3b869921223caafc

186. Boone, Timothy, "CB&I Completes Shaw Acquisition," *The Advocate*, February 21, 2013, at theadvocate.com/home/5176586-125/cbi-completes-shaw-acquisition

187. WNA, "GE Hitachi Looks to Generate Sales," *World Nuclear News*, September 29, 2010, at www.world-nuclear-news.org/c_ge-hitachi_looks_to_generate_sales_2909101.html

188. Osborne, James. "NRC Shoots Down Texas Nuclear Plant Expansion," *DallasNews* (*Dallas Morning News*), April 30, 2013, at www.bizbeatblog.dallasnews.com/2013/04/nec-shoots-down-texas-nuclear-plant-expansion

189. Haber, Gary, "Feds Deny Appeal for Third Calvert Cliffs Nuclear Reactor," *Baltimore Sun*, Match 11, 2013, at www.bizjournals.com/baltimore/news/2013/03/11/feds-deny-appeal-for-third-calvert.html

190. Bailey, April, "Construction Begins on MOX," *Aiken Standard*, August 22, 2007; Horner, Daniel, "DOE Set to Award Contract to Cogema for Data to Design MOX Plant in Russia," *Inside Energy*, January 30, 2006, p. 11.

191. Horner, Daniel, "DOE Set to Award Contract to Cogema for Data to Design MOX Plant in Russia," *Inside Energy*, January 30, 2006, p. 11; Ying, Yuan and Wang Haotong, "China's Nuclear Waste Rush," in *Chinadialogue*, March 21, 2011; WNA, *Nuclear Power in Japan*, September 2012, p. 15, at www.world-nuclear.org/info/inf79.html;

Wingfield, Brian, "Reprocessing Atomic Waste Slows Repository Need, Areva Says," *Bloomberg.com*, June 6, 2011.

192. Cary, Annette, "Report Finds Vit Plant Got Off on Wrong Foot from Start," *Tri-City Herald*, February 3, 2006, pp. B1-2.

193. Enormous expansions are underway in almost every aspect of the nuclear industry in nations other than the U.S. See Chapter 2 for a discussion of this situation.

194. WNA, *Nuclear Power in Russia*, September 2012, at world-nuclear-org/info/inf45.html; Weir, Fred, "Russia Plans Big Nuclear Expansion," *Christian Science Monitor*, July 7, 2007, at www.csmonitor.com/2007/0717/p01s04-woeu.htm; "Ukraine, Russia Sign Nuclear Pact," *United Press International* (UPI), June 5, 2007 at www.upi.com/Energy/Briefing/2007/06/05/ukraine_russia_sign_nuclear_pact/7346/; WNA, "Nuclear Power in Russia," September 2012, at world-nuclear-org/info/inf45.html; WNA, "USA and Russia Commit to Expand Nuclear Power," *World Nuclear News*, September 21, 2011, at www.world-nuclear-news.org/NP_USA_and_Russia_commit_to_expand_nuclear_power

195. Yemelyanenkov, Alexander, "Russia Takes First Step in Bid to Build UK Nuclear Plants," *The Telegraph*, July 2, 2012, at www.telegraph.co.uk/sponsored/russianow/business/9370958/russia-uk-nuclear-plan; NUKEM Technologies, 2012, at nukemtechnologies.de/270.0.html?&L=1

196. WNA, *Nuclear Power in Japan*, September 2012, p. 15, at www.world-nuclear.org/info/inf79.html

197. WNA, *Nuclear Power in the United Arab Emirates*, January 2014, at www.world-nuclear.org/info/Country-Profiles/Countries-T-Z/United-Arab-Emirates/

198. Pomper, Miles, Ferenc Dainoki-Veress, Stephanie Lieggi, and Lawrence Scheinman, "Nuclear Power and Spent Fuel in East Asia: Balancing Energy, Politics and Nonproliferation," *The Asia-Pacific Journal: Japan Focus*, June 21, 2010, at www.japanfocus.org/-Stephanie-Lieggi/3376

199. Pomper, Miles, Ferenc Dainoki-Veress, Stephanie Lieggi, and Lawrence Scheinman, "Nuclear Power and Spent Fuel in East Asia: Balancing Energy, Politics and Nonproliferation," *The Asia-Pacific Journal: Japan Focus*, June 21, 2010, at www.japanfocus.org/-Stephanie-Lieggi/3376; Yemelyanenkov, Alexander, "Russia Takes First Step in Bid to Build UK Nuclear Plants," *The Telegraph*, July 2, 2012, at www.telegraph.co.uk/sponsored/russianow/business/9370958/russia-uk-nuclear-plan

200. CANDU Owners Group, www.candu.org/; Pomper, Miles, Ferenc Dainoki-Veress, Stephanie Lieggi, and Lawrence Scheinman, "Nuclear Power and Spent Fuel in East Asia: Balancing Energy, Politics and Nonproliferation," *The Asia-Pacific Journal: Japan Focus*, June 21, 2010, at www.japanfocus.org/ Stephanie Lieggi/3376

201. French, Paul, "China to Saudi Arabia—the Nuclear Silk Road," *Nuclear Energy Insider*, February 12, 2012, at analysis.nuclearenergyinsider.com/new-build/china-saudi-arabia-%E2%80%93-nuclear-silk-road; Byung-koo, Kim, *Nuclear Silk Road: Koreanization of Nuclear Technology*, ISBN: 978-1456422585.

202. GDF Suez, *Energy Services*, 2011, at www.gdfsuez.com/en/businesses/srvices/energy-services/

203. EDF Energy, *EDF Energy is Part of EDF Group*, 2012, at www.edfenergy.com/about-us/about-edf-energy

204. Babcock International Group, *The UK's Leading Engineering*, 2012, at www.babcockinternational.com/about-us/

205. "Don't Mention the Atom," *The Economist*, June 23, 2012, at www.economist.com/node/21557363

206. Yemelyanenkov, Alexander, "Russia Takes First Step in Bid to Build UK Nuclear Plants," *The Telegraph*, July 2, 2012, at www.telegraph.co.uk/sponsored/russianow/business/9370958/russia-uk-nuclear-plan

207. Vattenfall, 2012, at www.vattenfall.com/en

208. CEZ Group, "From a Czech Corporation to a Multinational Group," 2012, at www.cez.cz/en/cez-group/cez-group.html; Meyer, Jacy, "Czechs Forge Ahead with Nuclear Power Expansion," *New York Times*, September 2, 2010.

209. WNA, *Nuclear Power in China*, July 2013, at world-nuclear.org/ info/Country-Profiles/Countries-A-F/China—Nuclear-Power/#. Ud3NHDrn-Uk

210. "Onkalo Underground Rock Characterization Facility," *Posiva*, 2006, www.posivafi/files/375/Onkalo_Eng_290306_kevyt.pdf

211. Overbye, Dennis, "Finland's 100,000-Year Plan to Banish Its Nuclear Waste," *New York Times*, May 10, 2010; Ford, Matt, "Finland's Nuclear Waste Bunker to last 100,000 Years," *CNN. com*, November 2010, www.printthis.clickability.com/pt/cpt?action=cpt&title=Finland%27s+nuclear+waste; "Nuclear Waste Management in Finland," *Posiva*, 2012, www.posiva.fi/en/nuclear_waste_management/nuclear_waste_management in_finland; "Onkalo Underground Rock Characterization Facility," *Posiva*, 2006, www.posivafi/files/375/Onkalo_Eng_290306_kevyt.pdf; Fagerholm, Torsten, "Finland Builds Nuclear Dump at Island as Obama, Merkel Lag," *Bloomberg.com*, October 30, 2012, www. bloomberg.com/news/2012-10-29/finland-builds-nuclear-dump-at-island-as-obama-lags-with-merkel.html; WNA, "Forsmark for Swedish Nuclear Waste," *World Nuclear News*, June 3, 2009, www.world-nuclear-news.org/WR_forsmark_for_Swedish_nuclear_waste_0306091; "Common Sense Prevails? One Nation May have Found a Better Way to Store High-Level Nuclear Waste," *Las Vegas Sun*, April 9, 2010, www.lasvegassun.com/news/2010/apr/09/ common-sense-prevails/; National Agency for Management of Nuclear Waste (ANDRA—France), *Mastering Radioactive Waste*, ANDRA International, July 12, 2012, at www.andra.fr/international/pages/en/menu21/international-consultancy/operational; Capitol Press, "France," *Nuclear Waste News*, February 9, 2006, p. 23; WNA, "Next Phase for French Geological Disposal," *World Nuclear News*, January 5, 2012, at www.world-nuclear-news.org/ WR-Next_phase_for_French_geological_disposal-0501

212. Zhou, Yun, "China's Spent Nuclear Fuel Management: Practices and Future Strategies," Center for International and Security Studies, University of Maryland, March 2011; Pomper, Miles,

Ferenc Dainoki-Veress, Stephanie Lieggi, and Lawrence Scheinman, "Nuclear Power and Spent Fuel in East Asia: Balancing Energy, Politics and Nonproliferation," *The Asia-Pacific Journal: Japan Focus*, June 21, 2010, at www.japanfocus.org/-Stephanie-Lieggi/3376; Wang, Ju, "High-Level Waste Disposal in China: Update 2010," *Journal of Rock Mechanics and Geotechnical Engineering*, Vol. 2:1, March 2010, pp. 1-11

213. Ying, Yuan and Wang Haotong, "China's Nuclear Waste Rush," in *Chinadialogue*, March 21, 2011.

214. Ray, Kalyan, "India Keen on Having Nuclear Waste Repository," *Deccan Herald*, February 14, 2012, (Bangalore, India) at www.deccan-herald.com/content/227293/india-keen-having-nuclear-waste.html; WNA, *Nuclear Power in India*, September 2012, at www.world-nuclear.org/info/inf53.html; Bhabha Atomic Research Centre (BARC), "Nuclear Fuel Cycle," *BARC Highlights* (Mumbai, India), 2006-2007, at wwwbarc.ernet.in/publications/eb/golden/nfc/toc/...6.pdf

215. WNA, *Russia's Nuclear Fuel Cycle*, August 30, 2012, at www.world-nuclear.org/info/inf45a_Russia_nuclear_fuel_cycle.html.

216. *Ibid*, pp. 13-15.

217. WNA, "UK Waste Committee Proposes Repository Site Incentives," *Nuclear Waste Review*, Vol. 2:7, August 2006, pp. 1-2; Black, Richard, "Nuclear Waste Store Gains Public Backing," *BBC News*, May 22, 2012, at www.bbc.co.uk/news/science-environment-18144720; "Report on High-Level Nuclear Waste Storage for Cumbria," *BBC News*, July 20, 2012, at www.bbc.co.uk/news/science-environment-18927945

218. National Agency for Management of Nuclear Waste (ANDRA—France), *Mastering Radioactive Waste*, ANDRA International, July 12, 2012, at www.andra.fr/international/pages/en/menu21/international-consultancy/operational; Capitol Press, "France," *Nuclear Waste News*, February 9, 2006, p. 23; WNA, "Next Phase for French Geological Disposal," *World Nuclear News*, January 5, 2012, at www.world-nuclear-news.org/WR-Next_phase_for_French_geological_disposal-0501

219. U.S. DOE, "EM Delegation Shares Lessons Learned on Tour in France," *EM News Flash*, June 5, 2013.

220. "German Nuke Waste Storage Site Dead," *United Press International*, August 26, 2009, at www.upi.com/Energy_Resources/2009/08/26/ German-nuke-waste-storage-site-dead/; GNS, "Management of Spent Fuel from the Perspective of German Industry," presented at IAEA International Conference on Management of Spent Fuel from Nuclear Power Reactors," May 31-June 4, 2010, pp. 20-21, at www-ns.iaea.org/downloads/rw/conferences/spentfuel2010/opening-presentation-graf-gns-germany.pdf.

221. Overbye, Dennis, "Finland's 100,000-Year Plan to Banish Its Nuclear Waste," *New York Times*, May 10, 2010; Ford, Matt, "Finland's Nuclear Waste Bunker to last 100,000 Years," *CNN.com*, November 2010, www.printthis.clickability.com/pt/cpt?action=cpt&title=Finland%27s+nuclear+waste; "Nuclear Waste Management in Finland," *Posiva*, 2012, at www.posiva.fi/en/nuclear_waste_management/ nuclear_waste_management in_finland; "Onkalo Underground Rock Characterization Facility," *Posiva*, 2006, www.posivafi/ files/375/Onkalo_Eng_290306_kevyt.pdf; Fagerholm, Torsten, "Finland Builds Nuclear Dump at Island as Obama, Merkel Lag," *Bloomberg.com*, October 30, 2012, www.bloomberg.com/news/2012-10-29/finland-builds-nuclear-dump-at-island-as-obama-lags-with-merkel.html; WNA, "Forsmark for Swedish Nuclear Waste," *World Nuclear News*, June 3, 2009, www.world-nuclear-news.org/ WR_forsmark_for_Swedish_nuclear_waste_0306091.

222. WNA, *Nuclear Power in Belgium*, July 27, 2012, p. 4, at www. world-nuclear.org/info/inf94.html; IAEA, *Country Nuclear Waste Profile: Belgium*, 2007, at newmdb.iaea.org/profiles.aspx?ByCountry=BE; CEZ Group, *Waste Management*, 2010, at www.cez.cz/en/ power-plants-and-environment/nuclear-power-plants/temelin/ potential

223. Van der Zwaan, Bob, "Nuclear Waste Repository Case Studies: The Netherlands," *Bulletin of the Atomic Scientists*, May 19, 2008, at www.thebulletin.org/web-edition/reports/

nuclear-waste-repository-case-studies/nuclear; WNA, *International Nuclear Waste Disposal Concepts*, April 2012, pp. 2-3, at www.world-nuclear.org/info/inf21.html; Fieveson, Harold, Zia Mian, M.V. Ramana, and Frank von Hippel, *Managing Spent Fuel from Nuclear Power Reactors: Experience and Lessons from Around the World*, ISBN 978-0-9819275-9-6, IPFM, September 2011, pp. 117-120, at www.fissilematerials.org.

224. WNA, *Nuclear Power in Japan*, p. 20, at www.world-nuclear.org/info/Country-Profiles/Countries-G-N/Japan/

225. Nakagawa, Toru, "Ministry to Request Funding to Study Burying Spent Nuke Fuel," *Asahi Shimbun* (Tokyo), August 14, 2012, at ajw.asahi.com/article/0311disaster/fukushima/AJ201208140061

226. Pomper, Miles, Ferenc Dainoki-Veress, Stephanie Lieggi, and Lawrence Scheinman, "Nuclear Power and Spent Fuel in East Asia: Balancing Energy, Politics and Nonproliferation," *The Asia-Pacific Journal: Japan Focus*, June 21, 2010, pp. 4-5, at www.japanfocus.org/-Stephanie-Lieggi/3376.

227. "Nuclear Waste: Time to Learn," *Regina Leader-Post*, August 11, 2011, at http://www.leaderpost.com/story_print.html?id=5239024&-sponsor=; NEI, "The Canadian Plan," *NEI Magazine*, January 19, 2012, at www.neimagazine.com/story.asp?storyCode=2061617; Spears, John, "Nuclear Waste Storage Attracts Southern Ontario Towns," *The Star.Com*, February 20, 2012, at www.thestar.com/printarticle/1134081

228. NEI, *Nuclear Waste: Amounts and On-Site Storage*, at nei.org/resource-sandstats/nuclear_statistics/nuclearwasteamountsandonsitestorage; U.S. NRC, "Spent Fuel Storage in Pools and Dry Casks: Key Points and Questions and Answers," March 29, 2012, at www.nrc.gov/waste/spent-fuel-storage/faqs.html

229. Yucca Mountain Development Act, Public Law 107-200, U.S. Congress, Washington, D.C., July 23, 2002.

230. "Yucca Mountain: The Most Studied Real Estate on the Planet," Report to the Chairman, Senator James M. Inhofe, U.S. Senate

Committee on Environment and Public Works, March 2006 at epw.
senate.gov/repwhitepapers/YuccaMountainEPWReport.pdf

231. Valverde, Janice, "Administration to Withdraw License Bid for Yucca Mountain, Eliminates Funding," *BNA Daily Report for Executives*, Bloomberg BNA, February 2, 2010; U.S. NRC, *U.S. Department of Energy's Motion to Withdraw, In the Matter of the U.S. Department of Energy*, Atomic Safety and Licensing Board Panel, U.S. NRC, ASLBP No. 09-892-HLW-CAB04, March 3, 2010.

232. Nuclear Waste Strategy Coalition, *Lawsuits/Contentions*, 2012, at www.thenwsc.org/; Ferguson, Robert L., "Promising Developments in Yucca Mountain Lawsuit," *ANS Nuclear Café*, May 5, 2011, at ansnuclearcafe.org/2011/05/05/promising-developments-in-the-yucca-mountain-lawsuit/

233. U.S. DOJ, *Response to Request for Information from the Blue Ribbon Commission on America's Nuclear Future*, December 20, 2011, at www.brc.gov/sites/default/files/comments/attachments/doj_response.12.20.11_0.pdf; NEI, *Damage Awards Expected from Taxpayer-Funded Judgment Fund*, July 2012; Turner, Channing, "Liability for Scrapping Yucca Mountain Could Run in the Billions," *Main Justice*, July 27, 2010, at www.mainjustice.com/2010/07/27/liability-for-scrapping-yucca-mountain-could

Chapter 3

234. Wald, Matt, *Yucca Mountain: Chronology of Coverage, New York Times*, at topics.nytimes.com/top/news/national/usstatesterritoriesand-possessions/nevada/yucca-mountain/index.html

235. Kishi, Stephanie, "Topic: Yucca Mountain," *Las Vegas Sun*, October 27, 2013, at www.lasvegassun.com/news/topics/yucca-mountain/

236. U.S. DOE, *Viability Assessment of a Repository at Yucca Mountain*, DOE/RW-0508, December 1998, p. 36, at energy.gov/downloads/viability-assessment-repository-yucca-mountain-1

237. Organisation for Economic Co-operation and Development (OECD)/Nuclear Energy Agency (NEA)-International Atomic Energy Agency (IAEA), *Joint International Peer Review of the Yucca*

Mountain Site Characterization Project's Total System Performance Assessment Supporting the Site Recommendation Process, Final Report, December, 2001, p.4, at energy.gov/sites/prod/files/edg/media/NEA-iaeaPRTSPA12-01.pdf

238. Anzelc, Meghan, "Gregory Jaczko, Ph.D. Physics, Commissioner, U.S. Nuclear Regulatory Commission," APS Physics, American Physical Society (College Park, Maryland), 2013, at www.aps.org/units/fgsa/careers/non-traditional/jaczko.cfm

239. Nuclear Waste Policy Act, 42 U.S.C. 10101: Public Law (P.L.) 97-425; 96 Stat.2201, Jan. 7, 1983, as amended by P.L. 100-203, December 22, 1987, P.L. 100-507, October 18, 1988, and P.L. 102-486 (The Energy Policy Act of 1992), October 24, 1992; Yucca Mountain: Most Studied Real Estate on the Planet, Report to the Chairman, Senator James M. Inhofe, U.S. Senate Committee on Environment and Public Works, Majority Staff, March 2006, at www.epw.senate.gov/repwhitepapers/YuccaMountainEPWReport.pdf

240. Nevada Commission on Nuclear Projects (NCNP), Report to the Governor and Legislature of the State of Nevada, State of Nevada, December 2000, p. 2, at www.state.nv.us/nucwaste/news2001/commrpt2000.pdf

241. Christensen, Jon, "Can Nevada Bury Yucca Mountain?" High Country News, Vol. 33:13, July 2, 2001, p. 11 (citing Harry Reid), at www.hcn.org/issues/206/10604/print_view

242. U.S. Government Accountability Office (GAO), Technical, Schedule, and Cost Uncertainties of the Yucca Mountain Repository Project, GAO-02-191, December 21, 2001, at www.gao.gov/assets/240/233244.pdf.

243. Associated Press (AP), "Report Deals Yucca Nuclear Dump Severe Blow," Tri-City Herald, December 2, 2001 (citing Harry Reid).

244. Beattie, Jeff, "Bechtel: GAO Got it Wrong on Yucca Mountain Project," Energy Daily, December 6, 2001 (partially citing Spencer Abraham), .

245. U.S. DOE, Final Environmental Impact Statement for a Geologic Repository for the Disposal of Spent Nuclear Fuel and High-Level Radioactive Waste at Yucca Mountain, Nye County, Nevada, Document EIS-250, U.S. DOE,

Office of Civilian Radioactive Waste Management (OCRWM), Washington, D.C., February 2002, pp. S-83-84, at energy.gov/nepa/downloads/eis-0250-final-environmental-impact-statement

246. "Bush Greenlights Yucca Mountain Nuclear Waste Dump," *Environment News Service*, February 15, 2002, at www.ens-newswire.com/ens/feb2002/2002-02-15-01.asp

247. "Bush Hears Arguments Against Nevada Waste Dump," *Environment News Service*, February 8, 2002 (citing Spencer Abraham, at www.ens-newswire.com/ens/feb2002/2002-02-08-02.asp

248. Nieves, Evelyn, "Not Under Our Mountain, Nevada Says of Nuclear Dump," *New York Times*, April 2, 2002, at www.nytimes.com/2002/04/02/us/not-under-our-mountain-nevada-says-of-nuclear-dump.html; "Desert Storm," *Knight-Ridder News*, reprinted in *Seattle Times*, May 9, 2002.

249. *Yucca Mountain: Most Studied Real Estate on the Planet*, Report to the Chairman, Senator James M. Inhofe, U.S. Senate Committee on Environment and Public Works, Majority Staff, March 2006, at www.epw.senate.gov/repwhitepapers/YuccaMountainEPWReport.pdf

250. Yucca Mountain Development Act, Public Law 107-200, U.S. Congress, Washington, D.C., July 23, 2002.

251. Hilger, John, and Bernard Menke, *Report of the Nevada Committee for the Utilization of State Resources to Meet National Needs*, Nevada Committee for the Utilization of State Resources to Meet National Needs, Las Vegas, NV, October 1978.

252. "Nevada Takes Yucca Fight to Court," *Inside Energy*, December 9, 2002.

253. U.S. GAO, *Persistent Quality Assurance Problems Could Delay Repository Licensing and Operation*, GAO-04-460, U.S. GAO, April 30, 2004.

254. "Court Upholds Yucca Mt's Selection as Repository," *Inside Energy*, July 12, 2004.

255. Jeffery, Simon, "Bush to 'Spend Political Capital'," *The Guardian*, November 4, 2004 (citing George Bush), at www.theguardian.com/world/2004/nov/04/uselections2004.usa20.

256. Dennis, Steven, "NRC Chief Gregory Jaczko Resigns–With a Catch," *Roll Call*, May 21, 2012, at www.rollcall.com/news/nrc_chief_gregory_jaczko_resigns_with_a_catch-214683-1.html

257. Tetreault, Steve, "'Fix' Vow for Yucca: Energy Chief Admits Past Process 'Broken'," *Las Vegas Review-Journal*, March 9, 2006.

258. U.S. DOE, *Technical Report Confirms Reliability of Yucca Mountain Technical Work*, February 17, 2006, at energy.gov/articles/techni cal-report-confirms-reliability-yucca-mountain-technical-work

259. Associated Press, "DOE Makes New Push for Yucca Mountain Nuclear Dump," *Channel 8 News Now* (CBS News: Las Vegas), March 6, 2007, at www.8newsnow.com/story/6187260/doe-makes-new-push-for-yucca-mountain-nuclear-dump

260. Mulik, Katie, "Six Years On, Yucca Mountain Nuclear Repository Slows Moves On," *PBS News Hour*, May 16, 2008, at www.pbs.org/newshour/updates/science/jan-june08/yucca_05-16.html

261. Werner, Eric, "NRC Rejects Nevada's Challenge to Yucca Mountain Database," *Las Vegas Sun*, December 12, 2007.

262. Tetreault, Steve, "Yucca Mountain Research Leaves Doubt," *Las Vegas Review-Journal*, December 20, 2007.

263. Ball, Molly, "Clinton Declares Yucca Mountain will be 'Off the Table Forever'," *Las Vegas Review-Journal*, January 17, 2008, at www.reviewjournal.com/news/elections/clinton-declares-yucca-mountain-will-be-table-forever; Seattle Time Editorial, "NRC Must Finish Work on Yucca Mountain Nuclear-Waste Site," *Seattle Times*, August 13, 2013, at seattletimes.com/html/editorials/2021604805_edityuccamountain14xml.html

264. U.S. NRC, *DOE's License Application for a High-Level Waste Geologic Repository at Yucca Mountain*, March 29, 2012, at www.nrc.gov/waste/hlw-disposal/yucca-lic-app.html

265. World Nuclear Association (WNA), "Yucca Mountain Application Docketed," *World Nuclear News*, September 9, 2008, at www.world-nuclear-news.org/WR-Yucca_Mountain_application_docketed-0909087.html

266. U.S. NRC, "Statement of NRC Chairman Dale E. Klein on the Confirmation of Gregory Jaczko to a Second Term," *NRC Press Release 08-057*, March 14, 2008.

267. U.S. NRC, *Consideration of Environmental Impacts of Temporary Storage of Spent Fuel After Cessation of Reactor Operation*, NRC-2008-0404, October 9, 2008.

268. Tetreault, Steve, "Ruling Reopens Debate on Yucca Mountain," *Las Vegas Review-Journal*, June 8, 2012.

269. "Demise of Yucca Project Predicted," *Las Vegas Review-Journal*, November 21, 2008, at reviewjournal.com/news/yucca-mountain/demise-yucca-project-predicted

270. Rogers, Keith, "Yucca Mountain: Nevada Objects—229 Times," *Las Vegas Review-Journal*, December 20, 2008.

271. "Mountain of Trouble," *Washington Post*, March 8, 2009, at articles.washingtonpost.com/2009-03-08/news/36882975_1_nuclear-waste-yucca-mountain-nuclear-repository

272. "FY2010 Energy Budget Shuts Down Yucca Mountain Nuclear Dump," *Environment News Service*, May 8, 2009, at ens-neswire.com/ens/may2009/2009-05-08-092.asp

273. U.S. DOE, *A Sustainable Energy Future: The Essential Role of Nuclear Energy*, U.S. DOE, Office of Nuclear Energy, August 2008, www.nuclear.gov/pdfFiles/rpt_SustainableEnergyFuture_Aug2008.pdf

274. Bullis, Kevin, "Q&A Steven Chu," *MIT Technology Review*, May 14, 2009 (citing Steven Chu), at www.technologyreview.com/news/413475/q-a-steven-chu/

275. U.S. GAO, "Nuclear Waste: Disposal Challenges and Lessons Learned from Yucca Mountain," GAO-11-731T, GAO, June 1, 2011, at www.gao.gov/new.items/d11731t.pdf.

276. Hannah Northey, "GAO: Death of Yucca Mountain Caused by Political Maneuvering," *New York Times*, May 10, 2011, at www.nytimes.com/gwire/2011/05/10/10greenwire-gao-death-of-yucca-mountain-caused-by-politica-36298.html?pagewanted=all.

277. Garvey, Todd, *Closing Yucca Mountain: Litigation Associated with Attempts to Abandon the Planned Nuclear Repository,*

Congressional Research Service, Report R41675, March 4, 2011, at www.legistorm.com/reports/view/crs/121561/Closing_Yucca_Mountain_Litigation_Associated_with_Attempts_to_Abandon_the_Planned_Nuclear_Waste_Repository.html

278. Peterson, Spencer, *OCRWM Contracting Officer Direction to Stop Contract License Application Contract Tasks to USA Repository Services LLC (USA RS), Contract Number DE-RW0000005*, Letter to Douglas Cooper, U.S. DOE - Office of Civilian Radioactive Waste Management, June 7, 2010.

279. "Unemployment Rate Increases Slightly in Nye County," *Pahrump Valley Times*, March 14, 2012; Robison, Jennifer, "Job Scene Stays Sluggish," *Las Vegas Review-Journal*, April 12, 2012.

280. Tonopah, Nevada, City Data, p. 3, at www.city-data.com/city/Tonopah-Nevada.html; Pahrump; Nevada, City Data, p. 3, at www.city-data.com/city/Pahrump-Nevada.html; Beatty, Nevada, City Data, p. 3, at www.city-data.com/city/Beatty-Nevada.html

281. Waite, Mark, "The Year in Review," *Pahrump Valley Times*, December 31, 2010.

282. Mascaro, Lisa, "Feds File Request for Suspension of Yucca Mountain License," *Las Vegas Sun*, February 1, 2010, at www.lasvegassun.com/news/2010/feb/01/feds-move-withdraw-yucca-mountain-license-applicat/

283. "Special Bulletin: NRC Licensing Board Rejects DOE Attempt to Pull Yucca Application," *Radwaste Monitor*, June 29, 2010.

284. House of Representatives Committee on Energy and Commerce, "400 Days and Still No Decision on NRC Atomic Safety Board Yucca Vote—Chairman Jaczko Continues Stonewalling—Tally of 5 Votes," Press Release, U.S. House E&C Committee, August 3, 2011, at http://energycommerce.house.gov/press-release/400-days-and-still-no-decision-nrc-atomic-safety-board-yucca-vote-chairman-jaczko

285. U.S. NRC, Memorandum to Office Directors and Regional Administrators from J.E. Dyer, Chief Financial Officer, NRC, *Guidance Under A Fiscal Year 2011 Continuing Resolution*, October 4, 2010.

286. Senator Patty Murray et al., *Letter to Stephen Chu*, July 6, 2010, at www.murray.senate.gov/public/_cache/files/f849572d-f3eb-44f2-931d-3a0129eb32d5/Yucca%20Letter.pdf

287. *Ibid.*

288. U.S. NRC, *Congressional Budget Justification: Fiscal Year 2011 (NUREG-1100, Volume 26)*, February 2010, at www.nrc.gov/reading-rm/doc-collections/nuregs/staff/sr1100/v26/

289. Kristine L. Svinicki, Commissioner, U.S. NRC, Letters to Congressman Jo Barton and others, November 1, 2010.

290. Majority Staff Report, Committee on Oversight and Government Reform, *A Crisis of Leadership: How the Actions of Chairman Gregory Jaczko Are Damaging the Nuclear Regulatory Commission* (December 13, 2011), at oversight.house.gov/wp-content/uploads/2012/02/12-13-11-NRC-Report-Final-1.pdf.

291. Letter from Congressman Fred Upton and Congressman Ed Whitfield to Hubert T. Bell, Inspector General, Nuclear Regulatory Commission (October 19, 2010).

292. Hubert T. Bell, Inspector General, U.S. NRC, *NRC Chairman's Unilateral Decision to Terminate NRC's Review of DOE Yucca Mountain Repository License Application*, OIG Case No. 11-05, at www.gpo.gov/fdsys/pkg/CHRG-112hhrg71695/pdf/CHRG-112hhrg71695.pdf

293. Ferguson, Robert L., *The Cost of Deceit and Delay: Obama and Reid's Scheme to Kill Yucca Mountain Wastes $Billions*, first edition, pp. 18-27, ISBN: 978-1449978921, Crosby-Ferguson Publishing, Richland, WA, 2012, at www.crosby-ferguson-publishing.com

294. Kristine Svinicki, George Apostolakis, William Magwood IV, and William Ostendorff (NRC Commissioners), Letter to William Daley, White House Chief of Staff, October 13, 2011.

295. "Nuclear Commission Chief 'Abusive' Fellow Members Testify," *McClatchy Newspapers*, December 14, 2011, at www.mcclatchydc.com/2011/.../nuclear-commission-chief-abusive.html

296. Grim, Ryan, "Bill Magwood, NRC Democrat, Is 'Treacherous, Miserable Liar' And 'First-Class Rat,' Says Harry Reid," *Huffington*

Post, July 30, 2012, at www.huffingtonpost.com/2012/07/30/bill-magwood-nrc_n_1712181.html

297.   Tetreault, Steve, "Final Report Mixed for NRC Chairman Jaczko," *Las Vegas Review-Journal* June 26, 2012 at www.reviewjournal.com/news/yucca-mountain/final-report-mixed-nrc-chairman-jaczko

298.   Broder, John, and Matt Wald, "Chairman of N.R.C. to Resign Under Fire," *New York Times,* May 21, 2012 at http://www.nytimes.com/2012/05/22/us/gregory-jaczko-to-resign-as-nrc-chairman-after-stormy-tenure.html?_r=0

299.   U.S. NRC, *Chairman Allison M. Macfarlane,* July 16, 2013, at www.nrc.gov/about-nrc/organization/commission/macfarlane.html

300.   "Let's Rally for Dr. Gregory Jaczko Legal Fund to Help Make a Difference," *Searchlight Leadership Fund* at www.jaczkolegalfund.com/; Dixon, Darius, "Reid's Leadership PAC to Donate $10,000 to Jaczko Legal Defense Fund," *Politico,* July 19, 2012, at www.politico.com/news/stories/0712/78746.html

301.   Two of my most trusted friends and longtime business colleagues, Bill Lampson, President and CEO of Lampson, International, with headquarters in Kennewick, WA, and operations worldwide; and Gary Petersen, Vice-President of Hanford Programs at the Tri-Cities Development Council in Kennewick, WA.

302.   U.S. GAO, *Commercial Nuclear Waste: Effects of a Termination of the Yucca Mountain Repository Program and Lessons Learned,* GAO-11-229, April 2011 at www.gao.gov/assets/320/317627.pdf

303.   Attorney Barry M. Hartman, K&L Gates, LLP

304.   Reid, Harry, *U.S. Senator for Nevada, Issues: Yucca Mountain,* at www.reid.senate.gov/issues/yucca.cfm

305.   Reid, Harry, *Reid Statement on Blue Ribbon Commission Draft Report,* July 29, 2011, at www.reid.senate.gov/newsroom/pr_072911_blue-ribbon.cfm

306.   Reid, Harry, *Reid Statement on Blue Ribbon Commission's Final Report,* January 26, 2012, at www.reid.senate.gov/newsroom/pr_012612_reidstatementonblueribboncommissionsfinalreport.cfm

307. On June 8, 2012, the D.C. District Court of Appeals sent the NRC's 2010 Nuclear Waste Confidence decision, which stated that dry cask storage at nuclear plants would be safe for many decades, back to the NRC for "deficiency."

308. Bullis, Kevin, "Q&A Steven Chu," *MIT Technology Review*, May 14, 2009 (citing Steven Chu), at www.technologyreview.com/news/413475/q-a-steven-chu/

309. *Ibid*, p. vii.

310. Ferguson, Robert L., *The Cost of Deceit and Delay: Obama and Reid's Scheme to Kill Yucca Mountain Wastes $Billions*, first edition, pp. 70-72, ISBN: 978-1449978921, Crosby-Ferguson Publishing, Richland, WA, 2012, at www.crosby-ferguson-publishing.com

311. Tetreault, Steve, "DOE Unleashes Bureaucrats on Post-Yucca Report, *Las Vegas Review-Journal*, March 26, 2012, at www.reviewjournal.com/columns-blogs/political-eye/doe-unleashes-bureaucrats-post-yucca-report

312. Lando, Ben, "Analysis: Reid's Yucca and Nuke Waste Plan," *UPI.com Energy Resources*, December 4, 2006, at www.upi.com/Business_News/Energy-Resources/2006/12/04/Analysis-Reids-Yucca-and-nuke-waste-plan/UPI-18721165275507/#ixzz1wrySH1Ei

313. "Republicans Open Inquiry on YM Shutdown," *New York Times*, April 5, 2011, at green.blogs.nytimes.com/2011/04/05/republicans-open-inquiry-on-yucca-mountain-shutdown/?_r=0

314. U.S. Court of Appeals for the D.C. Circuit, Case No. 11-1271, Aiken et al. vs. Nuclear Regulatory Commission, On Petition for Writ of Mandamus, August 13, 2013, at www.cadc.uscourts.gov/internet/opinions.nsf/BAE0CF34F762EBD985257BC6004DEB18/$file/11-1271-1451347.pdf

315. Straub, Bill, "Reid Isn't Quite in the Yucca Mountain Clear," *PJ Media*, September 1, 2013, at pjmedia.com/blog/reid-isnt-quite-in-the-yucca-mountain-clear/

316. Raju, Manu, "Harry Reid's Gambit," *Politico*, November 21, 2013, at www.politico.com/story/2013/11/harry-reid-senate-fillibuster-100243.html

317. "NRC Released Redacted Draft of Yucca Safety Report," *Las Vegas Review-Journal*, February 18, 2011, at www.reviewjournal.com/news/ nevada-and-west/nrc-releases-redacted-draft-yucca-safety-report.

318. Reid, Harry, *Yucca*, at www.reid.senate.gov/issues/yucca#. UtxtltjTncs

319. Northey, Hannah, "Jaczko Inks Book Deal," *Greenwire*, April 17, 2013 at www.eenews.net/search/stories?keyword=Jaczko+ Inks+Book+Deal&commit=go%21

320. Colman, Zack, "Reid Appoints Former NRC Chief Jaczko to Nuclear Panel," *The Hill*, April 18, 2013, at thehill.com/blogs/e2-wire/e2-wire/294795-reid-appoints-former-nrc-chief-jaczko-to-nuclear-panel

321. Guillen, Alex, "Inhofe on Jaczko Appointment: How Much Damage Can He Do?" *Politico Morning Energy*, April 19, 2013, at www.politico. com/morningenergy/0413/morningenergy10482.html

322. McConnell, Michael W., "Obama Suspends the Law," *Wall Street Journal*, July 9, 2013, at online.wsj.com/news/articles/SB1000142412 7887323823004578591503509555268

323. Hall, Kevin G., and Anita Kumar, "Analysis: Tens of Millions Could be Forced Out of Health Insurance They Had," *McClatchy D.C.*, at www.mcclatchydc.com/2013/11/07/207909/analysis-tens-of-millions-could.html

324. Obama, Barack, "Remarks," at the M. Luis Construction Co., Rockville, Maryland, October 3, 2013, at www.c-spanvideo.org/ program/ObamaonGo

325. Issa, Darrell, and Dave Camp, "The IRS Scandal's Inconsistencies," *Washington Post*, August 6, 2013, at articles. washingtonpost.com/2013-08-06/opinions/41112134_1_tea-party-cincinnati-irs-inspector-general

326. Theissen, Marc, "How Obama's IRS Scandal Harms National Security," *Washington Post*, August 5, 2013, at articles.washington-post.com/2013-08-05/opinions/41075747_1_irs-scandal-president-obama-national-security-agency; Todd, Chuck, Kelly O'Donnell, and Carrie Dann, "Snowden's Revelations Force Obama's Hand on Surveillance Program," *First Read*, August 9, 2013,

at firstread.nbcnews.com/_news/2013/08/09/19950803-snowden-revelations-force-obamas-hand-on-surveillance-program?lite

327. The Associated Press is a multinational news agency headquartered in New York.

328. U.S. Constitution, *Bill of Rights, Amendment One*, National Archives, Washington, D.C., 1791.

329. Downie, Leonard, and Sara Rafsky, "The Obama Administration and the Press," *Committee to Protect Journalists*, October 10, 2013, at www.cpj.org/reports/2013/10/obama-and-the-press-us-leaks-surveillance-post-911.php

330. Reibus, Reintz, "Where's Obama as IRS, EPA Compete for Most Bizarre Scandal in Washington?" *FoxNews.com*, June 7, 2013, at www.foxnews.com/opinion/2013/06/07/where-obama-as-irs-epa-compete-for-most-bizarre-scandal-in-washington/; Hayward, John, "Your Next Obama Scandal Factory: The EPA," *Human Events*, June 7, 2013, at www.humanevents.com/2013/06/07/your-next-obama-privacy-scandal-factory-the-epa/

331. Roy, Avik, "Yet Another White House Obamacare Delay: Out-of-Pocket Caps Waived Until 2015," *Forbes*, August 13, 2013, at www.forbes.com/sites/theapothecary/2013/08/13/yet-another-white-house-obamacare-delay-out-of-pocket-caps-waived-until-2015/

332. Ball, James, "NSA Monitored Calls of 35 World leaders After Official Handed Over Contact," *The Guardian*, October 24, 2013, at www.theguardian.com/world/2013/oct/24/nsa-surveillance-world-leaders-calls; Sherwell, Philip, and Louise Barnett, "Barack Obama 'Approved Tapping Angela Merkel's Phone 3 Years Ago'," *The Telegraph*, October 27, 2013, at www.telegraph.co.uk/news/worldnews/europe/germany/10407282/Barack-Obama-approved-tapping-Angela-Merkels-phone-3-years-ago.html

333. Wehner, Peter, "Barack Obama's Lawlessness," *Commentary Magazine*, July 20, 2013, at www.commentarymagazine.com/2013/07/12/barack-obamas-lawlessness/; Williams, Joseph, "President Obama Appoints Three to NLRB," *Politico*, January 4, 2013, at www.politico.com/news/stories/0112/71086.html

334. Landler, Mark, and Thom Shanker, "Leaving Military Aid Intact, U.S. Takes Steps to Halt Economic Steps to Egypt," *New York Times*, August 18, 2013, at www.nytimes.com/2013/08/19/world/middle-east/leaving-military-aid-intact-us-takes-steps-to-halt-economic-help-to-egypt.html?pagewanted=all&_r=0

335. Yan, Holly, "Billions in Aid on the Line: What Will the U.S. Do about Egypt?" *CNN*, August 20, 2013, at www.cnn.com/2013/08/15/world/meast/egypt-us-what-next

336. Noyes, Richard, "Broadcast Networks Drop the Ball on Obama's Smarmy 'Phony Scandal' Mantra," *Newsbusters*, August 9, 2013, at newsbusters.org/blogs/rich-noyes/2013/08/09/broadcast-networks-drop-ball-obama-s-smarmy-phony-scandal-mantra

337. Richard Nixon, "Address on the State of the Union," Washington, D.C., January 30, 1974, the *American Presidency Project*, University of California at Santa Barbara, at www.presidency.ucsb.edu/ws/?pid=4327

338. "When the President Does It, That Means It is Not Illegal," Interview with David Frost, May 19, 1977, citing Richard Nixon, *Think Progress, Center for American Progress*, at thinkprogress.org/politics/2007/05/19/13066/nixon-bush-

339. "LBJ: Program Transcript," *The American Experience*, *PBS*, at www.pbs.org/wgbh/americanexperience/features/transcript/lbj-transcript/

340. Mitchell, Alison, "Impeachment: the Overview; Clinton Impeached—He Faces a Senate Trial; 2nd in History; Vows to Do Job Till Term's 'Last Hour'," *New York Times*, December 20, 1998, at www.nytimes.com/1998/12/20/us/impeachment-over-view-clinton-impeached-he-faces-senate-trial-2d-history-vows-job.html?pagewanted=all&src=pm

341. Noah, Timothy, "Bill Clinton and the Meaning of 'Is'," *Slate*, September 13, 1998, at www.slate.com/articles/news_and_politics/chatterbox/1998/09/bill_clinton_and_the_meaning_of_is.html

342. "FDR's Losing Battle to Pack the Supreme Court," *NPR*, April 13, 2010, at www.npr.org/templates/story/story.php?storyId=125789097;

Shesol, Jeff, *Supreme Power: Franklin Roosevelt vs. the Supreme Court*, W.W. Norton & Co., 2010.

343. McConnell, Michael W., "Obama Suspends the Law," *Wall Street Journal*, July 9, 2013, at online.wsj.com/news/articles/SB1000142412 7887323823004578591503509555268

Chapter 4

344. World Nuclear Association (WNA), *World Energy Needs and Nuclear Power*, 2013, at www.world-nuclear.org/info/ Current-and-Future-Generation/World-Energy-Needs-and-Nuclear-Power/

345. Exelon Corp. is headquartered in Chicago, Illinois.

346. Next Era Energy's American headquarters is in Juno Beach, Florida.

347. Arizona Public Service Co. is headquartered in Phoenix.

348. Dairyland Power Cooperative is headquartered in LaCrosse, Wisconsin.

349. Garvey, Todd, *The Yucca Mountain Litigation: Liability Under the Nuclear Waste Policy Act of 1982*, Congressional Research Service, Report R40996, March 8, 2010; Zabransky, David, U.S. DOE Office of General Counsel, "Liability Estimate," *Memorandum to Owen Barwell*, October 26, 2011; Hertz, Michael, U.S. DOJ, *Statement Before the Blue Ribbon Commission on America's Nuclear Future*, Washington, D.C., February 2, 2011.

350. Garvey, Todd, *The Yucca Mountain Litigation: Liability Under the Nuclear Waste Policy Act of 1982*, Congressional Research Service, Report R40996, March 8, 2010; Hertz, Michael, U.S. DOJ, *Statement Before the Blue Ribbon Commission on America's Nuclear Future*, Washington, D.C., February 2, 2011, p. 10.

351. Hertz, Michael, U.S. DOJ, *Statement Before the Blue Ribbon Commission on America's Nuclear Future*, Washington, D.C., February 2, 2011.

352. Adams, Ron, "Opening Yucca Mountain Would Require Exelon to Write a $1 billion Check," *AtomicInsights.com*, October 4, 2013, at atomicinsights.com/opening-yucca-costs-exelon-a-billion/; "Form 10-K," filed with U.S. Securities and Exchange Commission, Exelon

Corp., December 31, 2012, p. 194, at www.sec.gov/Archives/edgar/data/9466/000119312513069749/d474199d10k.htm#toc474199_51

353. Lipton, Eric, "Ties to Obama Aided in Access for Big Utility," *New York Times*, August 22, 2012, at www.nytimes.com/2012/08/23/us/politics/ties-to-obama-aided-in-access-for-exelon-corporation.html?pagewanted=1&_r=0

354. Data Distribution Centre for the Intergovernmental Panel on Climate Change (IPCC), United Nations (UN) and World Meteorological Organization (WMO), 2012, at www.ipcc-data.org/

355. Guzman, Andrew, *Overheated: The Human Cost of Climate Change*, Oxford University Press, 2013, p. 31, partially citing IPCC Assessment Report Four, 2007.

356. *Ibid*, p. 34.

357. *IPCC Fifth Assessment Report Climate Change 2013: The Physical Science Basis: Summary for Policymakers*, IPCC and WMO, September 27, 2013, pp. SPM-3-21, at www.ipcc.ch/report/ar5/wg1/

358. *Ibid*, p. 12-6.

359. *Ibid*, pp. SPM-3-21.

360. Guzman, Andrew, *Overheated: The Human Cost of Climate Change*, Oxford University Press, 2013, pp. 36-39, partially citing IPCC Assessment Report Four, 2007; Wright, Judith, and James Conca, *The Geopolitics of Energy: Achieving a Just and Sustainable Energy Distribution by 2040*, BookSurge Publishing, 2007.

361. *Ibid*, p. 80.

362. "Bangladesh Fears Climate Change Will Swallow a Third of Its Land," *Washington Times*, September 18, 2009, at www.washingtontimes.com/news/2009/sep/18/bangladeshi-fears-land-will-vanish/?page=all

363. Bala-Gbogbo, Elisha, "Nigerian Oil Companies Boost Production as Majors Retreat," *Bloomberg.com*, September 18, 2013, at: www.bloomberg.com/news/2013-09-17/nigerian-oil-compa-nies-boost-production-as-majors-retreat.html; U.S. Energy Information Administration (EIA), *U.S. Imports of Nigerian Crude Oil Have Continued to Decline in 2012*, April 10, 2012, at www.eia.gov/todayinenergy/detail.cfm?id=5770; Guzman, Andrew, *Overheated:*

The Human Cost of Climate Change, Oxford University Press, 2013, pp. 163-167, partially citing IPCC Assessment Report Four, 2007.

364. Harvey, Fiona, "Caribbean has Lost 80 Percent of its Coral Reefs Due to Climate Change and Pollution," *The Guardian*, August 1, 2013.

365. "Environmentalists Sue on Ocean Acidification," *Tri-City Herald*, October 17, 2013.

366. Baumik, Subir, "Fears Rise for Sinking Sunderbans," *BBC News*, September 15, 2013, at news.bbc.co.uk/2/hi/south_asia/3102948.stm

367. Guzman, Andrew, *Overheated: The Human Cost of Climate Change*, Oxford University Press, 2013, pp. 173-174, partially citing IPCC Assessment Report Four, 2007.

368. Shuman, Emily, "Global Climate Change and Infectious Diseases," *International Journal of Occupational Environmental Medicine*, Vol 2:1, January 2011, p. 16, citing World Health Organization, at www.theijoem.com/ijoem/index.php/ijoem/article/viewArticle/65

369. *Recent Monthly Average Mauna Loa CO_2*, National Oceanic and Atmospheric Administration (NOAA), 2013, at www.esrl.noaa.gov/gmd/ccgg/trends/; Gillis, Justin, "Heat-Trapping Gas Passes Milestone, Raising Fears," *New York Times*, May 10, 2013, at www.nytimes.com/2013/05/11/science/earth/carbon-dioxide-level-passes-long-feared-milestone.html?_r=0

370. *IPCC Fifth Assessment Report Climate Change 2013: The Physical Science Basis: Summary for Policymakers*, IPCC and WMO, September 27, 2013, pp. 26-27, at www.ipcc.ch/report/ar5/wg1/

371. *IPCC Fifth Assessment Report: Summary for Policymakers*, Intergovernmental Panel for Climate Change, Potsdam, Germany, April 2014, p. 23.

372. U.S. EIA, *What is U.S. Electricity Generation by Energy Source?* 2012, at www.eia.gov/tools/faqs/faq.cfm?id=427&t=3

373. *IPCC Fifth Assessment Report: Climate Change: Mitigation of Climate Change*, Intergovernmental Panel for Climate Change, Potsdam, Germany, 2014, p. 25.

374. "A Look at Natural Gas Production in Texas," *KUT Radio* (*National Public Radio Network*: Austin), 2013, at stateimpact.npr.org/texas/tag/natural-gas-production-in-texas/

375. Begos, Kevin, "Marcellus Shale Natural Gas Output Rising Fast," *Christian Science Monitor*, August 15, 2013, at www.csmonitor.com/Environment/Latest-News-Wires/2013/0815/Marcellus-Shale-natural-gas-output-rising-fast

376. "Bakken Shale," *Unconventional Oil and Gas Report* (PennWell Corp: Houston), 2013, at www.ogj.com/unconventional-resources/bakken-shale.html

377. U.S. EIA, *Repeal of the Powerplant and Industrial Fuel Use Act (1987)*, 2003, at www.eia.gov/oil_gas/natural_gas/analysis_publications/ngmajorleg/repeal.html

378. Downing, Bob, "Utica, Marcellus Shales are Ripe with Natural Gas to Benefit Ohio, Pennsylvania," *Ohio.com* (*Akron Beacon Journal*: Akron, Ohio), September 18, 2013, at www.ohio.com/news/local/utica-marcellus-shales-are-ripe-with-natural-gas-to-benefit-ohio-pennsylvania-1.429684

379. "What's the Difference Between Wet and Dry Natural Gas?" *WITF Radio* (*National Public Radio Network*: Harrisburg, Pennsylvania), 2013, at stateimpact.npr.org/pennsylvania/tag/natural-gas-prices/

380. U.S. EIA, *U.S. Crude Oil and Natural Gas Proved Reserves*, August 1, 2013, at www.eia.gov/naturalgas/crudeoilreserves/

381. U.S. EIA, *How Much Natural Gas Does the United States Have and How Long Will it Last?*, August 29, 2012, at www.eia.gov/tools/faqs/faq.cfm?id=58&t=8

382. Soraghan, Mike, "Baffled About Fracking? You're Not Alone," *New York Times*, May 13, 2011, at www.nytimes.com/gwire/2011/05/13/13greenwire-baffled-about-fracking-youre-not-alone-44383.html?pagewanted=all

383. Committee Staff, *Chemicals Used in Hydraulic Fracturing*, Committee on Energy and Commerce, U.S. House of Representatives (Washington, D.C.), April 2011, at democrats.energycommerce.

house.gov/sites/default/files/documents/Hydraulic-Fracturing-Chemicals-2011-4-18.pdf

384. "Pipeline Explosions Since 2001," *FracDallas.org*, 2013, at fracdallas.org/docs/pipelines.html

385. Clayton, Mark, "West Virginia Gas Pipeline Explosion—Just a Drop in the Disaster Bucket," *Christian Science Monitor*, December 12, 2012, at www.csmonitor.com/Environment/2012/1212/West-Virginia-gas-pipeline-explosion-just-a-drop-in-the-disaster-bucket

386. Caldwell, Carla, "Planned Gas Pipeline Concerns Landowners," *Atlanta Business Chronicle*, September 30, 2013, at www.bizjournals.com/atlanta/morning_call/2013/09/planned-gas-pipeline-brings-safety.html; Minter, George, "Shifting Natural Gas Supplies Adding to U.S. Pipeline Constraints," *Black and Veatch*, 2013, at bv.com/Home/news/thought-leadership/energy-issues/shifting-natural-gas-supplies-pipeline-constraints; "Natural Gas Pipelines: Problems from Beginning to End," *Food and Water Watch*, January 23, 2013, at www.foodandwaterwatch.org/factsheet/natural-gas-pipelines-problems-from-beginning-to-end/; Katz, Matthew, "Spectra Pipeline in NYC Approved By Federal Government to Start Natural Gas Pumping," *Huffington Post*, October 21, 2013, at www.huffingtonpost.com/2013/10/21/spectra-pipeline-nyc-natural-gas-approved_n_4135428.html

387. Johnson, Tim, "Mexico Runs Low on Natural Gas," *Tri-City Herald*, September 19, 2013.

388. U.S. Environmental Protection Agency (EPA), *Electricity from Natural Gas*," September 25, 2013, at www.epa.gov/cleanenergy/energy-and-you/affect/natural-gas.html

389. Fisher, Danielle, "Are There CO_2 Emissions from Natural Gas?" *How Stuff Works*, 2013, at science.howstuffworks.com/environmental/energy/emissions-natural-gas.htm

390. Nelder, Chris, "Why Carbon Capture and Storage Will Never Pay Off," *SmartPlanet.org*, March 6, 2013, at www.smartplanet.com/blog/take/why-carbon-capture-and-storage-will-never-pay-off/534

391. "Coal: The Fuel of the Future, Unfortunately," *The Economist*, Vol. 411, #8883, April 19-25, 2014, p. 56)

392. Kramer, David, "Scientists Poke Holes in Carbon Dioxide Sequestration," *Physics Today*, August 2012, at scitation.aip.org/content/aip/magazine/physicstoday/article/65/8/10.1063/PT.3.1672

393. Zeller, Tom, "Carbon Capture and Storage: Global Warming Panacea, or Fossil Fuel Pipe Dream?" *Huffington Post*, August 19, 2013, at www.huffingtonpost.com/2013/08/19/carbon-capture-and-storage_n_3745522.html

394. "Bubbles of the Future: Is Carbon Sequestration Really Green?" *Newsweek*, November 24, 2009, at mag.newsweek.com/2009/11/24/bubbles-of-the-future.html

395. Gies, Erica, "Solar Waste Recycling: can the Industry Stay Green?" *Spot.us*, at www.spot.us/pitches/352-solar-waste-recycling-can-the-industry-stay-green/story

396. Woody, Todd, "Solar Industry Anxious Over Defective Panels," *New York Times*, May 28, 2013, at www.nytimes.com/2013/05/29/business/energy-environment/solar-powers-dark-side.html

397. Atkins, Gavin, "Green Deaths: The Forgotten Dangers of Solar Panels," May 17, 2011, at www.asiancorrespondent.com/54571/green-deaths-the-forgotten-dangers-of-solar-panels; *Solar Panel Hazards*, SA Publications, February 13, 2011, at www.scienceray.com/technology/solar-panel-hazards

398. Bryce, Robert, "The Real Problem with Renewables," *Forbes*, May 11, 2010, at www.forbes.com/2010/05/11/renewables-energy-oil-economy-opinions-contributors-robert-bryce.html; Layton, Bradley, "A Comparison of Energy Densities of Prevalent Energy Sources in Units of Joules per Cubic Meter," *International Journal of Green Energy* Vol. 5, 2008, pp. 438-455.

399. "What is the Energy and Carbon Payback Time for PV Panels in the UK?" *Centre for Alternative Technology*, 2009, at info.cat.org.uk/questions/pv/what-energy-and-carbon-payback-time-pv-panels-uk

400. "Germany's Energy Poverty: How Electricity Became a Luxury Good," *Der Spiegel*, September 4, 2013, at www.spiegel.de/

international/germany/high-costs-and-errors-of-german-transition-to-renewable-energy-a-920288.html

401. Carlyle, Ryan, "Should Other Nations Follow Germany's Lead on Promoting Solar Power?" *Forbes*, October 4, 2013, at www.forbes.com/sites/quora/2013/10/04/should-other-nations-follow-germanys-lead-on-promoting-solar-power/

402. Amiel, Geraldine, "Energy Bosses Call for End to Subsidies for Wind, Solar Power," *Wall Street Journal*, October 11, 2013 at online.wsj.com/news/articles/SB10001424052702303382004579129182510803694

403. Small, Vernon, "Greens's Solar Pledge Would 'Push Up Prices'," *The Dominion Post*, February 17, 2014, at www.stuff.co.nz/dominion-post/news/politics/9729839/Greens-solar-pledge-would-push-up-prices-Key

404. "Washington Incentives/Policies for Renewables and Efficiency," *Database of State Incentives for Renewables and Efficiency*, North Carolina State University, July 9, 2013, at www.dsireusa.org/incentives/incentive.cfm?Incentive_Code=WA15R

405. Smith, Erik, "Windpower Purchasing Rules Spark Another Fight in Olympia—Green Groups Balk at Changes," *WashingtonStateWire.com*, February 7, 2013, at washingtonstatewire.com/blog/windpower-purchasing-rules-sparking-another-fight-in-olympia-green-groups-balk-at-changes/

406. Gray, Louise, "Wind Farms are Inefficient, Says New Environment Secretary, as DECC Prepares to Launch Review," *The Telegraph*, September 18, 2012, at www.telegraph.co.uk/earth/earthnews/9535165/Wind-farms-are-inefficient-says-new-Environment-Secretary-as-DECC-prepares-to-launch-review.html

407. "What if Your Life Were as Unreliable as Wind Power," *Institute for Energy Research*, October 9, 2013, at www.instituteforenergyresearch.org/2013/10/09/what-if-your-life-were-as-unreliable-as-wind-power/

408. Associated Press, "Man Sues Over Noisy Turbines," reprinted in *Tri-City Herald*, August 12, 2013; Yardley, William, "Turbines Too Loud?

Here, Take $5,000," *New York Times*, July 10, 2010, at www.nytimes. com/2010/08/01/us/01wind.html?_r=0

409. Pace, Julie, "Obama Blocks Chinese Wind Farms Purchase Near Navy Base," *NBC News*, September 28, 2012, at www.nbcnews.com/ id/49216985/#.UmbrjRBoCM8 Note: President Obama has since lifted the suspension on Oregon wind farms.

410. Cockle, Richard, "Wind Farm Faces Oregon Fight: Union Joins the Resistance to Turbines," *The Oregonian*, March 4, 2010; Woolacott, Emma, "Wind Farms Could Raise Temperatures," *TG Daily*, March 12, 2010; Upham, B.C., "Pentagon Puts Hold on Nation's Largest Wind Farm," *TriplePundit*, April 21, 2010, at www.triplepundit. com/2010/04/pentagon-puts-a-hold-on-nations-largest-wind-farm; Learn, Scott, "Oregon Public Health Office Decides It's Time to Study Health Effects of Wind Turbines," *The Oregonian*, October 21, 2010; "Safeguards Needed to Prevent Population Declines in the Whooping Crane and Greater Sage-Grouse, and Reduce Mass Mortality Among Eagles and Songbirds," *Salem-News*, December 29, 2010, at www.salem-news.com/print/17335

411. "Study Looks at Wind Farm Eagle Deaths," *Tri-City Herald*, September 12, 2013, partially citing American Bird Conservancy.

412. Garman, David, and Samuel Thernstrom, "Europe's Renewables Romance Fades," *Wall Street Journal*, July 30, 2013.

413. Bryce, Robert, "The Real Problem with Renewables," *Forbes*, May 11, 2010, at www.forbes.com/2010/05/11/renewables-energy-oil-econo-my-opinions-contributors-robert-bryce.html.

414. Romm, Joe, "We're Already Topping Dust Bowl Temperatures—Imagine What'll Happen if We Fail to Stop 10°F Warming," *ThinkProgress.org.*, at www.thinkprogress. org/climate/2012/07/08/512596/already-topping-dust-bowl-temperatures-imagine-if-we-fail-to-stop-10f-warming/

415. Deutch, John, "Biomass Movement," *Wall Street Journal*, May 10, 2006, at heartland.org/sites/all/modules/custom/heartland_migra-tion/files/pdfs/19037.pdf

416. Ausubel, Jesse H., "Renewable and Nuclear Heresies," *International Journal of Governance, Economy, and Ecology* Vol. 1:3 (2007), pp. 229-43, at phe.rockefeller.edu/docs/HeresiesFinal.pdf

417. Heyes, J.D., "Burning Up Food Prices: More Corn Going to Ethanol Production Now than Food Production," *NaturalNews.com*, August 19, 2011, at www.naturalnews.com/033369_corn_ethanol_food; Bryce, Robert, "The Real Problem with Renewables," *Forbes*, May 11, 2010; Smith, Rich, "Record Drought May Be a Good Time to Stop Using Corn for Fuel," *dailyfinance.com*, August 18, 2012, at www.dailyfinance.com/2012/08/18/drought-corn-ethanol-fuel/

418. Loveday, Eric, "John McCain Gives Ethanol Blender Pump Subsidies a Big 'No'," *autobloggreen.com*, October 19, 2011, at www.green.autoblog.com/2011/10/19/john-mccain-gives-ethanol-blender-pumps-a-big-no; Thornton, Jim, "Ethanol from Corn—Burning Both Money and Oil," *igreens.org.uk*, January 2004.

419. Lipton, Eric, and John Broder, "In Rush to Assist a Solar Company, U.S. Missed Signs," *New York Times*, September 22, 2011; McCarty, Dawn, "Beacon Power, Backed by U.S. Loan Guarantees, Files Bankruptcy," *Bloomberg BusinessWeek*, October 31, 2011; Amarnath, Nish, "Abound Bankrupt: Third Government-Backed Solar Firm Goes Bust Within A Year," *International Business Times*, June 28, 2012; Finley, Allysia, "How Government is Making Solar Billionaires," *Wall Street Journal*, October 21, 2013.

420. Amiel, Geraldine, "Energy Bosses Call for End to Subsidies for Wind, Solar Power," *Wall Street Journal*, October 11, 2013 at online.wsj.com/news/articles/SB10001424052702303382004579129182510803694

421. Ferguson, Robert L., *The Cost of Deceit & Delay: Obama and Reid's Scheme to Kill Yucca Mountain Wastes $Billions*, p. 144. Crosby-Ferguson Publishers, Richland, WA, at www.crosby-ferguson-publishing.com.

422. Smil, Vaclav, *Energy Myths and Realities*, American Enterprise Institute (Washington, D.C.), 2010; *Energy Transitions: History,*

Requirements, Prospects, Praeger (an imprint of ABC-CLIO Inc.: Santa Barbara, CA), 2010.

423.   Obama, Barack, *Remarks by the President on Climate Change,* Georgetown University, Washington, D.C., June 25, 2013, at www.whitehouse.gov/the-press-office/2013/06/25/remarks-president-climate-change

424.   Bacevich, Andrew, *The Limits of Power,* Metropolitan Books (division of Henry Holt: New York), 2008.

425.   Tassava, Christopher, *The American Economy During World War II,* Economic History Association, University of Arizona, Tucson, AZ), February 5, 2010, at eh.net/encyclopedia/article/tassava.WWII

426.   U.S. EIA, *U.S. Net Imports of Crude Oil and Petroleum Products,* September 2013, at www.eia.gov/dnav/pet/hist/LeafHandler.ashx?n=PET&s=MTTNTUS2&f=M

427.   Organization of Petroleum Exporting Countries, *Brief History,* 2013, at www.opec.org/opec_web/en/about_us/24.htm

428.   "OPEC Enacts Oil Embargo: October 17, 1973," *History.com,* a division of Arts and Entertainment Television LLC (New York), 2013, at www.history.com/this-day-in-history/opec-enacts-oil-embargo; U.S. EIA, *U.S. Net Imports of Crude Oil and Petroleum Products,* September 2013, at www.eia.gov/dnav/pet/hist/LeafHandler.ashx?n=PET&s=MTTNTUS2&f=M

429.   U.S. Debt Clock at www.usdebtclock.org/

430.   Labonte, Marc, and Jared Nagel, *Foreign Holdings of Federal Debt,* Congressional Research Service, Report RS22331, June 24, 2013, at www.fas.org/sgp/crs/misc/RS22331.pdf

431.   Gellman, Larry, "Pay it Backwards—the Greatest Wealth Transfer in History," *Huffington Post,* November 4, 2008, citing T. Boone Pickens, at www.huffingtonpost.com/larry-gellman/pay-it-backward--the-grea_b_140530.html

432.   Ferguson, Niall, *The Great Degeneration,* Penguin Press (New York), 2013, pp. 2-40; Chantrill, Christopher, "U.S. National Debt and Deficit History," *usgovernmentspending.com,* at www.usgovernmentspending.com/debt_deficit_history; "Eurozone Crisis

Explained," *BBC News*, November 27, 2012, at www.bbc.co.uk/news/business-13798000.

433. Gellman, Larry, "Pay it Backwards—the Greatest Wealth Transfer in History," *Huffington Post*, November 4, 2008, pp. 5-7, citing T. Boone Pickens, at www.huffingtonpost.com/larry-gellman/pay-it-backward--the-grea_b_140530.html.

Chapter 5

434. Congressman Lee Hamilton and General Brent Scowcroft, co-chairs of the Blue Ribbon Commission on America's Nuclear Future (BRC), *Testimony Before the Committee on Energy and Natural Resources*, U.S. Senate, 112th Congress, February 2, 2012, at www.energy.senate.gov/public/index.cfm/files/serve?File_id=d1881c53-9805-4cb0-a4c8-b3495f0873f4

435. Andrews, Anthony, *Nuclear Fuel Reprocessing: U.S. Policy Development*, Congressional Research Service, Report RS22542, March 27, 2008, at wayback.archive-it.org/1078/20080922204830/http://ncseonline.org/NLE/CRSreports/08Apr/RS22542.pdf.

436. The difficulties being experienced with vitrifying liquid waste at the government's Hanford Site in Washington State that have received so much media and Congressional attention occur in large part because the waste has been generated, co-mingled, and stored for about 70 years. The chemical and physical interactions that have occurred within the waste over these years make them much more difficult to vitrify.

437. Nuclear Waste Policy Act, 42 U.S.C. 10101: Public Law (P.L.) 97-425; 96 Stat.2201 Jan. 7, 1983, as amended by P.L. 100-203, Title V, Subtitle A, December 22, 1987, P.L. 100-507, October 18, 1988, and P.L. 102-486 (The Energy Policy Act of 1992), October 24, 1992, Section 148, Part D. Note: The NWPA also defines nuclear fuel withdrawn from a reactor after irradiation as spent nuclear fuel. Thus, spent nuclear fuel is not technically a waste, but it is a byproduct of irradiation and, like high-level waste, and must be disposed of to the highest

standards of safe packaging, handling, transportation, and environmental isolation.

438. Andrews, Anthony, *Radioactive Waste Streams: Waste Classification for Disposal*, Congressional Research Service, Report RL32163, December 13, 2006, at wayback.archive-it.org/1078/20081113231856/ http://ncseonline.org/NLE/CRSreports/07Jan/RL32163.pdf; U.S. EPA, *What is Low-Activity Radioactive Waste?* Washington, D.C., at www.epa.gov/radiation/larw/larw.html

439. U.S. DOE, *Radioactive Waste Management*, Order 435.1, Washington, D.C., July 9, 1999; U.S. DOE, *Radioactive Waste Management Manual*, Manual 235.1-1, July 9, 1999.

440. Note that low-level waste (LLW) is not the same at low-activity waste. The LLW is waste that is not high-level waste, not uranium mill tailings or residues, and not containing more than specified concentrations of transuranic elements. Transuranic elements are those elements with higher numbers than uranium on the Periodic Table of the Elements. See LLW Fact Sheet, Environmental Sciences and Training Center, Rutgers University (New Brunswick, NJ), November 1996 at www.nj.gov/dep/rpp/llrw/download/fact10.pdf

441. Class C waste is a form of LLW that contains less than certain concentrations of specific radionuclides. Since the allowed concentration is different for each radionuclide, there is no simple way of expressing the Class C limits. A Table in 10 CFR 61.55 provides the specifics for each radionuclide.

442. U.S. DOE, Manual 235.1-1, Chapter 2, Part B.

443. Transuranic waste contains more than 100 nanocuries per gram of weight. A nanocurie is one-billionth of a curie. A curie is a measurement unit of radioactivity.

444. Harden, Blaine, and Dan Morgan, "Debate Intensifies on Nuclear Waste," *Washington Post*, June 2, 2004, partially citing Maria Cantwell.

445. Melfort, Warren, ed., *Nuclear Waste Disposal: Current Issues and Proposals*, Nova Science Publishers, Hauppauge, NY, 2003, pp. 111-113.

446. Natural Resources Defense Council (NRDC) v. Abraham, 2003, 271 F. Supp 2nd 1260, Idaho, 2003.

447. NRDC v. Abraham, 2004, No. 03-35711, District Court No. CV-01000413-BLW Opinion, November 5, 2004.

448. Ronald W. Reagan National Defense Authorization Act of 2005, Public Law 108-375, Section 3116, 108th Congress, 2004; Lobsenz, George, "Congress Backs DOE on Residual Waste, Advanced Nukes," *Energy Daily*, Vol. 32:195, October 12, 2004, pp. 1-2.

449. *Blue Ribbon Commission on America's Nuclear Future: Report to the Secretary of Energy*, January 2012 at cybercemetery.unt.edu/archive/brc/20120620220235/http://brc.gov/sites/default/files/documents/brc_finalreport_jan2012.pdf

450. Bullis, Kevin, "Q & A: Steven Chu." Interview with Steven Chu. *Technology Review* (MIT), May 14, 2009, at www.technologyreview.com/business/22651/?a=f

451. *A Sustainable Energy Future: The Essential Role of Nuclear Energy*, August 2008, signed statement of Directors of the U.S. DOE national laboratories, including Steven Chu, at www.thenwsc.org/ym/DOE%20Lab.%20Dirs%20Rpt%20Sustainable%20Energy%20Future%200808.pdf

452. *Blue Ribbon Commission on America's Nuclear Future: Report to the Secretary of Energy*, January 2012, p. vii, at cybercemetery.unt.edu/archive/brc/20120620220235/http://brc.gov/sites/default/files/documents/brc_finalreport_jan2012.pdf

453. Note: The BRC's first recommendation is the most controversial because the Congress will not delegate a constitutional responsibility. Implementing the recommendation may be useful in final decisions of the Congress.

454. *Blue Ribbon Commission on America's Nuclear Future, Report to the Secretary of Energy*, January 2012, at cybercemetery.unt.edu/archive/brc/20120620220235/http://brc.gov/sites/default/files/documents/brc_finalreport_jan2012.pdf

455. *Ibid*, p. vii.

456. *Energy and Water Development Appropriations Bill*, 2012, Senate Report (S.R.) 112-75, 112th Congress, 1st Session, p. 81, Government Printing Office (GPO), 2011, at www.gpo.gov/fdsys/pkg/CRPT-112srpt75/pdf/CRPT-112srpt75.pdf (The BRC final report was issued January 26, 2012.)

457. U.S. DOE, Office of Nuclear Energy, Nuclear Waste Plan Working Group Announcement, at www.ne.doe.gov/newsroom/BRC_info.html

458. U.S. DOE, *Strategy for the Management and Disposal of Used Nuclear Fuel and High-Level Radioactive Waste*, January 2013, at energy.gov/downloads/strategy-management-and-disposal-used-nuclear-fuel-and-high-level-radioactive-waste

459. *Ibid*, p. 2,

460. *Ibid*.

461. Nuclear Energy Institute (NEI), *Amounts and On-Site Storage*, 2012, at www.nei.org/resourcesandstats/nuclear_statistics/nuclear/wasteamountsandonsitestorage

462. U.S. Senate Committee on Energy and Natural Resources, "Senators Release Discussion Draft of Comprehensive Nuclear Waste Legislation," U.S. Senate, April 25, 2013, at www.energy.senate.gov/public/index.cfm/featured-items?ID=dd4c2028-b451-4000-8b13-b2c177886338

463. *Nuclear Waste Administration Act of 2013*, Senate Bill (S.B.) 1240, 113th Congress, 1st Session, Washington, D.C., 2013.

464. *Ibid*.

465. U.S. DOJ, *Response to Request for Information from the Blue Ribbon Commission on America's Nuclear Future*, December 20, 2011, at www.brc.gov/sites/default/files/comments/attachments/doj_response.12.20.11_0.pdf

466. Mufson, Steven, "Court Orders Government to Stop Collecting Fees for Discontinued Waste Dump," *Washington Post*, November 19, 2013, at www.washingtonpost.com/business/economy/court-orders-government-to-stop-collecting-fees-for-discontinued-nuclear-waste-dump/2013/11/19/c7172bf0-5165-11e3-a7f0-b790929232e1_story.

html; NEI, *DOE Proposes Suspending NWF Fee But Asks Court for New Hearing,* January 9, 2014, at www.nei.org/News-Media/News/News-Archives/DOE-Requests-Suspending-Nuclear-Waste-Fund-Fee-But?feed=News

467. "Reid Ready to Put Americans at Risk," *Intelligencer-Wheeling News-Register,* Aug. 26, 2013, partially citing Harry Reid, at www.theintel-ligencer.net/page/content.detail/id/588819.html

468. Daly, Matthew, "Obama Administration Violating Law on Nuclear Waste Dump Decision Delay: Appeals Court," *Huffington Post,* August 13, 2013, at www.huffingtonpost.com/2013/08/13/obama-nuclear-waste-dump_n_3749254.html

469. Wald, Matthew, "Government Must Continue Review of Nevada Nuclear Waste Site, Court Says," *New York Times,* August 13, 2013, partially citing Keith Chu, for Ron Wyden, at www.nytimes.com/2013/08/14/us/politics/government-must-continue-review-of-nevada-nuclear-waste-site-court-says.html?_r=0

470. Strassel, Kimberly, "Harry Reid's Yucca Bluff," *Wall Street Journal,* August 15, 2013, at stream.wsj.com/story/latest-headlines/SS-2-63399/SS-2-302636/

471. *Ibid.*

472. Nuclear Waste Policy Act, 42 U.S.C. 10101: Public Law (P.L.) 97-425; 96 Stat.2201 Jan. 7, 1983, as amended by P.L. 100-203, Title V, Subtitle A, December 22, 1987, P.L. 100-507, October 18, 1988, and P.L. 102-486 (The Energy Policy Act of 1992), October 24, 1992, Section 148, Part D.

473. *Blue Ribbon Commission on America's Nuclear Future, Report to the Secretary of Energy,* January 2012, p. xvi, at cybercemetery.unt.edu/archive/brc/20120620220235/http://brc.gov/sites/default/files/documents/brc_finalreport_jan2012.pdf

474. U.S. DOE, *Environmental Impact Statement for the Tank Waste Remediation System, Hanford Site,* DOE/EIS-1089, February 1997.

475. U.S. DOE, *Environmental Impact Statement, Disposal of Hanford Defense High-level, Transuranic and Tank Wastes, Hanford Site,* DOE/EIS-0113, December 1987.

476. U.S. DOE, *Tank Closure and Waste Management Environmental Impact Statement for the Hanford Site*, DOE/EIS-0319, November, 2012.

477. "Hanford Waste Plant Will Cost $4.4 Billion, Bechtel-WGI Predicts," in *Weapons Complex Monitor* (Washington, D.C.), April 30, 2011; Office of the Inspector General (OIG), *The Department of Energy's $12.2 Billion Waste Treatment and Immobilization Plant—Quality Assurance Issues—Black Cell Vessels*, DOE/IG-0863, U.S. DOE (Washington, D.C.), April 2012.

478. The Integrated Disposal Facility.

479. U.S. DOE/Nuclear Waste Partnership, LLC, Press Release on WIPP Radiation Release: "Follow-up Testing Shows No Health Risk for Exposed Employees," at www.wipp.energy.gov/pr/2014/Second%20 Bioassay%20Sample%20Results.pdf. Note: The incident under investigation is operational and does not put into question the decision to dispose of transuranic waste in the WIPP facility.

480. U.S. DOE, *Tank Closure and Waste Management Environmental Impact Statement for the Hanford Site*, 2012, DOE/EIS-0391, p. S-167.

481. *Ibid*, Foreword, p. 12.

482. Nuclear Waste Policy Act, 42 U.S.C. 10101: Public Law (P.L.) 97-425; 96 Stat.2201 Jan. 7, 1983, as amended by P.L. 100-203, Title V, Subtitle A, December 22, 1987, P.L. 100-507, October 18, 1988, and P.L. 102-486 (The Energy Policy Act of 1992), October 24, 1992, Section 148, Part D.

483. *Blue Ribbon Commission on America's Nuclear Future, Report to the Secretary of Energy*, January 2012, Executive Summary, p. ix, at cybercemetery.unt.edu/archive/brc/20120620220235/http://brc.gov/sites/default/files/documents/brc_finalreport_jan2012.pdf

484. *Ibid*, p. 59.

485. *Ibid*, p. 32.

Afterword

486. Patterson, Thom, "Climate Change Warriors—It's Time to Go Nuclear," *CNN.com*, November 3, 2013, citing Hansen, Caldeira,

Emanuel, and Wigley at www.cnn.com/2013/11/03/world/nuclear-energy-climate-change-scientists/

487. Leahy, Stephen, "Japan Bails out on CO_2 Emissions Target," *Climate Connections, Global Justice Ecology Project*, November 15, 2013, at climate-connections.org/2013/11/15/japan-bails-out-on-co2-emissions-target/

488. U.S. NRC, *NRC Directs Staff to Complete Yucca Mountain Safety Evaluation Report*, Document 13-097, NRC News Releases, 2013, at www.nrc.gov/reading-rm/doc-collections/news/2013/

489. U.S. Court of Appeals, District of Columbia Circuit, "On Petitions for Review of Final Actions or Failures to Act by the United States Department of Energy," No. 11-1066 consolidated with 11-1068 (Washington, D.C.), November 19, 2013.

490. Schlesinger, James, draft speech delivered to the *Oxford Energy Forum* on December 7, 1992.

Index

About the Authors

Bob Ferguson has more than 50 years of experience in the field of nuclear energy, both in government and industry. He is a former Deputy Assistant Secretary for Nuclear Energy for the U.S. Department of Energy, and former Managing Director for the Washington Public Power Supply System. Ferguson has been married for 56 years to Catherine Crosby Ferguson. They have two daughters, Catherine Kolinski and Colleen Lowry; and three grandchildren, Ashley, Michael, and Keefe.

Bob Ferguson in the control room of B Reactor, the world's first full-scale nuclear reactor built during the Manhattan Project (photo by Richard Breshears)

Ferguson is the author of *The Cost of Deceit and Delay: Obama and Reid's Scheme to Kill Yucca Mountain Wastes $Billions*. The book is about the cost to the country and the nuclear industry of the unlawful termination of the Yucca Mountain Project, and Ferguson's legal efforts—suing the President to hold him and his administration accountable for violating the law for their self-serving political agendas. He and his wife split their time living in Richland, Washington, and Lake Oswego, Oregon.

D r. Michele S. Gerber has had a long and distinguished career as a World War II and Cold War historian. With 36 years of experience, she has become an authority on operations, environmental and waste management practices throughout the history of the Department of Energy (DOE) and the nuclear facilities that are the legacy of World War II and the Cold War.

Dr. Gerber has appeared in more than 66 television programs and interviews about Hanford Site issues, including feature-length films televised nationally. She is the author of *On the Home Front: The Cold War Legacy of the Hanford Nuclear Site*, the first and only comprehensive history of America's largest nuclear defense site. She has published more documents about Hanford's operations and facilities than any other author, and has won numerous awards, honors, and commendations. She lives with her family in Richland, Washington.

CPSIA information can be obtained at www.ICGtesting.com
Printed in the USA
BVOW04s2115081014

370099BV00001B/62/P